M000084103

Me and E:
A Baseball Odyssey
David Bornstein

David Bornstein

Copyright © 2012 David Bornstein
All rights reserved.
ISBN- 13: 978-0615914985
ISBN-10: 0615914985

Dedication

To Ethan

David Bornstein

Contents

David Bornstein

Acknowledgments

This book, and in fact this entire experience, would not have been possible were it not for the great coaches and trainers we have been blessed to know who imparted at least a bit of the mystical lore of baseball to us: Rob Haben, Todd Bellhorn, Vic, Matthew and Jared Incinelli, Chip Gierke, Matt Gerber, and Sal Lombardo. A special thanks to the Orlando Scorpions baseball organization, who proved that a good team experience can make all the difference between mediocrity and greatness. And to everyone who believes in second chances and fresh starts, thank you.

Does the road wind uphill all the way?
Yes, to the very end.
Will the day's journey take the whole long day?
From morn to night, my friend.
Christina Rossetti

Preface

I love baseball. I also hate it. I'm not sure if that makes me schizophrenic or a masochist. I love sitting in the bleachers talking with parents of other players, or in a folding chair behind the backstop behind home plate, watching young pitchers and catchers work. I hate that it consumed me, taking precedence over basic needs like food and sleep. I love the ping of metal bats, the smell of early morning dew on fresh cut grass fields, the grimy feel of worn leather gloves. I hate the way my car always stunk of old cleats, filthy equipment bags, sweat-stained socks. I love the familiar feel of the Florida sun baking my face, poring onto my bald head through my baseball cap. I hate the cost, the time commitment, the injuries, the pressure, the crazy parents, the paranoid coaches, the recruiting, the player-as-commodity philosophy. I hate skin cancer and sunburn. But mostly I've loved watching my son Ethan play and grow from the time he started to now. To today. How he got where he is, and what we've been through to get him there, well, that's the story. And it's a long and convoluted one.

What began as a father's whim became a painfully all consuming job that overwhelmed our family life for more than a decade, taking us to the great cities and backyard pig farms of America, orchestrating our schedules, dividing us, wounding us, and bringing us back together at last. It's been long. It's been arduous. It's been an enormous learning curve. And ultimately, it's been worth it, though the jury had been out on that verdict until recently.

I predicted many things about our children before we had them, few of which came true. I don't think this is particularly unusual, though perhaps the fact that Ethan has been the opposite of nearly everything I imagined counts in some category like "farthest from expectations" or "wouldn't have considered in wildest dreams." I could have foreseen a violinist or a chess player, or maybe even a short, clumsy writer with curly dark hair and big brown eyes, looking at the world with a deep curiosity and hiding away in his room after school to write dark poetry and fantasize about girls he'd never have.

But that was me. That was me assuming my wife and I would produce clones. What we got instead, with our first born, was a jock. A goofy, oversized, left handed jock with a big heart and an unexpected talent. He could play baseball, and he loved it. He wasn't the best. Not five tools. But he had some things I never had – raw talent and passion for the game, and in following the current parental mantra of "helping one's children reach their full potential" I became consumed by the bat, the glove, and the little stitched ball.

Ethan's story, and by default, mine for the past fifteen years, has been all about the highs and lows inherent in a game based more on failure than on success. I'm not sure which we've had more of. I only know that there have been huge accomplishments and incredible disasters, and where Ethan's journey has been, in part, to figure out who he is with baseball and despite it, mine has been a rediscovery of who I am outside my son's reflection. It has been a long process of individualization and separation, all while dedicating my evenings, weekends, and vacations to furthering his baseball ability and career.

Through all this I exposed myself and my family to an unknown world. A world of life changing choices and mistakes, often coming on the heels of one another. A world of ex-pro players, overzealous coaches, scouts, recruiters and trainers, scouting combines, weekend games and weeklong tournaments, not to mention parents who were as involved and over the top as I was and knew far more than I about what it meant to have a high level athlete in the house. So we learned as we went, and made our fair share of boneheaded mistakes and asinine assumptions and half-baked decisions. Miraculously, some of them turned out ok, while others remained the messy stew they started out as. And that's what this book is about – what we all experienced and learned, the good, the bad, and the really bad, in all aspects of this most unique of American sports from little league to travel ball through the recruitment process by major colleges.

I hope, in the end, that this is more than just another sports story. It's really about what I've learned as a father, what Ethan and I have been through together, what has shaped him as he has grown up with both the blessing and curse of always knowing what you are, doing some things well, and some things terribly, both on and off the field. It's about falling into the parental trap of vicarious thrills, of living through one's children, and finally, after many indulgent years, figuring a way out. I hope that there is something here worth anyone's reading, and that you get a smidgeon as much out of it as I have in the telling and living. Play ball.

CHAPTER 1
The Littlest League

It is early January, a beautiful Florida late afternoon, and I am driving home from work. There are a number of ways I could choose to go, but today I'm in the mood to take my time. There's a light, cool breeze in the air, the sky a clear, cloudless blue. My windows are rolled down, and I go the slow, lazy way, winding down Delaney Avenue past Delaney Park, an old, inner city four block park with a couple basketball courts, two tennis courts, a playground, and two baseball fields. On the chain link fence that runs the perimeter of the smaller minor league field is a sign that, for some reason, I notice. I don't know why I bother looking up at it, but I do. Little League registration. Huh, I think. That would be fun.

My son is five years old and I'm looking for things to do with him. Somewhere in the back of my head is the misplaced notion, in the form of a Norman Rockwell magazine cover, that it would be great to play catch with my boy. Just that. Father and son playing catch in the backyard. And what better way to start, what better form of motivation, than joining a little league team, right in the neighborhood park where I grew up?

In some ways my own childhood was circumscribed by Delaney Park. We lived just a few blocks away, and my brother and I would ride our bikes down to the park to climb in the patch of bamboo and the big low hanging camphor tree, see how high we could swing on the old metal swing set, play tennis when we were older and laugh at the kids on the baseball fields.

I was the archetypal fat little boy with thick glasses who sat around reading books all day. My brother was a good natural athlete, but I was thick, clumsy, slow, the cliched last kid to be picked for everything except neighborhood games of tackle football, where I was so big I could carry three boys on my back and literally walk across the field to the end zone. I scored at will, but every time I did the humiliation swelled inside. In third grade my pants split open in the rear during a game of duck duck goose at recess, and I had to stand with my teacher outside the circle until my mother came and delivered another pair of pants.

My father and I never played catch. A busy local attorney and citrus man, he had no interest in it. He could have cared less what grade I got in Phys. Ed. It was all about academics. My parents' free time was spent involved in politics and the local Jewish community. When my extended family got together for brunch on Sundays, we joked about our combined lack of any athletic ability. We were the non-conformists, the cultured Jews in a southern wasteland. The idea of being beholden to a team, to scheduled practices, having to showcase our ineptness (mine in particular), was about as appealing as running a mile in gym class, or eating gefilte fish after Passover. Play baseball? It never crossed my mind.

It has been a challenging five years raising our firstborn. While my wife Pat has always been the model of loving patience, I have struggled with Ethan's energy and impulsiveness. He came to language awkwardly, and though he started talking at a normal age no one could understand him but us. We were his perpetual translators as he jumbled language and ran words together, talking more like Fred Flintsone than a two year old. "Iwafoo." He wants some fruit. "Stahdoomee." Stop doing that to me. It's as if he speaks in shorthand, getting the main sounds and forgetting the rest, and it obviously frustrates him when the only people who understand him are Pat and I, and even we struggle. We can tell he's bright, and activity is not an issue. He's big for his age and always into something. It's his follow through that drives me nuts. Asking him to do the simplest task is anything but. It's a constant test of my patience and his thought process. "Ethan, get your shoes and come to the kitchen. It's time to go." Ten minutes later I walk into his bedroom only to find his building blocks strewn across the floor, stuffed animals sitting in a semi-circle as if they're having a debate, and he's watching a Disney video with his shoes nowhere in sight.

This happened so often once, in a blind anger, I tossed him over my shoulder while he was screaming and thrashing. As we walked through the swinging door that led from our kitchen to the dining room he bashed the side of his head so hard against the doorframe his ear turned purple. He's screaming. My wife's screaming at me. And I don't care. He deserved it. He couldn't even put on his shoes when I asked.

Part of me wondered what I'd gotten into as a parent. None of this was what I bargained for, and even though I knew I loved him, I was more aware of my exhaustion, my impatience. My faults were magnified, my strengths diminished. I was crabby. I was angry. Everywhere I turned I was doing damage control. I loved him and felt burdened, heavily, unconscionably burdened at the same time. His coordination was slow to develop, so we got him physical therapy for fine motor skills. His speech impediment wasn't getting better with age, so he went to a speech therapist. We took him to afternoon therapy appointments four days a week after school. He was a bundle of anxiety, aggravation, and behavioral issues wrapped in the oversized body of a beautiful blonde boy with sweet intentions and an inability to carry them out.

It's been a tough time in more ways than just dealing with Ethan. My father had been sick with lung cancer for two years, and had died 9 months earlier on my 36th birthday. I had taken over his real estate development business which had slow sales, a huge payroll, and major cash flow issues. Then one day we got a package in the mail from an elderly couple who had been close friends of my parents.

The Rosenthals, a childless German Jewish couple married fifty years, had unofficially adopted my wife and I. They had us over for dinners and took us out to restaurants near their house. They baked a plum pie with our names written in dough. They made me executor of their estate and their trustee. Now we got the strangest package in the mail, a pair of good German binoculars, keys to their house, a pass into their gated community, and in the most meticulous German manner, a detailed map of their file cabinet showing where they kept personal files, business matters, even extra cash and postage stamps. And there was a letter that began, "Dear David and Pat, we have decided to take our lives." It took me a few moments to figure out what I held. Then I told Pat I thought the Rosenthals were planning to commit suicide.

We dropped Ethan off at my mother's house, and rushed over to the gated community where the Rosenthals lived. My hands shook as I held out the pass at the guard gate so we could be let in. Pat and I nearly flew over the speed bumps as I drove too fast on the winding road to their house, jumped out of the car and hurried into their bedroom where we expected to find them. They weren't there. Then we caught our breath, slowed down, and began to search the house, checking the spare bedroom, walking through the kitchen, until we found them in a back room of their house, leaning against one another with plastic bags over their heads. On a table nearby, a book on planned suicide was opened to a page that described what they did, highlighted in yellow marker. They had been dead at least a day. At that point, realizing we shouldn't touch or move anything, I called the police.

Hours later, after being interviewed and released by the police (we were immediately potential murder suspects, and then not), we went back to my mother's to pick up Ethan. He was gone. My mother had let him go for a car ride with her granddaughter – my niece – and my niece's boyfriend in a convertible, without a carseat, without saying a word about their plans.

"Do you know where they went?" I asked my mother.

"No."

"Did they say how long they'd be gone?"

"I didn't think to ask."

On a normal day this might have been worrisome, but nothing more. As it came on the heels of one of the strangest, most bizarre days of our lives, after finding this sad, lovely couple embraced in death, after dealing with the shock and the police, and then being forced to wait at my mother's house for an hour, then another, sitting, waiting, pacing for several hours until the teenagers showed up, two things occurred. First, I blew up. If I'd been a volcano my head would have exploded. I would have been the cause of massive air traffic disruptions across the western hemisphere. There was my little guy, happily, dangerously bouncing around in the back seat. I grabbed him. I yelled at them. I yelled at my mom. What were they thinking, letting him ride off like that while we were dealing with a life and death crisis? What if something had happened to him, to them? What then?

I realized, later, that I was yelling as much out of fear as I was out of anger, as much out of misplaced anxiety as out of real concern. But I also realized I was yelling out of love, pure, unlimited, unqualified love for my little boy. It was the first time I acknowledged that there was nothing more precious in the world to me than him.

When our nanny suddenly deserted us and we enrolled him in the childcare program at the local Jewish Community Center we found out what was going on with Ethan, through someone else's eyes, and even his pre-K teacher missed it. He covered it up well, almost brilliantly in an intuitive way. He would hop from one activity station to another, never staying anywhere for long, but acting involved and interested wherever he was. And he was sweet and polite and not a discipline issue.

It wasn't until we enrolled him in the JCC's summer camp that we discovered what was going on, and who he really was. His teacher had children with learning disabilities, and when she started tracking him she realized Ethan couldn't sit still, couldn't focus on anything in class for more than thirty seconds, couldn't follow the simple direction to put his backpack in the cubby, grab a square of colored carpet and come sit down for circle time. She called us to discuss what was a completely unexpected diagnosis by a summer camp counselor. Ethan had a learning disability, a big one. After further evaluation a child psychologist confirmed: Ethan had a severe case of attention deficit hyperactivity disorder - ADHD.

Now I replaced my intolerance and lack of patience with enormous guilt. No wonder he couldn't follow more than one request in a row. His brain wasn't wired to follow instructions. He got distracted. And quickly, without any choice in the matter, our guilt grew when we were told the only way for him to have any sort of success learning and behaving was to put him on drugs – in particular, on Ritalin, the old ADHD standard. Now we had to deal with the fact that not only had we been uninformed parents, and that I especially had treated Ethan with a complete lack of understanding, but we were going to put our four year old on a stimulant with mood altering, appetite suppressing, sleep troubling side effects.

Ethan already had a short fuse, blowing up in fits of anger when he was misunderstood, asked to do what was naturally difficult for him. Directions that involved more than two steps. Remembering to stop what he was doing at a certain time. Sitting at the dinner table. Add amphetamines to the equation, and we were in severe anger management with our little boy. We struggled getting him to sleep every night, and every morning Pat had to bring his breakfast to him and dress him in bed he was so tired, and then drag him to school. Ethan took himself so seriously we worried that he didn't have a sense of humor. He spoke in a deep voice with a soft lisp, was a head taller than the other children in his preschool, and because he stood out in so many ways was an easy target for the quicker (one could say meaner) wits in his class. He never knew how to respond when kids teased him. He'd stand there stunned, wondering if they were really talking about him, and he'd come home knowing he didn't fit in, and not understanding why. On top of that he'd melt down every day around five, throwing temper tantrums and exploding into a rage at the smallest incidents. We turned the TV off. We forgot his water. We were out of his favorite snack.

His little sister (Jerica, born when he was 2-1/2, happy and easy going), teased him then played innocent until he went berserk. It wasn't until I decided to try one of his 5 mg Ritalin tabs to see what it felt like that I understood what he went through every day. My brain turned into a pile of fried eggs by the afternoon. It wasn't fun.

Keep in mind that I was exactly the opposite of an ADHD kid. I'd always been a good student. I could sit for hours reading a book, engrossed to the point where I was unaware if someone was talking to me or a Gemini rocket was taking off outside. I assumed I'd have bright, top of the class kids. But a learning disorder that required drugs? Never entered my mind. It was an impossibility. Until Ethan.

🎾

I get an emergency call from the Jewish Community Center. Ethan is sitting listlessly on a chair in his classroom. He won't move, won't budge, and his left arm hangs dead at his side. Every time they try to move him he shouts out in pain and starts to cry. They've tried to contact Pat, but she's not answering her phone, so Dad is up next. They're scared to do anything, and if they hadn't reached me they would have called an ambulance. I know what's going on, or at least I have a hint.

A few months earlier I'd been playing with Ethan and lifted him up by his hands. When I put him down he couldn't raise his left arm, and when I tried to move it the pain was unbearable. I dashed him to our pediatrician, who promptly popped his elbow back into joint by holding his arm at a 90-degree angle, placing thumb and forefinger on either side of the elbow and turning his hand inward. You could feel the joint pop back into place. He showed me how to do it, in case it happened again, and he said it probably would. Ethan's joints were loose and popped in and out easily.

Ethan wasn't double jointed exactly, but his arms could bend backwards slightly, and his elbows were flexible, loose and wobbly. So when I got to the JCC I did what the doctor had shown me, popped his elbow back in and sent him off, after a few minutes and a few more tears, to the sandbox on the playground.

These weren't the only times it happened. Once, in New York City we were rushing for an elevator and I grabbed him by the hand and pulled him in. Same thing. I felt the elbow stretch and pop. He

16

cried out in pain, dropped his arm to the side, and just as quickly I lifted it up, set my fingers against his elbow, turned his hand, and fixed him. What I didn't think of then, and what I honestly didn't think of until many years later, was what that might mean to a child who took up a throwing sport that put excessive strain on that exact joint. It was a condition, I was told, that would disappear over time as the bones fused and the tendons and ligaments tightened. I believed that, and so I forgot.

So here I am, a year later, still trying to figure out what to do, how to have a father/son relationship with my little boy. And what could be more perfect than baseball? Throwing the ball back and forth, him to me and me to him at the park, in our backyard. It will be idyllic. It will be something fun for him, and for me, I can see the memories already, the scrapbook in my mind, our own little Field of Dreams where years later we'd reminisce about how we played catch and grew close, just like a dad and his boy ought to be. I sign him up.

First discovery. Ethan needs equipment. I go to the local Sports Authority for a bat and glove. At this level they use t-balls, lightweight safety balls that are softer than regular baseballs and don't leave quite as deep a black and blue mark on little kids when they get hit. There are tons of everything: bats, balls, gloves, bases, hitting tees, teaching aids, and dozens of other items I've never heard of. And the prices! This is supposed to be a game, not an investment strategy. I figure the way to go is to buy the smallest of everything, since he's just starting out, and I count on the one fact I know: he's a lefty. So I get him a cheap little left handed glove and a $20 aluminum bat. I hope it'll do and not be too embarrassing. More than anything, I don't want to put him in another humiliating situation.

Second discovery. He is really slow. Really, really slow. Oh well, there goes my first dream. No track star here. No stolen base records in danger. If kids can be divided into tortoises and hares, Ethan is a tortoise. Their first practice they do two things. They run around the bases to learn which direction to go, from home to first to second to third and back to home. They run in a pack, like hounds chasing a rabbit, and Ethan is chasing them all, trailing them like a wagging tail, chasing them doggedly and wildly, not giving up but far, far behind. Then they break into pairs and play catch, some with other fathers, a few with one another, me with Ethan.

Ethan can't catch. I am throwing from five feet away. He stands with an open glove pointing to the sky like he's trying to catch sunlight. I toss the ball into his glove. I hit the glove and the ball stays in. That's a catch. Otherwise he misses. It bounces out. He lunges and the ball hits the ground. Our coach looks at me, dismayed. He takes the bat I just bought and asks Ethan to hold it out from the knob end at arm's length for 10 seconds. Ethan does so easily. "The bat's too small," he says. "You can use one of the team bats." I remind myself that Ethan is five years old, and the coach is thirty years older. "Go home and play catch with your boy," he tells me.

"You think?" I say to myself. "Play catch with my boy? Brilliant idea." We are in the car on the way home, and I am thinking of catch and nothing else.

As parents we think that all the choices we make are critical. Where our kids go to school, who their friends are and which friendships we encourage or discourage, what they do with their free time, and how much and where we direct them. Baseball or piano? Chess or soccer or both? How much do they read each day? How much do we make them read? At the time, every decision, every move feels almost as forced and weighted as the next because, truth is, we don't know which ones will be important and which ones won't. It's only in hindsight, of course, only in the looking back do we see the critical path, the divergence in the yellow woods, some more obviously than others. If I had gone home a different way. If I hadn't looked up and seen the little league sign. If I hadn't followed through. If we had gone to the field and the coach had been a real jerk. If if if. But the real if here is what if baseball hadn't happened for Ethan. Who he would have otherwise been is the great unknown for him and us. The greater unknown at the time was that we had taken the first step down a very long path that we knew nothing about.

Recognizing a child's loves (not our own) is, I'm more and more convinced, one of the great, maybe the greatest challenge of parenting. For some children the joy lies in diversity. Our daughter, three years younger than Ethan, hopped from dance to singing to roller blading to swimming before finding horses and lacrosse and now, boys.

Our youngest, ten years removed from his older brother, enjoys anything creative. Ethan focused. He found baseball, and there was no room for anything else.

But that sort of intensity creates its own questions. Do you encourage that kind of passion to the exclusion of all else? What if someday it just ends? Where are you then? Do you go from playing ball to hanging out on street corners smoking pot and raiding 7-11s when the munchies hit? Is it better to treat your children like a mutual fund, and dabble in a wide array of investment opportunities, limiting loss if one doesn't work out while increasing the odds of finding something that will be beneficial long term?

The answer, I think, is that some children are more like hot stocks and others follow the S & P 500, and the parent's job is not to sway their child one way or the other, but to be sensitive enough to acknowledge the unique drive of each one's soul. Does this child like to stick his/her toe in the water, pull it out and try another pond, or do they jump in headfirst? And once in, do they love the water, the fish, the lilypads, or do they come up gasping for air and scrambling for the shore?

There's always a fear there, that you're limiting your child in some way, that when they get into something they're giving up something else, and there's truth to that. We all have these visions of our kids that we can't easily get away from, ideas that are formed at their birth (or often earlier) that they force us to reshape or forget altogether. I expected a poet, but deep down I think I always wanted a stud, someone who would get everything I didn't have, then rise above it all and instead of being the asshole jock, befriend the nerd and the geek and partner with them in the class science project.

The gist of it is, as parents we fly blind. There may be developmental markers, books written that tell us when to expect our child to walk, to talk, how to give a time out or understand the importance of limits. But no one has written a good book about what it's like to go through five years of sleep deprivation, or what to do when your child is quieter than you'd like around the grandparents, or what you should say or do when they're so different that you don't even feel like a parent at all. There hasn't been a great book that answers the question, "What do you do with the unexpected?" Rolling with it isn't answer enough. Being flexible, mirroring, empathizing, all may help a child, may let them know they're loved, nurtured, that they're safe with you, but none of it helps you. When the only constant

is change, what is there to hold onto? When the only thing you can
readily expect is the unexpected, and you realize parenting is more like
being cast adrift in a lifeboat on rough seas, and you can neither
navigate nor swim, that's when you're truly ready to plunge ahead willy-
nilly, naïve, unaware. Excitement built in me for no reason other than
that I was in uncharted waters, and my son was opening up a hidden
world.

I was getting what I wanted, playing catch with Ethan in the
backyard, and he was going to practices twice a week and games on the
weekends. He didn't want to miss a thing. And he wanted to play catch
more than I did. Every day in the backyard. "Can we fwow the ball?"
"Can we pway catch?" "C'mon, Dad, pwease?" Five year old Ethan,
blonde, lisping, slow afoot but beginning to show an indomitable
determination to get better, who had been unable to tie his shoes and
put his clothes away, now wanted to catch and throw and catch and
throw.

I'd give in every time, change into a t-shirt and go out in our
little napkin of a backyard and throw the ball for a half hour or so with
him. 10 foot tosses. Then 20, 30, until we'd backed up about as far as
the yard would allow, and he began to get adept with the glove, getting
used to its weight, understanding that his left hand covered the ball
after it hit the glove, not before, realizing that the goal was for me to
catch, not chase the ball when he threw it. Catch the ball and toss it
back. Aim for my chest. Field the ground ball. Cradle it between your
legs. Pop up, and throw it back. Hundreds of times a day. I'd never
really thought about where your fingers go when you throw (thumb
and ring finger underneath the ball), where your hand and throwing
arm should be (back, not by your ear). I'd never understood the effect
of the seams, throwing with your top fingers following the two seams
or crossing them, and how important it was for Ethan to start feeling
the ball that way. Step and throw. Step and throw. We'd go out and
sweat in the heat, put bug spray on to keep the mosquitoes at bay, and
throw and throw and throw. The monotony of the ball hitting the
glove, the soft, repeating thunk every time it sunk in, the satisfying pop
when the ball hit just so in the mitt, all became a spring ritual, a
synchronous rhythm of father and son, boy and man. I hadn't realized
that the real joy of playing catch was more than the time spent with my
son. It was the feeling that we were working in unison for a simple,
common goal. Keep the flight of the ball going. Make it smooth and

easy. The less effort, the more accurate the better. And when we were both throwing well, hitting the mitt, aiming for the head, the chest, and hitting the spot again and again, the shared satisfaction was immensely, strangely fulfilling.

I looked at books. I listened to the coach, because I wasn't sure Ethan, watching the red clay on the infield dribble through his fingers and chasing other players around the bases, was. But he was relentless. He wanted to go out and throw every day. So we did, and he absorbed the repeated drills and learned fast.

He learned to hit the ball off a T. At this level of little league the object is simply to make contact with the ball as opposed to knocking the T into the ground. All the coach wanted was contact. Hit the ball. Swing through. Hold the bat right (finger knuckles of the right hand on the bottom, hand knuckles of the left lined up with them on top for a lefty), and swing, head down, eyes on the ball. Everything else was left for later.

And maybe this is why Ethan became so attached, so young, to such a strange team game, a game whose greatest cliche is that it teaches about failure more than success, a game that is way too complicated for a five year old, but broken down into its basic components is simple, and full of lessons that make sense, even when you're that young. Take the right steps. Do things in the correct order. After you've made it to first, go to second, and then third, and feel good about making it all the way home. But make it to first safely. Don't try to do more than you can. Don't worry about things you'll learn later, or can't control. Follow a few basic rules and you can do something amazing. You can hit a ball hard and far. You can be part of a team. You can score. Pay attention. Keep your eyes on the ball, and good things will happen. You can feel good about yourself, and if things don't go right, you'll have another chance in a little while.

I only have a little bit of video from Ethan's first season, a minute or so. He is playing first base. There's a runner on first, and the ball is hit. The runner goes to second. Ethan is agitated. He waves his glove, bouncing up and down. He hops two-thirds of the way to second base, yelling "Fwow the ball! Fwow the ball!" You can't see where the ball is thrown, but now Ethan is running home, yelling "Fwow it home! Fwow it home!" I remember fretting that Ethan is everywhere he's not supposed to be. He's abandoned first base. He's hopping. He's yelling at his teammates. I don't know whether it's the

ADHD or little boy excitement. "Get back to first base," I'm thinking desperately, mouthing the words to myself. "Get back to first." And Ethan, I know, could care less. He's too into the game.

Amazingly, Ethan's coach votes him most improved player. I wasn't sure if this was because he had started at the bottom and risen somewhat, or because he had actually become decent, but it doesn't matter. He is acknowledged for his improvement, and I get an attaboy for a good job playing catch.

The minor league ball field at Delaney Park was my first experience with an iconic American baseball setting. A neighborhood field, backed by houses on a brick street, modestly maintained with almost no pitcher's mound, hard packed clay in the infield that wandered through weeds and thin grass into an outfield unfettered by fences or other manmade boundaries. Left field went on forever. If someone could hit a ball hard enough it would have rolled the length of two football fields, past a playground, past the fences of the major league field and into the distant brick street that bordered the farthest edge of the park. Right field ended with a scattered, haphazard row of azalea bushes, and beyond them, basketball courts that almost always had an inner city game in progress. Ethan's first, and one of his only home runs in little league came in his second season, when he hit the ball hard enough and with the right spin to roll past the right fielder all the way into the azaleas, wedging itself somewhere beneath a pile of shriveled up pink flowers and leaves. There was no one to call a ground rule double, so Ethan kept chugging around the bases while parents cheered, running with painfully slow, small steps as he hauled his big frame to second, to third as the outfielders finally fished the ball out of the leaves, carefully avoiding the yellowjackets that hung out in the bushes. When he finally made it home, exhausted, his teammates didn't know what to do. Instead of going out to high five him, they all stood in the dugout, hanging onto the fence as he stomped on home, as if they had tired and aged while he rounded the bases and returned to them.

$$\textcircled{D}$$

Ethan is nine years old, and I am coaching little league. I don't know how this happened. Maybe they were short on volunteers, or maybe it's because Ethan has become one of his age group's better players, but I've been handed the job. I still don't know much about baseball beyond the rules, but now, even though I really don't know what I'm doing, I am Coach to a dozen seven and eight year olds. I am fair, and consistent and that's about it.

My team is diverse: mostly poor, mostly white, with a couple Hispanic boys, and one black kid who gets dropped off and picked up every practice and game by staff from the juvenile detention center where he currently lives. His name is Ralph. He is athletic, eager to please, quick to shrink into despondency at a hint of criticism or the slightest mistake on his part, and no baseball experience whatsoever.

There's David, whose parents are appreciative that he's even on a team, tiny as a mouse and quick. Maybe he'll be a good base runner. There's freckle-faced Sy, a neighbor and a friend of Ethan's who already has more swagger than ability, not a half-bad athlete, but not half as good as he thinks. There's shaggy blonde Johnny, who desperately wants to be a key player on the team, but can't catch the ball. It scares me every time he puts his glove up to block a throw. There's Brett, a chubby pitcher/outfielder who right now is the only boy who can throw the ball over the plate, and DJ, our second best pitcher and a decent third baseman who at least is not afraid to step in front of a ground ball. I teach them how to hold a bat, how to keep your weight back when you swing. I show them how to throw. In fact, I show all these kids how to hold a bat and ball. That's where we start, every season in little league. And I start with the realization that these children are not just temporary players of mine. They are wards, and I have to treat them accordingly.

I have two weeks, four practices to get them ready for the first game. I have plans, practices outlined, drills to go over, but I realize, this first day, that I'll be spending most of my time just working on the fundamentals and keeping these boys safe. Safe when they catch. Safe when they run the bases. Safe emotionally when they do poorly, and we lose.

There are two kinds of little league coaches, those who teach and those who win. Of course, there's a spectrum in between, but it's rare for there to be a coach at this level who both knows the game and wants to help the six, seven, eight year old, and one who is fiercely competitive and wants to win at all costs. Most of the competitive coaches don't want to waste their time on the youngest players, many of whom will only play for a season or two anyway. They won't put the weaker hitters high up in the lineup, just so these kids know what it feels like to bat third or fourth. They won't put them in the infield where they botch plays, just so they experience the action once in their lives. They want to win. The best kids bat first. The best fielders are in the infield. The strongest arm (at this level, at least) is in center field, and he is told to catch EVERYTHING. Don't worry about the left or right fielder. They're just here to fill up space. They may start like I did, a dad coaching his son, but they know enough strategy, enough nuances to keep moving up the age ladder. My counterpart, my nemesis for the year, Doug Doudney, the coach of the other minor league team, is a winner, and his son is on his team. He is an entrepreneur, a banker and businessman with an angular face, thinning hair, a quick, eager smile, and a banter that always makes me feel like he's responding to me without ever listening to what I say. He's basically a good guy, just more intense with his team than I am with mine. His boys do push-ups when they make a mistake. They throw relays from the outfield in to the cut off man. They beat every team they face.

I quickly discover I can teach. I struggle teaching how to win. Winning comes with greater difficulty, and though I may feel good about how fair and reasonable I am, losing has its own high costs. Understand, first of all, that even at this young age kids know that whoever bats in the first four spots in the lineup is special. They all want to play infield, and beyond that, they all want to play first or shortstop, the glory positions. No one wants to play right or left field. Every time a play is made by the shortstop, parents cheer and applaud. Every time the first baseman catches the ball, it's the same thing. Instant gratification. Heroism. The spotlight. It's a child's dream of fame and fortune come true time after time, three or more times an inning. The corollary is also true. Missing the ball, not making the throw, comes with groans and shaking heads from the bleachers.

So I decide, early on, to do a few things in the name of fairness. I stagger my batting order, one good hitter, one not so good. Every kid gets a chance one game to bat first. This kills a lot of rallies and opportunities to score runs, but it does away with any hitting hierarchy on the team. I also give every boy the chance to play short or first, with two conditions. The shortstop has to be able to field ground balls, and make the throw to first. The boys understand this, and it limits the volunteers. At first base, my rule is simple: you have to be able to catch the ball, because I won't put someone there who can't and gets hit in the face. I come to this conclusion after putting Johnny at first. He begs me to play first every practice. I am concerned because he acts scared of the ball. Half the team is scared of the ball. They flinch when it's thrown to them, turn their heads away from ground balls. Johnny is one of the worst, but he wants to play first. I put him there. He gets hit in the face. I make a new rule.

I tell the parents my plan, and for the most part they understand. There are a few scowls, some muttering from those who realize this will cost us games, but there are an equal number of parents who appreciate the fact that their child will be given a chance, a first for many of them. That's about what I figured would happen, and all I can really expect.

Lefty Ethan has had a lot of experience at first, and is already pretty good. Several dads have volunteered to help, and I make them my first and third base coaches. They're talking about the great season ahead, but I'm looking around wondering who will play where? Who can hit? How do I handle having my son on the team, not showing favoritism even though he's probably the best player I've got? And what do I do about a shortstop? I don't have anyone who can consistently field the ball.

Delaney Park has a small little league, only two teams per division, so I'm comparing Ethan's talent level to a total pool of twenty-five boys. He might be top dog in our tiny corner of the world, and dog shit everywhere else. I have no point of comparison. He hits the ball with authority. He catches almost everything that's thrown to him at first base, and a few people with baseball experience tell me he's got a live arm. A live arm, as opposed to a dead one. I assume that's a good thing. I imagine Ethan bouncing around the bases with a dead arm flopping at his side. Not a pretty picture. He does seem to throw it with more pop than most of the other boys, who still throw rainbows with high, slow looping arcs across the field. I'm not sure where that really puts him in the bigger baseball world, but for now, it's fine.

Ethan complains the most about running, even two times around the bases. He dawdles in the back of the pack. I yell at him to keep up and he frowns back at me, his eyes furrowing together angrily.

I stare back at him, and keep staring, glaring, the whole time he runs. We're going to have a little father-son chat after practice. It proves to be the first of many.

"We need to have a talk" I say as soon as he enters the car.

"About what?"

"About you dogging it today around the bases."

" I wasn't dogging it."

"Ethan, yes you were. How can you say that? You were last by a mile."

"I was doing my best, dad."

"I find that hard to believe. You could've been in the middle of the pack easy."

"I was doing my best."

"Ethan, I'm your coach and you're supposed to be one of the leaders on the team. You can do better. I'd like you to try to at least stay in the middle. That won't be embarrassing for you or me."

"I'm not embarrassed."

" Well, just try to do better."

" Yessir."

At the point Ethan says "Yessir," I know I've lost him. He isn't listening anymore. His mind's off on something else, and like a bad song on the radio, he's turned me off, switched channels to something he likes more – rolling the window up and down, picking at the laces on his glove, anything to distract him from me. I am sitting there, driving and stewing. I know he's shut me off, and I'm caught between wanting to explode and letting him have it, making him realize that he was giving a half effort, that it was embarrassing for me, his father-coach, to be standing there on the field while other parents in the bleachers noticed him shuffling around the bases. They didn't have to say anything. I knew. I knew what they were thinking. I could feel the whispering. The son of the coach is getting away with something. And then there's another part of me that wants to just give it up, let it go, put this minor incident in the lost battle category and move on. But it's gnawing at me, and even as I park the car, turn off the engine and sit in our carport, I know that Ethan has already forgotten it and has run off to play with his neighborhood buddies for the last half hour of daylight before dinner. I walk inside with nails in my stomach, knowing I've been blown off, gotten nowhere as either a father or coach with the one player who it means the most for me to reach.

I didn't understand, right then, that Ethan's response, aside from being typical lockdown defensive father/son ADHD, was the perfect prescription for both his future success and failure, and if I'd by some chance known this, perhaps I would have pursued the matter, albeit in a different way.

Baseball is one of the few sports that can drive its participants mad with futility. Almost all other sports are based, to some degree or another, on productivity and usefulness. In tennis if you win 55% of the points in a game, or, even less, win a majority of the key points, you can win every set, every match handily. In basketball a player who shoots around 50% can be a superstar. In football a quarterback wants to complete 60% or more of his passes. In professional baseball if a batter gets a hit 30% of the time they are considered great.

The slow pace of a baseball game can be attributed, by and large, to the time it takes a pitcher to pitch the ball. The time between pitches, while the pitcher walks back up the mound, feels the seams of the ball in his glove, kicks the dirt off his cleats, and turns back to the catcher takes an inordinate amount of time. Even though some pitchers work much faster than others, there is still always significant time between pitches. This time is critical to the pitcher. His ability to succeed, to throw the next pitch how and where he wants, is often determined not by how he's feeling physically, but by what he's going through mentally. It is based on an obvious, straightforward line of thought that can go in two different directions. Is the pitcher thinking about his last pitch, or the next one he's going to throw? If a pitcher thinks about what just happened, he is doomed. Unless the ball is hit or bunted right back to the pitcher, he gives up control the moment it leaves his hand. It is up to the batter to swing, the fielders to make a play. When a pitcher dwells on the mistake pitch, the spot he missed where the catcher held his glove, the base hit, the error, by focusing on the past he is distracting himself from the task at hand, and thus making its completion more doubtful. That task, easy as it sounds and incredibly difficult to achieve, is to throw the next pitch right. And the only way to do this over and over is to believe, in a game of failure, of one's virtual infallibility.

The two basic components of baseball are two of the most difficult in all of sports. Hitting is widely considered the most difficult task, reacting to the speed, location, spin of a baseball in tenths of a second, making the necessary adjustments and then hitting it where fielders aren't. Second most difficult by a hair is consistent pitching. If you've ever tried to hit a tree with a rock you know what I mean. Most of the time you're proud if you come close. A pitcher is asked to throw a ball the size of a large round rock at near peak velocity into a space the size of a small box again and again with complete confidence, even as the hitter on the opposite end stands there ready to crush the ball in the most humiliating way, sometimes right back at him.

The players who succeed are, almost inevitably, the ones who focus on their successes and disregard their failures. The hitters who have greatness etched in them contain both the physical attributes necessary to play at a high level, and the mental ability to not only emphasize their positives, but evaluate their faults and mistakes and adjust, learning and developing as they go. And the pitchers who succeed are the ones who, after each pitch, focus on the next. It doesn't matter, it can't matter what just occurred. If an error was made behind the pitcher, so be it. He had no control over that. If the hitter hit a bomb, the pitcher might tell himself not to throw it there to that hitter again. He might think, for a half second, "bad pitch," or "mistake," but then he shrugs it off and moves on. If he dwells on it, if he lets himself get flustered, he's lost before he throws. His shoulder freezes. He holds the ball too tightly. His timing goes off. He drags his arm, his body, steps forward too soon. He swallows too hard, and chokes a little bit. Something, anything, one of the many miniscule movements required for a successful pitch go haywire. He blows it. Or he blows it off, makes a minor adjustment, and moves on. That spells success.

Ethan has both the best and worst inside him: the ability to shrug off, disregard, even ignore the strikeouts, the errors, the mistake pitches. He can act like his failures don't exist and perform brilliantly. And, when he is less than composed, bothered by teasing teammates, frustrated on the field, mad at his overwrought, in his face father, he implodes and falls apart. Of course, ignoring one's weaknesses also makes it more difficult to overcome them. And listening to them ad nauseum from the one person you only want praise from makes it all the more problematic. Ethan believed wholeheartedly that he was never responsible for anything bad that happened. As I coached I began to obsess over every detail on the field. Most of the time Ethan was in the mix, and I couldn't get that out of my head. I wanted to talk to him, review the games, figure out the way things should have gone and why they didn't. Ethan was over it the moment he left the field.

It is right before our first game, and a new player is added to each team. I get Andrew Bell. Doug gets Trey.

I take Ethan aside and ask him to throw with Andrew. Andrew catches the ball, and throws it back to Ethan. I watch him closely. I can tell in the first three throws he knows how to play. He is smooth. He can throw. He can catch. He takes batting practice and makes good contact. He glides easily, gracefully side to side, flowing between second and third, fielding ground balls and moving like a player. He's not very big, but he's thin and athletic. I have a bona fide infielder. Doug, I find out, got a pitcher.

It is the last game of the regular season, and we are playing Doudney's team. We have had an up and down time, winning just over half our games. Some of the parents are appreciative of my approach, while others resent the fact that because of it we've lost games. I know how they feel. When we lose it rankles me for days. I go over every play, every mistake I made, every what if again and again. What if I'd had Andrew and Ethan hitting in the 3 and 4 spots consistently? What if I hadn't shuffled my infield so much? What if I had a consistent lead off hitter? And of course when I talk to Ethan about this, or try to, he typically answers with an "It doesn't matter, Dad. I had a good time," and runs off to play with friends. All the boys on the team do this. When we lose they may hold their heads low for a minute, but after that they're laughing and yelling and chasing one another to their cars. It drives me nuts. It drives the angry parents nuts. We all want them to be more upset, like us.

Andrew is very good at everything he does. He has played every position on the field. He is our best shortstop, our best catcher, and he pitches well. He swings a bat with consistency and gets the timely hits. And he's quiet bordering on shy. He's done it all with a big smile, with humility and acceptance.

Ethan, on the other hand, has become, during the second half of the season, the go to pitcher on our team and our big power hitter. In mid season a coach from the little league majors gave our team a one-shot lesson on pitching – the power position with the throwing arm back and the other arm out in front, the leg kick and stride, the

29

final fielding position. Something clicked. Instead of just heaving the ball, Ethan got a glimpse, for the first time, of how his flailing arms and legs could work together. He started throwing strikes, an accomplishment at this age even with the exaggerated little league strike zone (knees to armpits, 6-8 inches off the plate in either direction). The coach showed the boys three pitches: the four seam and two seam fastball, and a changeup, or palm ball, held with fingers spread and the palm open wide against the ball. Ethan developed a deceptive changeup, and at this level it was all he needed. When he was on and throwing around the plate, he was very hard to hit.

Ethan has become a good teammate, and a terrible one. He's first to tell someone good job, and he's the first to tell them how and where to play on the field, a job that belongs to the coaches, not him. He pounds his glove when he's at first base and shouts encouragement to the pitcher. "Good pitch, way to go. Go get him." And he struggles to keep his mouth shut. He moans, he mutters "come on" when someone makes an error. He kicks the dirt. He shakes his head. He's always talking, and he also wears his frustration for all to see. It's great that he's so invested, but the toll it takes on everyone else is problematic.

Ethan and Andrew have become friends on and off the field. Ethan's also in unbridled competition with Andrew. When Andrew gets a good hit and comes back in the dugout and other boys congratulate him, Ethan bursts in and says, "Yeah, but did you see my hit last inning?" When Andrew is pitching I can see that, while Ethan wants him to do well, however well Andrew does, Ethan's new goal is to do better.

Doudney's team has only lost a few games to teams in other larger little leagues. I decide, in this final regular game of the season, to be competitive. Both Andrew and Ethan have pitched in the previous week, so I give DJ the ball. Ethan's at first, little David, Mr. Hustle, is at second, with Andrew at short and Brett, who can field the ball and throw it with a single hop over to first, at third. In the outfield I'm rotating everyone else, with Sy in center. Ralph is behind the plate. He's a big boy with a strong arm, and he likes throwing the ball back to the pitcher. It makes him smile. I also let the boys know this is the one game of the year we're going to play a little differently. We're going with a batting order based on who's hit best during the season, so our lineup is Sy, Brett, Andrew, Ethan, and Ralph to start us off.

Doug comes out with both barrels loaded. Trey, unhittable Trey, is on the mound. Trey throws strikes. He throws hard. He makes batters swing and miss. He is, by far, the best pitcher in our league. And so the game goes. They are the home team, and in our first time up Sy and Brett don't even touch the ball. Andrew makes contact, a weak grounder to second base. Three up three down.

DJ struggles from the get go. He throws balls in the dirt. He looks tired, anxious. He walks the first two batters, and Trey comes in and hits a bomb over Sy. Sy is running, running to stop the rolling ball. By the time he retrieves it and runs it back in (it's too far to throw) two runs score, and Trey is at third. Trey scores on a ground ball to Ethan, then Andrew catches a pop fly and DJ gets a strikeout against a flailing hitter who swings at everything. 3-0.

The next inning is more of the same. Ethan gets a hit, a seeing eye single that dribbles past the first baseman, but he is stranded there as Trey handles the rest of our hitters with ease. Ralph gets mad when he strikes out and throws his helmet. Anger has been a recurring issue, and he is warned by the lone umpire behind the plate not to do it again or he'll be ejected. I have to squat down beside him and comfort him just to get him to put his catcher's gear back on. When they get up to bat they score three more runs - an error at third, a throw in the dirt from Andrew to Ethan that Ethan can't handle, three walks. I have no choice. I take DJ out and put Andrew in to pitch. DJ goes to third and Matt moves to short. Andrew wastes little time taking charge. He doesn't throw hard, but he throws the ball over the plate, forcing the batters to swing. A strikeout on a head high pitch. A ground ball that Ethan bobbles, then controls and makes the out. A weak hit back to Andrew, who tosses the ball to Ethan. We're out of the inning, and down 6-0.

Trey mows us down once again, and we get out of the next inning with no runs scored. Andrew isn't quite as commanding. He walks one, and appears visibly tired. The ball begins to sail. He takes longer with each batter. Even though he gets two slow grounders and a pop fly that he catches, I am concerned. I look over at his father, Tom Bell, an easygoing dad with a thick gray mustache. Tom looks worried, too. That's it for Andrew. I decide to close with Ethan.

Then something happens. Doug, confident as he is of the easy win, has taken Trey and moved him to shortstop. Their new pitcher is, well, not Trey. He's just another little league pitcher. Little David, who I have batting down in the order, gets hit by the ball. He runs down to first, crying and smiling at the same time. Johnny, who I've had to beg all season to swing the bat, gets walked. Sy beats out a ground ball to the shortstop, who automatically throws the ball to first instead of getting the force at second. We have the bases loaded. Brett gets walked. 6-1. Andrew hits a shot, a line drive double into left field that scores two. 6-3. The pitcher is waiting on the mound for Doug to take him out, his arm drooping, holding the ball listlessly. Disgustedly, Doug walks to the mound, takes the ball away from the boy, and calls in his center fielder. Ethan hits a towering fly ball the right fielder misjudges. It sails over his head. Andrew scores. Where any other kid might have had a home run, Ethan chugs his way to second, and remains there. Strikeout. Strikeout. Fly ball. We're back in it, 6-4.

Ethan takes over where Trey left off. He is on. Everything he throws is around the plate. His ball has begun to show signs of a lefty's movement, spinning slightly away from righthanded batters, and his imperfect control makes his pitches unpredictable enough. Ethan strikes out all three batters he faces.

Doug's center fielder remains on the mound, but he has completely lost control. He walks four batters in a row. Doug walks to the mound, tries consoling the boy who is on the verge of tears. He settles down. Brett strikes out. Andrew hits another line drive, but this one is right at Trey, who gloves it easily. The runners stay where they are. Ethan then hits a ground ball to Trey and is thrown out by six or eight steps. He is pissed. He takes his helmet and is about to throw it to the ground, when I grumble "Ethan!" from the dugout. He fixes me with a scowl, holds his helmet and stomps off the field.

Now he's pitching angry, even better, harder. The ball pops when it hits Ralph's catcher's mitt. The hitters are missing by so much I can see the air between the bat and ball. I smile, and wonder if this is a tactic I should use more often with him, piss him off and then throw him out to the wolves.

We're in the sixth inning, and it's up to the bottom of my lineup, my little guys, my wannabes. Doug, however, has run out of pitchers, and he makes it easy on us. Two more walks, and then Ralph is up. I've told Ralph to wait until the pitcher throws a strike, but he swings at the first pitch anyway, and hits a ball that's over his head. It goes over the pitcher, over second base into center. A run scores. We're tied. The pitcher walks the next batter to load the bases, and now he's crying on the mound. Doug walks out to talk to him. He asks the umpire if he can have a moment, then motions to me to join him on the mound. I look around. This is unusual. Me? On the mound with you and your pitcher? I walk out to talk to him.

"Listen," he says to me. "I don't want to put this poor kid through any more. Can I put Trey back in?"

Can he put Trey back in? It's clearly against the rules. I look at the teary boy. He is sobbing, shaking visibly. I can tell every pitch is tortuous for him now. If I say no, if I make him stay in his suffering is on me. I look back at my dugout. My boys are staring at me. Parents are staring at me. I look down at the clay on the mound, look at the streaks of sweat and tears on the boy's face, look at the plea in Doudney's eyes.

"I know it's an exception, but I don't have any more boys who can pitch."

I don't know what to do. I don't have to say yes. If I do, Trey will probably come in and shut us down. If I say no, I'm leaving this boy on the mound to suffer, and we'll probably win, though not the way I'd like. I make what I think is the right decision. I let Trey back on the mound. Doug's pitcher jumps gleefully away. Doug says, "Great!" and pats me on the back. I'm already feeling like I've been had. Trey takes the ball and I know the inning is already over. The next three batters strike out. It's Ethan's turn to hold them again.

Now it's a pitcher's duel. Ethan strikes out the first two batters he faces, walks the third, and the fourth gets a single before Ethan struggles through a full count to get a force out ground ball to Andrew, who fields the ball cleanly and makes the play himself at second. I can tell he's tiring. His ball is beginning to rise. He's throwing fewer strikes, but I have nowhere else to go.

We're in extra innings. My boys have played the best game of the season, and I have made a decision that makes it almost impossible for them to win. Trey mows us down again. It doesn't matter who he faces now. He strikes them out. He throws a strike. We swing and miss. End of story.

Ethan walks the first batter, strikes out the second. The next batter hits a ground ball to David, our second baseman. He makes the play at first, lobbing the ball nervously to Johnny, who catches it and feels like a hero. But Trey is up, and the runner is on second. Ethan's first pitch is right down the middle of the plate, and Trey hits the ball

33

hard between short and third. The run scores. We lose 7-6. Doug is beaming, high fiving his players. I am breathless, speechless. My shoulders slump. The ball is tossed in from the outfield. Ethan picks it up and hands it to me. He won't look me in the eyes.

Afterwards, I try to think of the right words to say to my boys. They're staring at the ground. Some of them are crying. Ralph runs off to his counselors before I have a chance to speak. I go over all the clichés in my head. Great job. Way to play. Best you've done all year. But I don't utter them. All I can say is I'm sorry. I thought I was doing the right thing. They don't say a word. I can see the parents in the bleachers talking amongst themselves. A few come up and shake my hand, but it's a halfhearted gesture. I feel like an idiot, a loser. This is the first time all season when a decision I made created wounds that will take a long time to heal. On the way home Ethan says one thing to me. "I wish you hadn't let Trey back in, Dad." I look around for a rusty blade, something to twist in my stomach that will make the pain I feel real. I made the right decision, just for the wrong team. I hurt my boys, and lose sleep that night going over it and over it in my head. I swear I'll never do something like that again. I blew it. I'm a loser. Misguided charity. It's not worth the price.

⚾

I am walking behind Ethan at the Bithlo baseball complex, carrying his equipment bag. Tall black chain link fences surround pristine, well-manicured ball fields. Perfect pitcher's mounds, shining bleachers with screens to shield spectators from the Florida summer sun make the new fields the nicest by far at which we have ever played. Hundreds of little league players in a rainbow of colored uniforms swarm around the fields, watching games in progress, huddled in team groups waiting for their time to play. Parents are shouting, cheering, carrying their son's equipment bags as they walk to the fields, standing in knots by the concession stand to catch a bit of cool air conditioning. It is the second round of the local little league tournament. Games are being played all around us. I stop and watch for a moment. The players look serious. On the field they're sharp, smooth, at a completely different level than what I'm used to. The winner of this goes off to regionals, and the winner of regionals plays for the state championship, then the southeast championship, and the winner of that plays in the Little League World Series at Williamsport.

We have no unrealistic aspirations here. Delaney Park is a small, a tiny little league. In order to field a team of twelve we took six players from my team and six from Doudney's. Of those, maybe four players would have earned spots no matter where they played: Trey, Ethan, Andrew, and Doug's son. The rest are here because we needed to field a team. Other little leagues choose twelve from six, eight, ten teams, and put together a real all-star roster. We feel lucky just to be here.

Somehow we win our two first round games against College Park little league, another small league like us, and advance to the next level of play. In the bottom of the last inning we scored two runs on a combination of two errors and two hits. Ethan got one of the hits, but it was nothing to brag about, just a ground ball that made its way out of the infield and landed him on first.

I am Doudney's assistant in the tournament, and though he asks for my opinion, he does so, it seems, only out of respect. "What do you think we should do?" he asks. "What do you think about this lineup?" He shows me the already made up lineup card and then hands it to the umpire. Case closed, decision made. I'm chafing silently. Trey starts every game and goes as long as he can. When he tires, Doudney puts Ethan in. So it goes. Trey starts our single elimination game against Windermere Little League.

We haven't heard much about Windermere. It's one of the more upscale towns around Orlando. The names we know, and fear, are the little leagues that have regularly represented Central Florida in the state tournament – the powerhouses, the organizations: Conway, Union Park, Apopka, Goldenrod. These are the storied programs with reputations I've heard whispered by parents at our games. "I wish we were in the Conway district." "Wait til you see how Goldenrod plays." Many of the boys in these districts, I'm told, play in other leagues as well, especially Pony League, where the style of play is more akin to real baseball. They play in two leagues year round - little league for the chance to go to Williamsport, and Pony League to play good baseball. Pony League is where the better ball players go when they outgrow little league, when they're ready to start playing real baseball.

Real baseball? What have we been playing the past four years? Real baseball – Pony League baseball – does a few things differently than little league. Runners are allowed to take leads off bases. In little league players have to stand on the base until the pitch crosses home plate, virtually nullifying the ability of a player to steal unless there's a passed ball or wild pitch, or the player is uncannily fast. There are no pick off moves in little league, because there is no need for them, so pitchers don't concern themselves with runners on first or second. And in Pony League the distance from the mound to home plate transitions back slowly as players get older, from 38' to 44' to 48' to 54' to the standard 60'6". In little league it leaps from 46' back to the big league distance, an adjustment for players that is enormous. Base paths get longer slower in Pony League as well, in 10' increments from 50' all the way back, finally, to the big league 90', making the adjustment, and the premium on speed, more transitional and less of a shock. And the strategies of baseball – the steal, the hit and run, the suicide squeeze – are all taken away by the rules of Little League, while other youth leagues teach baseball the way it's played by the pros. So what does Little League have? Broad public support. A globally broadcast tournament that pits the best overseas little league teams against the best little league teams from the United States, so the USA always has a 50% chance of coming out on top. Crazy parents screaming their heads off like it's the end of the world at Williamsport. And Little League is a great place to begin to learn baseball. But it's not real baseball.

Little League plays with bats skinny as toothpicks that more closely resemble girl's softball bats. The fields are, by and large, undersized by the time boys reach age 12. Short base paths. Short distances from the pitching mound to home plate. Short fences in the outfield. What does Little League have that no other youth baseball league has? Williamsport and television.

Since its founding in 1938, Little League has grown to more than 7,000 leagues and two and a half million participants. No other baseball program in the world comes close to this level of participation. It receives more municipal support than any other youth baseball organization. And in 1960 the final of the Little League World Series was broadcast live on ABC TV for the first time. That same year membership in Little League around the world jumped from 380,000 to 825,000 members.

The advent of greater coverage by ESPN and the cachet of playing at Williamsport and in front of a global television audience has given Little League an irresistible allure. With Brent Musberger, and later commentators who were professional players calling the action, with pitching velocity adjusted to account for the difference in distance between the mound and home plate from the pros and Little League to make Little Leaguers appear like 90 mph pitchers, the Little League

World Series has become an annual international sporting event. But let's face it. If a 70 mph fastball from 46 feet equates to a 90 mph fastball from 60'6", shouldn't a little leaguer who can hit a 70 mph fastball from 46 feet also be able to hit a 90 mph fastball from 60'6"? Of course, it doesn't work that way. It just looks good on TV.

⚾

Our game is starting. Trey is on the mound, Ethan at first, Doug's son at second, Andrew at short, another one of Doug's boys at third. We're confident with our starters and our infield, and our first five batters have some real ability. The Windermere boys look big. I wonder if anyone's checked their birth certificates. No need to, though. These kids are just huge. And polished, very polished. They throw the ball around the infield without missing. Their warm-up drills appear orchestrated.

The outfielders throw the ball a long way effortlessly. Our boys are watching from the dugout, and already I can see the intimidation growing in them. They're smiling nervously as they cling to the dugout fencing, peering out at the competition. In the top half of the first inning we go down one two three. The Windermere pitcher throws nothing but strikes, and we hit nothing but air.

When it's their turn to bat I can feel their confidence. They exude, not arrogance, but something close to it – it's obvious they assume they're going to win. I can see it in the way they swing their bats in the batter's box. I can see it in their eyes as they watch Trey warm up. There is no fear or awe in them. They're big time. We're small fry. They're jocks. We're wearing diapers. They're ready to go. We're wondering what we're doing here.

In the first inning Trey gets rocked. He's never been hit this hard before. They score five runs with only one out and we're up to bat again. Ethan leads off. He gets his bat on the ball, but it's a weak grounder to second, and we're out of the inning quickly again. Trey gets hit hard again as well. Bomb bomb bomb. His shoulders slump. He hangs his head between pitches, and keeps looking over to Doug with an unspoken plea to take him out. He's pitching without thinking, throwing the ball over the plate, waiting for them to score their runs so the inning can be over. Ten nothing. Doug tells Ethan to go warm up.

There is no miracle finish here, no amazing relief effort, no comeback. Ethan gets raked, too. The second batter Ethan faces hits a line drive that bounces off Ethan's right leg. He hops around in pain for a moment, and the umpire goes out to take a look at the welt, but Ethan refuses to be taken out. He continues to pitch, continues to get hammered. I'm struck by his tenacity. Ethan refuses to give in or give up. He competes with every pitch, even though he's losing every battle. Mercifully, the game ends after four innings. We're run ruled, and Ethan hobbles off the field, shaking his head. "Those guys were really good," is all he says. He has a bruise on his leg the size of my fist, but he's smiling just for having the chance to play here.

"Is there anything you could have done to stop them?" I ask. "Could you have pitched better?"

"Nope," he responds. And I leave it at that. Sometimes the loss is inevitable, and the victory comes in being brave enough to go back on the field.

We have a family picnic to celebrate the end of spring ball, and even though I had the players vote, I made sure every player wins an award for something. Fastest. Most Team Spirit. Best Outfielder. Best Hitter. Best Fielder. Best pitcher. Best Teammate. Funniest Player. Biggest Player in the Smallest Package. And there are two coveted awards. Most Valuable Player and Best All Around. There are only two players in the running for those awards: Ethan and Andrew, and they split the votes evenly, leaving me to cast the deciding vote. I give Andrew, who was our best catcher, infielder, and one of our two best pitchers the all around trophy, and Ethan MVP. Maybe I should have been more gracious. Maybe I shouldn't favor my son. Arguments could be made both ways. But I play a little daddy ball here to make Ethan happy. And when I call him up to accept his award, I place my hands on his shoulders and struggle to speak, not because I'm nervous, but because my tongue feels like it's swelling up. I am choking on pride.

CHAPTER 2
Pony Boy

I am up to bat. It's a hot day, the beginning of summer, and just standing out there on a shadeless field at home plate makes me sweat. I'm dripping. I'm drenched. I'm waiting for the pitch. No one thinks I can hit but me. I foul one off intentionally, dribbling it down the third base line, step out of the batter's box. I step back in. Now I know what to expect. That's fine. I'm ready. The pitcher throws one right down the middle of the plate. It comes in waist high and I crush it, sending it to deep left center. I run down the first base line, watching the center fielder back up, back up until he almost touches the fence. He barehands the ball. I make the turn around first and stop, shrug it off. The runner on third scored. I get the RBI and the sacrifice fly. I wipe my face off on my t-shirt, grateful that the softball game in gym class is almost over. I'm in eleventh grade. That is the extent of my baseball experience.

I could always hit the ball, and I could do a decent enough job fielding and throwing in pick up games that my lack of ability flew mostly under the radar. I was never a player, never that much of a fan, really, until I started watching the minutest details in Ethan's game. I could tell when he was standing too straight, when he was swinging a hair late, when his hands were slow or he bailed out too early. I attended every practice, every game. I worked with him on the days he didn't have practices, at the batting cages, throwing bullpens, working on his swing with a tee and net I set up in our backyard. I always knew if something was off in his pitching or his swing, though I wasn't astute enough to be able to pinpoint what exactly was wrong. I knew if he changed something he was doing, but I couldn't tell you why, or whether it was an improvement or not. I also knew, after two quick seasons, that I'd done all the coaching I could with him. I couldn't teach him how to score a game. I couldn't teach him signals. I couldn't take him to the next level, even if that next level was only the Majors in Little League. He had already passed me by, at age nine. He needed better training, greater knowledge, deeper understanding of the game. He needed a real coach and real instructors, not his dad. I learned all this by watching him time after time, so many times I lost count, but I never lost sight of him.

_____

39

Fall comes quickly, and with it a new season of challenges and expectations on my part. After the accomplishments of the last season, those expectations include a move up to one of Delaney's two major league teams, and an offer, to me, to coach again. Neither occurs. I go petulant, but it doesn't take much for me to realize not coaching is a blessing – for everyone. And realizing that, I also feel a wave of relief. No more lineups, or pressure to give everyone a chance. No more guilt. I can focus on my boy, which is what I want to do, for better or for worse.

But that focus has its' own hidden costs. I don't get why Ethan is left behind, when Andrew, Trey, and Doug's son all step up to the majors. I chew on it. I mull it over. I resent it. So what if they're older and Ethan is only nine? Isn't my boy good enough? What do these other boys have that Ethan doesn't? Is there something going on here that I don't know about? The truth is, there isn't. Ethan is young, and has plenty of time to move up, but I think he's ready. I know he's ready. We're told spots are limited, and if Ethan moves up an older player loses his place. That infuriates me. There's no finite number for players on a team. There's no reason there couldn't be thirteen, or fourteen instead of twelve. There's also no arguing, no changes. No exceptions. And I see conspiracies everywhere, at every level, even down to the Minors in Little League.

The team Ethan's put on is Minor League in all respects. Most of the boys can't catch, can't throw, can't hit. It's baseball for beginners all over again. On top of that, Ethan dwarfs the other boys on the team. He's Mongo among the Lilliputians. And the coach tells us he's counting on Ethan to carry the team. I'm scared he's being counted on to be the team. Out of frustration and resentment, out of believing, fairly or not, that we (not just Ethan) deserve better, I instigate our first act of baseball disloyalty. I search for alternatives, and find Pony League Baseball.

We'd been warned that Pony League was where the better boys played, that it was on a whole different level. But I'm not concerned. We're talking about Ethan here. Big E. Stud pitcher. Great hitter. MVP. Nine years old. He's boisterous, verbal, a leader. He's going to come in and dominate, just like he'd done at Delaney Park for years.

I don't know where these thoughts came from, but I know they were there. There may have been an inkling of fear, some trepidation that this would be more difficult than I imagined, but it wasn't very deep. I had inflated my perspective based on Ethan's performance at a small Little League comprised of 24 boys. I fully expected Ethan to go out and play big, whatever team he landed on. He was too good not to.

We are late arrivals to Pony League, so Ethan misses tryouts and gets placed on a team coached by Rob Haben. I didn't know that someone from Delaney had already called Pony League and spoken to Rob and told him I was a pain in the ass, that the only reason I was moving Ethan over was because they wouldn't let him play in the Majors – which was correct. I made a decision I thought was in my son's best interest. He needed tougher competition. But others didn't see it that way.

Rob told me later, when he and his son Robbie drove up to the ball field at Shenandoah Elementary School, Robbie spotted Ethan and said, "Look dad. That kid can catch," with some relief, because you never knew what kind of player would be dumped on you at this late stage of spring. Rob responded by saying, "Yeah, son, but what's better is he's playing catch with his dad." Rob preferred the involved parent to the ones who dropped their boys off and said "See you later." He didn't know what else he was getting with me.

Rob is a big guy with a barrel chest, a thin dark mustache, and thinning dark hair. He walks with a quick step, bouncing from behind home plate to second to show infielders how he wants them to smother a ball. He is generous with his gestures, his feelings, his likes and dislikes. All are an open book, written all over his face. When he wants something done in practice, he barks at his players. When he's unhappy he groans and grimaces. He turns his head to the side. He drops one shoulder, and leans on the fungo bat for a second before hitting another ball. "Oh come on," he'll say. "That's just plain ridiculous." He never swears, and he's always instructing. I haven't experienced anyone quite like him in our four years of Little League.

I walk up to Rob after the first practice Ethan attends, and tell him, "Ethan was one of the best players at Delaney Park. You'll be glad you got him."

Rob nods his head and smiles at me, a smile I didn't get until years later. "Oh, ok," Rob said. "We'll see." Translation: every dad thinks that about their son.

We'll see? Didn't he believe me? Didn't he see how big Ethan was, how he caught everything at first base, how he looked like a player. "We'll see?" I thought to myself. "We'll show you."

In the world of sports fans it's a common joke that when a team is winning, fans say "we," and when it's losing it's always "they." They suck. They played horribly. They need a new coach. As opposed to "we're one of the best teams in the league. We are loaded. We sure stuffed it down their throats tonight." The transition from first to third person is a dead giveaway. Somewhere I'd made the transition to first person with Ethan. It wasn't about him anymore. It was about us. It wasn't his accomplishments. They were ours. When he did well, we did well. I had jumped on the winning bandwagon, and I didn't see any reason to get off.

We had no idea how lucky Ethan was with Rob, but we soon learned that Ethan was on a very good team. Rob's son, Robbie, played short, caught, and pitched, much like Andrew from Little League. But Robbie was stockier, bigger, stronger. He threw harder and he pounded the strike zone. Robbie hit home runs. And he was a dominating right-handed pitcher. No doubt about it. His best friend, DeeJai Oliver, played second and also pitched. DeeJai was the son of Joe Oliver, all-star catcher and World Series MVP for the Cincinnati Reds. DeeJai was wiry and fast, a blur of blonde hair and smiles, a good all-around athlete. Kyle Mitchell, short, freckled, thickly built, wavy brown hair and glasses, played infield and pitched. He threw the ball hard. This team had players, and as I watched them I had the first inkling that I'd been evaluating Ethan in a tiny fishbowl, and now he was out among the sharks.

In some ways, Pony League was like Baseball 101. Ethan had to learn how to take a lead off first. How to steal a base (though when Rob saw Ethan run he didn't think there'd be too much of that going on). How to swing a big barrel bat. One of the key differences between Little League and Pony League is that Little League uses bats with narrow barrels, while Pony League (and virtually every level of competitive baseball) uses bats with wider, 2-5/8" barrels. The bats have more power, but they're also heavier and drag more. With a big barrel bat in his hands, Ethan's swing looked slow. And then there was the pitching. Real pitching. Competitive pitching. Hitting your spots with three pitches pitching, with a smaller, more realistic strike zone than Little League.

Rob puts Ethan at the bottom of the lineup the first game and, disgruntled as I am, he proves to be right. The closest Ethan comes to getting on base is a slow ground ball back to the pitcher, who throws him out by half the base path. He strikes out his other two times up, and more than that, he looks confused, overmatched, defeated. I begin to wonder if we made a mistake, if I pushed him in over his head. But after the game Ethan shrugs it off, and whether it's his blind spot or his perennial optimism, he says only, "I'll get it." I, of course, want to talk more, to dissect every swing, to figure out what the pitchers were doing, what they were throwing. I want to hear how different this was from Little League. I want to see the game through Ethan's eyes, to rewind, have an instant replay, but he's done, and wants to go home and play with the neighborhood boys.

We are in the tenth game of the season, and Ethan remains hitless. O for 20. This hasn't been a case of a hitters' bad luck, hitting the ball hard but right at someone. This has been about not being close. Rob has been good about it. Even though I've begun to sweat and choke and pace every time Ethan gets up to bat, Rob has been reassuring. "Don't worry," he's told me, "every kid gets a hit. He'll be all right." But it wasn't all right. I try to teach him how to swing a bat all over again. I listen to what Rob says at practice, and look up drills, catch phrases, important points online. Get your hands moving. Keep them inside the ball. Keep your weight back. Swing the bat like you're chopping wood. I even get out an ax and have Ethan swing it to get the feel of the heavy blade moving through air. Get the barrel moving. But Ethan's bat is way behind every pitch he sees. Something beyond bat and ball hasn't connected, and every at bat is more painful than the next, both for him and me. Ethan watches third strikes go by without swinging. He's way behind the next. He barely gets the bat on the ball, hitting dribblers that never make it out of the infield. He hangs his head, shakes his head, hits the ground with his bat. He knows not to throw anything. That's an immediate ejection by Rob. But it's not getting better. It's getting worse. He's gone from being the kid who might be good to the kid who thought he was. And now, instead of having pride catching in my throat, it's my heart every time he's up. I clench up. I hold my chin up with my hands. I barely watch. I sigh deeply. I shout encouragement. I shout instructions. But nothing helps.

Nothing works. I sit apart from other parents. I am the pariah dad who brought an unknown plague to the team, a sure out. I know Ethan has it in him, an antidote, a path to success. It's called a hit, and I'm dying inside, bit by bit, waiting for its arrival.

⚾

It is a night game, a Friday night game, a game on Shabbat, the Jewish Sabbath. We light candles beforehand, but let's face it, we rush through the blessings over the bread and wine and do so in the afternoon, because Ethan has to be at the ball field an hour early, and the field is a half hour, not five blocks away from the house. The message we're giving him – I should say I'm giving him because my wife Pat has voiced her concerns about playing on Friday nights (which I've countered by saying every kid in America who plays sports plays on Friday nights) – is that baseball comes first, faith second. This isn't the only time we're going to struggle with this message. It's the first of many.

We aren't very religious. In fact my wife hasn't converted, though she's getting more and more involved in the Jewish community and in our synagogue. It's something I never wanted to push or foist on her. If she chose to convert, I always wanted it to be her own decision, her own heart guiding her, not some demand that would turn into anger and resentment later on. But now even she realizes we're compromising something. We might not be going to synagogue on a Friday night, but going to watch our son play baseball instead makes any commitment we espouse seem hypocritical. I don't want to be hypocritical. I also don't want Ethan to miss any games. The knots in my stomach untangle. I bury my values. I call it a compromise, a temporary concession. We'll make it up by making sure he never misses an important holiday (though doesn't our rabbi tell us the Sabbath is an important holiday?). We go to the games.

Ethan is now 0 for 25. His first time up he lunged and hit a little fly ball to short. He's up again. It's getting to the point where I can't bear to watch, but I can't pull my eyes away either. "Come on Ethan!" I yell. He looks at me with pursed lips and knitted eyebrows. Not happy. Pat jabs me in the side with her elbow. She wants me to shush too. Ethan squares up. The pitcher throws a fastball down the middle of the plate, and Ethan gets around on it and hits a shot to right center field. Not a lazy fly, but a laser that one hops to the fence. The fences for Pony League at this age are 180 feet back. That seems a long way. Ethan's ball gets there before the outfielders have even moved.

Ethan is stunned. He stands in the batters box for a second before he remembers to run. I stand up and scream, "Run!" Pat elbows me again. Rob, who is coaching at first base, turns to me and Pat, shrugs his shoulders and says, "Where did that come from?" Ethan is lumbering down to first and Rob motions him on to second. A double for his first hit. Outstanding! But the outfielder has the ball and throws it to the second baseman. Ethan stumbles and rolls more than slides into second, kicking up a cloud of dust and looking up, bewildered at the umpire's signal. Out! Only Ethan could be thrown out at second after getting his first hit in 26 attempts.

Ethan forgets to build a model of an atom for a science project. Panicking in the classroom, he impulsively points to one hanging up that, as far as he can tell, doesn't have a name on it and says, "That's mine." His teacher turns it around to reveal the name of the student who made it on the other side. Ethan gets a zero, and we get a call from school. We make him build the atom out of styrofoam and pipe cleaners anyway, for no credit other than showing the teacher his work. After he does this, and talks to his teacher, it's over. Forgiven. Forgotten, even though his grade drops, and he barely scrapes by with a C. Should we, would we be stricter with a student who wasn't an athlete? Would we, would I be less forgiving? Is it the ADHD, or the focus on and prioritizing of sports? Ethan is like a sponge, absorbing all the time and attention we're willing to dish out his way. And it's not just the positive attention he gets from baseball. It's the negative attention he gets as well, when we get on him to spend more than 15 minutes on his homework, to read something besides what he has to for school, to get the grades he's capable of, instead of settling for grades that will just get him by. But he blows all this off, keeping his energy and attention focused in one direction only, to our frustration and chagrin.

It is the last game of the season. Robbie, DeeJai, and Kyle are all moving on to all-stars, competing for the state championship and, if they get so far, on to nationals. Ethan has gotten more hits. He's finally figured out how to swing these bats, how to get the big barrel around to meet the ball, and Rob has moved him up from the bottom to bat seventh in the lineup. He's also gotten some time at first base. But he hasn't pitched a lick. He's been begging Rob, and he's thrown a number of bullpens with Rob either catching or watching. He hasn't thrown well enough to convince Rob he's ready. But he's been promised a chance to pitch anyway, and he's warming up now.

There's a wide concrete walkway at the Pony League fields that connects all the fields to the parking lot, and on either side of the walk are the pitching mounds for warm ups and bullpens. I'm standing on the walkway watching Ethan loosen up, nodding my head as he throws. Everything looks right. The ball ends up in the catcher's glove. The sun is shining. The world is good. It's time for Ethan to show what he can do.

It doesn't work out quite that way. Ethan manages one out, and gives up 5 runs on three hits and three walks. He can't keep his pitches in the Pony League strike zone, and when he does they hit it. He walks off the mound after the fifth run scores, disconsolate, head down, hitting his leg with his glove. Rob takes him to the side. "Son," he says, "you want to pitch you work hard over the summer and try again this fall. This wasn't the end of the world. You'll get another chance. Now quit crying and get out of here." Ethan nods at Rob and wipes the sweat, and the tears, off his face. Season over. It's summertime.

𝔇

During the summer Ethan's standard week includes a pitching lesson, batting cages, long toss, soft toss, weighted balls and fielding drills. Our lives, even in the hot offseason, revolve around the stitches of a baseball.

I have often wondered, since shortly after Ethan's first season playing baseball, what it would be like to have a child involved in an activity they loved, but in which they didn't excel. I know this sounds arrogant and condescending, but it's not meant to be. I realized, early on, that when it came to Ethan getting a fair shake I had it easy. I never had to worry about his playing time. He got his time in the field.

He got his at-bats. I was never one of the parents in the bleachers who complained that my boy wasn't getting to play at first when he was obviously better than the boy stationed there. It's a joy, a snap, to parent a child who's always a success. When the attaboys come regularly, when the kid, in the most clichéd manner, steps up to the plate and gets the big hit more often than not, it's easy to overlook the bumbling errors, the mistakes, the strikeouts amidst the spotlight of expected heroism.

What does it mean, to help your child reach their potential? And what is potential? Is it what they can become if given the chance, or what's already in them that we as parents encourage them to release? And is it the one, or the few, or the many things they're really good at? Is it promoting the obvious skill, or helping the child become well rounded, capable in all the areas that life demands? Is it better to be great at one thing, or good at many? These were questions I was asking as Ethan focused all his energy on baseball, and more and more was becoming so much that I wasn't.

Ethan made it easy to praise him, easy to minimize all the little disasters, all the sacrifices, all the mistakes. I sacrificed faith, but gained recognition through him. He got by with minimal effort in school where I'd excelled, but he made it up, somehow, with a key hit. Would I have rather he did well at both? Sure, but it was easier to slough off the lack of effort in one area for the excessive effort in another.

Do we pay more attention to the child who excels or the problem child? What do you do if both are combined in one, as Ethan was, the star athlete with ADHD? How much attention do you focus on one child? Do we find ourselves attracted to, feeding off the light reflected by our kids? I know I did. And is the aphrodisiac enough to cause us to ignore, or if not ignore, lessen our attention to others? The sad example I have to look at is with my own children.

I am a member of the over involved parenting generation, and whether this is augmented by my being a doting Jewish parent, or is simply a reaction to my own parents, who were not nearly so involved, I don't know. But I have always been preoccupied with my childrens' development and activities to a heightened (some would say extreme) degree. I don't want any of them ever saying or thinking their dad wasn't involved, didn't care, didn't know who they were or what they were about. So I have gone to all the school plays in the middle of the day and helped with homework assignments at night. I praise the art projects and schlep them to and from afterschool play dates. I wake up early to make breakfasts, and if I don't, I feel terribly guilty. I go shopping for prom dresses with my daughter and Halloween costumes with my youngest son. I have tried to do it all, but in my heart I know it still doesn't compare to the time and attention I've given Ethan. And while I'm still not sure what I would change, or if I'd be willing to have given any of it up, I know I feel uncomfortable about the attention Ethan has sucked up, and though I don't think my other children feel neglected or less than, I can't help but wonder, and kick myself in the process.

I've spent more time at baseball practices than I have with my daughter Jerica, watching her dress up and dance the part of a red red robin, swim competitively and learn to speed skate, all with complete joy, showing some potential, but a lack of serious interest as well, abandoning them when they veered beyond fun and into the boredom of practice and repetition. Even when she found her true loves — horseback riding and lacrosse — and began to show real talent at both, we were loathe to make the same, or even a similar commitment to her that we made to Ethan and baseball. Are there rationalizations we can make? Is it more fun to watch a baseball game than to sit in a chlorine-filled gym waiting for four hours for your daughter to swim a 30 second race? Does it feel more like an obligation to help your daughter tack up a horse, when you first had to overcome your fear of being crushed, bitten, or stepped on by a 900 pound animal, when you can sit in the bleachers and carouse with other fathers, complaining about the bad umpiring, critiquing the inexplicable coaching decisions, praising the amazingly unexpected play by the player at second while the game takes place in front of you? It's almost not fair.

I ask myself what it would be like to have a child play a sport, enjoy it, but be average. It's something I haven't experienced. It's simple magnanimity to say to someone, "It doesn't matter if he bats fourth or fifth," when you know everyone else thinks he should. It's not a problem to keep your mouth shut with the coach when you know your kid's going to get what he wants. I had it easy in one respect. I never had to concern myself with Ethan's playing time, with his importance to the team. I could sit back and bask in the glow. But when everything is in doubt, and the doubt starts to gnaw, and you wonder what you're in it for, that's the real hurt. That's the most frustrating situation of all, and until Pony League, I'd been able to avoid it.

I can only wonder about all the children who rely solely on their parents' love to see them through because they don't get it from the outside world, all the children who depend on their parents adoration and attention, and I wonder what happens when it's not there, when they get dropped off and left at the field, when no one watches but the coach, when no one stays to play catch with them until the other players arrive, when no one showers them with positive reinforcement because they're not great, they're just ok. The kid who's average, the kid with uninvolved parents get lost, remain hidden, unseen. A kid like Ethan, between the positive attention he earned and the negative attention he brought down upon himself and my doting – Ethan was in the spotlight all the time.

I never had to be in it for the sheer joy of playing, not since Ethan was six years old. There was always an added bonus because he got to shine. I knew parents whose boy played for the sake of playing. I knew a lot of them. But I didn't understand them, and I still didn't understand them when Ethan struggled, because I wasn't sure what was going on. It was as if a cloud had descended on him, hiding the base paths, blurring his direction, my own clarity of purpose. I didn't know if he'd maxed out, if he'd reached his abilities' limits, if he was poised to make a leap, or if this was a test, something he had to overcome.

Ethan always had his detractors. He was slow (to which I responded, "yes but he hits the ball far"). His footwork was bad (but he makes the big plays). He could catch the balls thrown right at him, but ask him to pedal backwards to catch a pop fly and you were in trouble (but he makes the routine plays). And his distractibility makes him a challenge, at times, to coach. He talks too much. His doesn't pay attention. But it was impossible, up until his first season in Pony League, to deny the fact that he was an important player on the team. And I was the first to let everyone know. His exploits were always on the tip of my tongue. He was a good hitter. He threw the ball hard. He was a very good (little league) pitcher. And I could sit back and, if not bask in the afterglow, at least settle in and get a damned good tan. I could relax with my hands behind my head, a beatific smile on my face, and wait for the handshakes and accolades. "Tell Ethan great job today!" "You must be really proud." It was part of a dad's job, and his reward, to get congratulations from other parents when his son did well. It also felt, in a participatory way, gratifying, as if the accomplishment were part mine.

Now the shoe was on the other foot, and I didn't like the way it fit. I didn't know what to do with the message, "Go work over the summer and come back and try again next year." I didn't know what Ethan would do, or what he was capable of doing. Up until this point it had all been a natural progression. He kept growing. We kept playing catch, going to the batting cages, and he had done well – against limited competition. I had watched him progress. In fact, since the time he was about 7 and I was self-employed and in control of my own schedule I had watched nearly every practice he went to, sitting on the sidelines with the other dads in the late afternoon shade. Pat thought watching boys practice was ridiculous. It wasn't even playing, wasn't real, was a total waste of time But I enjoyed it more than almost anything else I did, and I could do as much business on my cell phone from a ball field as I could from an office or car. And besides, by the time I dropped him off and went home, I only had an hour to kill before I had to turn around and pick him up, so why not enjoy watching the boys work on their games? More particularly, watch Ethan. Make sure he worked hard, stayed focused, didn't goof around too much. But now it was summer, intensely hot, steaming, three shirt a day summer, and there are no baseball games except what's on TV. And Ethan has been challenged to get better.

I am no help. As much as we do together, Ethan has realized I have taken him as far as I can. We can play catch. He can even throw bullpens with me, but I can't make him better. When we go to the batting cages he gets angry if I make a recommendation. And I'm full of recommendations. You're dropping your hands. You're opening up too early. Get your hands back. Lock and load. Spread your feet further apart. Bring them closer together. Check your hands. Do you have the right grip? Keep your head down. Keep your eyes on the ball. I comment on virtually every swing, and at 20 balls a token x 10 rounds that's 200 comments per batting session. I think I'm being productive. In hindsight, I can see that Ethan was acting in self-defense, and what I really needed to do was shut up and step out of the picture. Any kid who says yessir to everything their dad says, takes in everything and tries to make adjustments would short out their baseball circuitry.

"Dad, zip it."

"Dad, please, can you just let me hit?"

"Dad, you promised you wouldn't say another word."

And, after getting into it one more time at the cages and stomping off to a silent ride home in the car, I did what any good parent would do. I got lucky.

Ethan spends the summer working hard with a pitching and hitting coach I found who, I was told, had been in the majors (though I could never find anything on line to confirm that was true). Ethan works on his stance, his control. He changes his changeup and learns how to throw a sort of half slider, thrown like you throw a football, one that's not supposed to hurt his elbow. He practices almost every day, hitting in batting cages, hitting off the tee. He throws bullpens with me, and I can see the improvement. His percentage of strikes is up. He hits his spots more often. High. Low. Inside. Outside. Not consistently. Not yet, but he's gaining the control Rob demands.

Something happens the next season, Ethan's second with Rob. A switch has been flicked on inside me, and I can't turn it off. Ethan's hitting again, and I can't shut up. After every at bat, good or bad, I try to contain myself, but can't. I have something to say to him. Something comes boiling out. I pace behind the wire mesh dugout until I get his attention. "Ethan," I say. Sometimes he ignores me. Sometimes he moves away. Sometimes he turns his head and says, impatiently, "What, dad?" And I tell him. If the first pitch is good go ahead and swing. You're a little late. That's why you got under that ball. You're dropping your hands again. You need to be more still. I have a million things I could say, and I hope one of them, any of them stick. Then I sit back down, wait until something happens, and an insight, something important, something he has to know that will help him boils up inside and gushes out until I connect it to him. I'm not the only dad who does this, but I'm one of the worst.

When I don't go over to him, he motions to me. He puts his hand to his mouth like a baby sucking on a bottle, indicating he's thirsty and needs a Gatorade. He mouths, "I'm hungry," and I go to the concession stand for cheeseburgers. When the game is done I help him collect his stuff, make sure everything is back in his baseball bag. Ethan can lose anything. We go through baseball gloves like water. Ethan teaches me what to say whenever he loses or misplaces a glove, because he knows how angry I get and how he explodes back at me.

"Just say, 'I'm sure you'll find it somewhere, Ethan,'" he tells me, and that becomes my catch phrase. I grab his bag so he doesn't have to carry it all the way to the car when he's tired and sweaty. Sometimes he insists on doing the carrying, but more often than not he's glad to let me be his valet. His bitch. I buy into the part. It fits me well.

♢

I am shouting instructions to Ethan from the stands. Rob has asked me privately not to do this. He's told me he's the coach, not me. He will make the changes or adjustments in Ethan's game. But I have forgotten or ignored what Rob has said. Ethan is up to bat, and I am shouting out instructions about his hitting stance and where his hands should be while he's in the box taking practice swings. I want him to swing level, not loopy. I want him to throw his hands out. I want him to take every practice swing seriously. I want him focused all the time. I want him to perform at a level that's unattainable, especially for an eleven year old. Rob calls time. He's coaching third base and he's stopped the game. He's angry, red faced, and shouts out. "If you don't stop coaching your son he can join you in the stands!" I shrink, shrivel up like a raisin wearing a baseball cap. I can't look anyone in the eye. I take up as little space as I can. I hunch over, huddled into a ball. Parents are staring at me, nodding at Rob. They can't believe he had the nerve to call me out publicly, but I don't see a hint of disagreement on any face. If anything, there's relief. Rob turns around and goes back to coaching first.

"I'd just had enough," Rob later says when I go up to apologize.

What I failed to realize then, and what took me many more years to really understand, was that there are two kinds of pressure in sports and life: internal and external. The internal pressures exist within the confines of the game, the field, the individual's mind, what we put on ourselves and how we cope with it. They are the pressures to perform when called upon, to do what you've practiced when you're up to bat, or onstage, or making a business pitch at an important meeting. And when you reach that point, either you're prepared or you're not, confident or scared, passive or aggressive, focused or confused. It's all about how you handle the moment, what you've brought to the plate.

The external pressure is what others try to impose on you the moment you're in the spotlight, and nothing anyone says at that point in time can truly affect how you do, other than make you worse. No directions, no hints, no last second drills or advice will change what you've prepared yourself to do. A pitch won't gain velocity. A swing won't transform. A mental state will not suddenly sharpen. Every parent who thinks they can have this kind of impact on the child who's about to perform is mistaken. Saying anything more than "go get them" falls on, if not deaf ears, then a body that can't incorporate what's being thrown at it, no matter how much it might want to. I didn't know that. I thought I could change Ethan in mid-swing. Not only wasn't it my job, it wasn't within my power. But I was the dad. I thought I had the right. Rob was the first person with the balls to tell me I didn't. It was a lesson I didn't learn overnight. It took years.

It is the middle of July, 2001, and Ethan is on the Orlando Pony League's Mustang All-Star team. For the first time in several years Orlando has won its way to the state semi-finals. Rob's team, Rossi's Pizza, has gone undefeated for the second season in a row. They are a combined 33-0, finally losing in a best team tournament to a powerhouse out of Tampa. During the spring season the pitching foursome of Robbie Haben, Deejai Oliver, Kyle Meredith, and Ethan have been dominating. Ethan has not allowed a run scored in fifteen innings covering five of the team's 17 spring games. All four of the boys make the all-star team, with Rob as head coach.

The Orlando SAY All-Stars have made it into the district finals with one loss. They have to beat West Volusia twice in a row to advance. They win the first game, and Rob tells the boys to relax in the shade and go have a hot dog and soda on him. All the boys get their food and drinks and sit down together. All except one. Rob hears the ping of a bat, and looks down to the far end of the ballfield where a tee and net are set up, and sees me doing soft toss with Ethan. While every other boy is resting, I have Ethan taking batting practice.

"This is just plain bullshit," Rob says to the group of parents milling around the concession stand, and marches off towards us.

I see him coming and think he'll be happy Ethan's getting some extra batting practice. I smile and say, "We just wanted to work on a few things before the next game," but Rob is not smiling. He scowls at me.

"Ethan is part of this team and he needs to be with the other boys resting." He storms away with Ethan jogging beside him. I am left with a baseball in my hand, a bucket of balls and Ethan's bat, which I dutifully, embarrassingly lug back with me.

The team wins the second game, and methodically plows their way through the state tournament field into the semis. Kyle Meredith is pitching. He has done well against a very tough team, but now the score is 6-5 in the fifth inning of a six-inning game, and the bases are loaded against us with no outs. Rob puts Ethan in to pitch.

With no room for error, Ethan steps on the mound. It's a sweltering summer evening. The lights are on, and if you look up you can see the swarms of moths and mosquitoes circling around the hot lamps. The Seminole Pony League fields are surrounded by swamp and wetlands, and the recommended equipment for all players and parents includes water bottles, sunscreen, and insect repellant.

Ethan does better in cooler weather. He sweats when he walks, when he breathes, and now I can see the perspiration beading on his forehead and dripping down his nose. He wipes his face, stares at the batter and sticks his tongue out of the side of his mouth, a la Michael Jordan. He's unaware he even does this, but it's become a trademark of his pitching. He strikes out the first batter on four good pitches. He's throwing hard. His two-seam is moving and his changeup is deceptive.

On an 0-1 pitch the next batter hits the ball sharply to center field. The runner on third prepares to tag up to score the tying run, but Cody Large, our center fielder, catches the ball and releases it quickly, making a spectacular throw right over Ethan's head to the catcher. The runner holds. Two outs. The next batter fights. He fouls off several balls, works the count to 2-2. Ethan rears back and throws his fastest pitch of the night, down at the knees, on the outside corner of the plate. The batter gets his bat on the ball, but it's a routine grounder to second. Inning over. Ethan comes off the field holding his left elbow. I don't know what's wrong, but I know something is. He talks to Rob, who puts him back on first the next inning. Robbie pitches to close the game. We win, but Ethan is out for three weeks with a hyperextended elbow.

Rossi's loses in the finals the next night to a Tampa team with Jaimie and Petey, two of the biggest, strongest, most highly touted ten year olds in Florida. Petey has already been featured in Sports Illustrated as the best ten-year old player in the country. During the game he hits a home run that not only clears the fence of the field we're playing on, but the far fence of the baseball field behind us. None of us have ever seen a ball hit so far by a ten-year old. The final score isn't even close.

◯

That fall, after that third season with Rob, the boys move up from Mustang to Bronco division, to a larger field and new teams. I fully expect Rob, who moves up to coach Broncos as well, to select Ethan in the Pony League draft, but he doesn't. He has a choice between Ethan and another pitcher, and he goes with the other boy. Ethan is scooped up by a first time coach and a new team. I am stunned. Ethan is no longer with Rob. I hear through the grapevine that Rob just thought the other pitcher was better than Ethan. Maybe, but I know now that Rob was not only choosing a different player, he was choosing a different parent. He was not choosing me.

Rob told me, years later, "You might have missed some of the "enjoyment" of just watching the baseball games Ethan played in. You were very focused on Ethan's performance - performance meaning each pitch he threw, each at bat he had, each play in the field he made. Sometimes it seemed like you lived or died with every moment of Ethan's activity. I don't think you realized the "effort" portion of Ethan's play as opposed to just reacting to the results of Ethan's play. I have also been guilty of this myself, so I do understand how this can happen though. You were trying to set the bar high all the time and some times it just can not be met."

◯

We are driving to a game, hurtling down Interstate 4 through downtown Orlando. We're late, and Ethan is scheduled to pitch. I am trying to talk to him about his hitting. I think he is too inconsistent, and tries any approach that anyone recommends - besides me. Hands lower. Hands higher. Stand straighter. Bend over the plate. Feet spread more. Feet closer together. I'm trying to get him to listen to me as I

55

explain the importance of doing the same thing right over and over, but he won't have any of it. I want him to pick his stance, pick the place he stands to hit. He says he's fine. He says there's nothing wrong with his hitting. He wants me to leave him alone. He yells at me to stop going on about how he hits. "I went two for three last game, Dad. What are you complaining about?"

But that last at bat, I'm thinking, could have been so much better. You were shifting around. You weren't mentally prepared. You got under the ball and hit a weak pop fly. I shout back at him. We're trying to "out loud" one another. He's yelling over me and I'm yelling at him, trying to get him to shut up and listen. All I want him to do is hear me out, and all he wants is for me to stop. We both lose.

Then, as if in response to our escalating anger, one of my rear tires blows, and we pull off the highway, frightened, chastised, silent. We're not going to make it to the game, and Ethan is terribly, unconsolably angry. Somehow the flat tire is my fault, and we start to get into it again. Miraculously, as if it were an angel sent by God, a Road Ranger, a service vehicle funded by the state, pulls up behind us. We both grow quiet, and in less than 15 minutes he has us back on the road. We make it to the Pony League fields with minutes to spare before game time. Ethan insists on taking batting practice before stepping onto the field. He and I run over to a tee for him to hit into a net. He hits quickly, furiously, and one of the balls bounces back and hits him in the mouth. His lip is cut, his mouth is full of blood, but he ignores it, runs over to his catcher to warm up before he has to go out and pitch. Then he runs onto the field, wiping the blood off his lips. It's obvious to me he's having a hard time concentrating. I can almost see his heart pounding its way out of his chest. He lasts two innings, pitches erratically, walks four, and the coach pulls him. Lesson learned. Stress doesn't help when a calm, commanding presence is required. We drive home without speaking, without looking at each other after the game.

The season ends abysmally. We are one of the worst teams in the league. Ethan is our best pitcher, but he is eleven in a league of eleven and twelve year olds, and the adjustments to a bigger field, a longer distance from the pitcher's mound to home, and a new team have taken their toll. Boys are bigger, faster, stronger. Many have hit their first growth spurt. Ethan throws the ball a respectable 60 mph, but there are twelve year olds clocking in the mid to upper 70s. This is Florida Pony League Baseball, after all.

Even so, Ethan is selected to the All-Star team, but the B team, not the A. And we have begun to hear about another level of play, the cream of the crop, so to speak, where only a handful of players get to go. It's not a league you join. It's a private selection to one of an elite, limited number of teams. It's like playing on a team of all-stars all the time. It's known as travel ball, and it's run nationally by the Amateur Athletic Union (AAU). I've only heard hints about it, spoken in whispers around the league. Supposedly there have been coaches with AAU teams scouting some of the boys at Pony. You have to be exceptional. You have to be asked. I'm wondering, of course, why Ethan hasn't been.

During the course of the all-star tournament Ethan is spotted during a game in which he pitches four shutout innings and goes two for four with a double and a home run. He gets noticed. Tony Moore, the coach of the Orlando Rock AAU team, invites him to play with them that spring. We jump at the chance.

CHAPTER 3
Have Ball Will Travel

The word that best describes AAU baseball is commitment. Money commitment. Time commitment. This is not league ball, where you pay a small seasonal fee and play all your games at a few home fields. This is travel ball, where each season the expenses run into the hundreds, sometimes thousands of dollars, and every weekend you play tournaments or double headers, and there are hours long practices two to three times a week, and the travel takes you anywhere in the country you can imagine.

The first practice with the Rock opens our eyes. In Little League you played with neighborhood boys who dreamt of being ballplayers. In Pony League you played within a bigger neighborhood concept, with better ballplayers in a more competitive environment, but it was still league ball, where anyone could play, so every team had kids who wanted to be but just weren't very good. Now we are part of a select group, where the players are hand picked to fill positions, and for the first time Ethan is on a team without a weakness. The outfielders run down fly balls and catch them. The infielders turn double plays regularly, easily. They make plays behind Ethan when he is on the mound. Hitters hit. Pitchers pitch. It's an inspiring group of eleven year olds.

The daunting part of AAU play is that we have no home. Leagues have home fields. We have each other. We struggle to find a place to practice, and wind up on a rocky, weedy, unkempt ball field behind a church off a major highway. It's the only field our coach can find for us to use on a regular basis.

Ethan still hasn't learned how to really run. In one hitting practice he hits a ball deep into the outfield. As he runs around the bases he is tagged out, not once, but a half dozen times by his teammates. It's the team joke. Ethan is the only kid who can turn a triple into a single.

We travel wherever games and tournaments take us - to Tampa, Sarasota, Winter Haven, Lakeland, Daytona, Gainesville. We spend nights, weekends on the road, fathers and sons huddled together, snoring under thin sheets with freezing, rattling air conditioning units in the windows of La Quinta Inns and Fairfield Inns and Holiday Inns, anywhere the group rates are less than $50/night and the rooms come with a breakfast buffet.

Unbeknownst to us, we have joined AAU baseball at its zenith, its peak of popularity and prestige. Until this point there have been a few choice teams, and membership on any of them puts you in a highly elite category, a group of ball players with potential, the ones who have a chance to star in high school, play in college, and dream of what lies beyond. Over the course of the next few years, however, a fundamental change occurs within the national organization. It becomes the dumping ground for disgruntled dads. Every father who gets upset at the way he or his son have been treated by local leagues, be they Little, or Pony, or Babe Ruth, every parent and child who have been caught by the favoritism and the politics of youth baseball, or shortchanged in some way, forms his own AAU team. There are no talent-level requirements to do this. All it takes is the time, the money, filling out the forms and joining, and the organization swells its ranks, going from a tightly knit group of the best, to myriad teams with a wide range of talent. This all takes place between 2000-2005, and ushers in both the pinnacle of AAU baseball and its demise. But for now, Ethan is happy on the Rock.

Baseball truly is America's game, not because of its popularity, which pales in comparison to football and basketball, but because it is everywhere, in every hidden nook and cranny and outpost of the country. There are ball fields tucked everywhere, not just in cornfields, but in backyards and by landfills and citrus packing plants. Wherever there is excess acreage, it seems, someone has decided to put a ball field or two. And that's where we play. That's what we discover each weekend when we play a doubleheader or a tournament somewhere in the state.

In one of the first tournaments of the season the Rock make it all the way to the final game which, because of rain delays and the length of games, doesn't start until 11 p.m. on Sunday night. These boys all have school the next day, and a one to two hour drive home, but no one has left. No one has packed up and said, "Enough. School and sleep are more important." Including us, though Pat is begging me to leave. She thinks it's crazy. She thinks this is nuts. It's a cold night. We're playing in 45 degree weather with a strong wind. We're wearing thin clothes, a lucky few shivering in sweaters and sweatshirts. The boys are freezing cold. We go through the hot chocolate and coffee at the concession stand until they run out. But Ethan is the starting pitcher in the final. How can we possibly leave?

"Are we out of our minds?" my wife asks me rhetorically. She is furious. "Are all these people nuts? Don't their kids have school tomorrow? Do you realize what you're putting us all through? Where are their priorities? Where are ours?"

And the truth is, I do realize it, and it doesn't matter. I ignore my family's needs, prioritize baseball over sleep, school, health. We argue until game time, and then it's too late. Ethan is on the mound. He struggles through three innings, and is replaced by Richard W., a skinny, blonde ball player with a good fastball. Richard pitches well. We win, and I drive home happy at 1 a.m., after the awards ceremony, thawing out while Pat, Ethan, my daughter and our bundled up baby all fall asleep huddled together in the back seat. My wife mutters grudgingly to me. In her mind there is no doubt this wasn't worth it. Today, no one has any idea what tournament it was or who we played.

⚾

The Rock make it out of their bracket – barely – in a tournament near the end of the season. All the big teams are here. To get out of our bracket we have to beat the Windermere Wildcats who are loaded with future stars – Chris Talladay (future University of Central Florida player), a catcher, infielder and a solid right handed hitter; Jabari Henry (future Florida Atlantic University player), a big, strong, fast kid whose father played in the NBA. Jabari is good at everything but great at nothing, and his coaches don't know where to play him. He pitches, catches, plays short, outfield, without concentrating on any one. He is one of the most feared right-handed hitters in Central Florida.

I entertain my daughter by walking her down to an adjacent pig farm between games to watch pigs wallow in dark Florida mud. She loves it. "It's a baseball zoo!" she tells me delightedly. She doesn't want to leave, squealing with the pigs as they roll around, snorting and seemingly smiling at her. But I know the next game is due to start soon, and my anxiety rises as I take her by the hand and lead her unwillingly away.

The Rock squeak by somehow and now, in the shadow of a massive county sewer plant with huge white containers looming over the field, play the Central Florida Mustangs in the first elimination game. The Mustangs - the 2001 national 10-under champions with a host of great players including a 10 year old with perhaps the best baseball name in the country: Beau Glorious. Winning an AAU national championship is a rare feat, playing through a weeklong tournament and beating the best teams in the country, and the Mustangs did it with this team just last season.

Ethan starts against them. He keeps them off balance with his changeup, and his fastball is moving with a lefty tail that weaves and dances around the plate. The Rock is winning 1-0. He is almost unhittable. But the game is seven innings long, and Ethan gets taken out after having thrown 81 pitches through six. The Rock can't hold the lead, losing 6-1 in the seventh. Whispers riffle through the tournament about his performance. Parents come up to me afterwards and tell me they heard how well Ethan threw. It is, in a way, his AAU coming out party. That summer the Mustangs go on to be runner-ups nationally as 11 year olds.

The Rock play in the state tournament and win the first two games of their bracket, but then run into a buzz saw called the North Florida Hurricanes from Jacksonville. They have a righthanded pitcher who throws harder than anyone we've seen with a big curveball no one can touch. A few years later he has elbow surgery at age 14. Ethan pitches and struggles with a low, tight strike zone. He can't keep the ball at the knees and gives up four runs. Richard comes in and pitches well, but the Rock lose 4-2, and we head home for the summer. A few weeks later we hear that several of the better players have bolted the Rock and joined a new team made up of half the members of the Florida Sun Devils, one of the best teams in the state. We don't know what this means for us or the Rock, but then I get a phone call from the dad of one of the departed players with the same invitation. Join us. The Rock is falling apart. The other three players who are leaving, Rafi Gonzalez, Jordan Mays and Jordan Dailey, are Ethan's friends. Rafi was the Rock's shortstop, Jordan Mays played with him in Pony League, and Jordan Dailey is the catcher/junk ball pitcher/third baseman on the team. I leave it up to Ethan, and for him there's no doubt. Ethan says go, and we leave for Team Easton.

We were at a point in time when the investment in Ethan's baseball had begun to spiral upward. It wasn't just the equipment, though every year there was another pitching glove ($100+), first baseman's glove ($100+), big barrel bat ($200+). It was the team fees ($1,000+ over two seasons), travel (hotels, meals - $2,000+), and private lessons ($2,500+). Without blinking, without taking everything else into consideration (uniforms, laundry, baseballs, tournament admission fees), we were spending more than $6,000/year on an 11-year old's pastime. And that doesn't include lost work time, lost family time, lost opportunities elsewhere. I had taken on a second profession – managing my son's career, and it was sucking me dry.

Just as he switched teams, Ethan switched private coaches and schools. He moved from his first hitting/pitching instructor to Todd Bellhorn, a lefthanded pitcher who played at the University of Central Florida and was Ethan's first real pitching instructor. Todd was the brother of Mark Bellhorn, a second baseman who played from 1997-2007 with the Red Sox, Cubs, Athletics, Padres and Rockies. Todd started each lesson with games, then mechanics, then simulated pitching to batters. Throwing to the head was 2 points, chest 3, waist 5, knees 3, game to 20. Ethan began to develop a new level of consistency and control, and I took him to nearly every lesson in Oviedo - a 45 minute drive - staying to watch every pitch he threw.

He also left the small, private Jewish school we'd had him in since kindergarten and went to Lake Highland Preparatory School, an 1800 student K-12 on a sprawling college-like campus with a full fledged baseball program, whose head baseball coach was Cy Young Award winning lefthanded pitcher Frank Viola. As a sixth grader Ethan made the middle school team, pitching well enough on a regular sized field to become the number 3 pitcher on the team. He set a school hitting record by starting the season 12 for 12, finishing with the second highest batting average ever at Lake Highland – a hair under .700. He also almost set a school record in futility for getting thrown out at first from every field – left, center, and right. The longer base paths coupled with Ethan's speed handicapped him if he hit the ball too hard and it got to the outfield too quickly. In one game he was thrown out at first after hitting a line drive to right, and then the same thing happened when the center fielder threw him out after stopping a sharply hit ball. His last at bat he hit the ball to left and beat the throw by a step. It was a feat of comic proportions - hitting prowess combined with turtle-like speed.

I began to feel a bit biblical in my commitment to Ethan. He was becoming Esau to my other children's Jacob. He was the hunter who killed the big game and brought it to the table, spiced with recognition and served steaming hot with the gravy of glory. I was the blind father who nodded appreciatively and looked around the table, seeing no one else with my limited sight. I loved them no less, but it didn't seem that way to the rest of the world, and I worried that it didn't seem that way to them.

I had two families. One consisted of my wife, daughter, and youngest son. That was my normal family. We had dinners together. We did homework. We went to movies and took bike rides. We wrestled. This family was sweet, funny, and managing them was a cinch. Except when it came to baseball. I was either gone or dragged everyone with me, and Gabriel, our youngest, learned to hate every hot afternoon game, every double-header, every tournament. He hated sitting around trying to get my attention while I kept score and counted pitches. He hated sweating in the sun, trying to find a cool shaded spot under someone's tent or umbrella. He hated the waiting, and he had no interest in watching. I bribed him with blow-pops and cheeseburgers and hoped that other children would be there, bored like him, ready and willing to play.

My second family was me and E.

I built a pitcher's mound in the front yard and had Ethan throw bullpens with me twice a week. Our house was known as "the house with the clay hill in front." I had a net set up in the backyard where he took batting practice and hit off a tee, which I oversaw, setting the balls on the tee and counting the good swings. I drove him to and from practice twice a week, now with Team Easton an hour away in Kissimmee, and I drove him to the weekend games and tournaments, staying with him when we had to spend nights in hotels.

Managing Ethan was anything but easy. In hotel rooms like a slug he left a trail of slime behind him. Stinking baseball clothes on the floor. Socks under the bed. Underwear thrown on the wet bathroom floor. He unpacked his duffel bag by dumping its contents out on the floor by his bed. Toothpaste and toothbrush dumped in the sink. He snored like a jackhammer, and the volume increased as the night wore on. Wherever we went he lost something. Whenever we left home he forgot something. I would go through his stuff and everything would seem in place, until we arrived at the hotel and I realized he wasn't wearing any shoes, nor had he packed anything besides his cleats. Or he'd leave his cleats, and I'd have to ask another parent who was arriving later to drive by our house and pick up the pair of $75 shoes he outgrew or tore through every season.

"We have to figure out how to be more balanced with the kids," my wife exhorted. "You spend 80% of your time with Ethan and 20% with the rest of us."

"You're right," I replied. "I'll make things even out. I'll take Jerica to more horseback riding lessons. I swear I will." Then I'd look at my calendar and recant.

"Except for this week. He's got a lesson and a midweek game. I'll start next week." And she'd roll her eyes and walk away, falling back into old patterns as she managed the two younger while I watched Ethan play ball.

Team Easton is mostly a team of working class and Hispanic boys, and Ethan. Fathers who work in warehouses, for UPS, for masonry suppliers, truck drivers and mothers who are secretaries, nurses, bookkeepers, front desk clerks at hotels. Three families besides us are wealthier. One father is a doctor from the Philippines, one owns several auto body repair shops, and one is a banker. The banker, Craig Hazen, is the coach. The repair shop owner is the money behind the team. Half the team is Puerto Rican. Ethan, the big lefty Jew, fits right in. He hangs with the working class boys easier than the rich snobs at his previous and current school. They accept him for what he can do on the field, and forgive him when he opens his mouth and says something unedited, unexpurgated, unnecessary, which they soon realize is a regular event. I mutter, yell, holler at Ethan from the stands. He yells, hollers, banters from the dugout. Both our voices buzz constantly, counterweights to one another, his for his team, mine for him.

The fall season proceeds unspectacularly. I still can't keep my mouth shut, but I'm not the only one on this team obsessed with my kid (though I may be the worst). Every dad talks to every other. Why isn't my boy higher up in the batting order? Why is he sitting so many innings on the bench? What's Craig thinking about by playing so and so ahead of my son, when everyone knows my boy is the better infielder? Why hasn't so and so been given a chance to pitch more? One bad outing doesn't mean he can't throw the ball.

This is my introduction to high level Bleacher Ball, the standard non-etiquette banter between dads who believe they know their sons better, see them more clearly, and understand the game and its subtleties with greater acumen than whoever might be coaching at that moment. Sandy Koufax could be the pitching coach, Mickey Mantle could be working with the hitters, and Tony LaRussa and Billy Martin could make the lineups and strategize together, and dads would still second guess them. I join in when the conversation isn't in Spanish. Craig may not be the world's greatest baseball coach, but he's a bright and decent guy with good enough baseball sense to put this group of boys on a field together, and boy can they play ball.

That first season together is a feeling out process. Ethan cements his spot on the team. When he's not pitching he's on first. Almost everyone pitches. Our centerfielder, Alex Burgos, is another lefty with a great arm from the outfield and a huge curveball. Josh Hazen pitches and plays first, third and outfield. Frances Halili, our Filipino, is another lefthanded pitcher and outfielder. Mirko Filippi, a boy with movie star good looks and silky moves on the field, plays second base and pitches. George's son Nelson, or Nellie, is a boxer, a baseball player, and a power-hitting outfielder. And Ozzie Perez, the team's starting shortstop, is one of the fastest players his age I've ever seen. He makes plays in the hole seem routine. He hits for average and power. This team turns double plays without a hitch. They cut runners down at home plate from center field. They work double steals. They've jumped into prime time. This is real baseball.

All the players are asked to submit their goals in writing at the beginning of the Spring season. Ethan wrote this:

"What I would like to accomplish this season is for me to become a dominant pitcher known by almost all of the teams in Central Florida. When I come to pitch I want the kids on the opposite team to know that Bornstein is coming to the mound and that they're going to have no chance of winning. I think my fielding is very solid right now, but I would like to make more of the hard plays that take running. I want to cover more area at first base. I want to improve my running, my hitting, and try to get a better relationship with some of the guys on my team. I want to be known as a team leader who leads by example.

———
65

"What I want this team to accomplish this year is to become one of the top four teams in the state, be known throughout Florida, and I want this team to go to Cooperstown and to come back the final week for the championship. I want us to finish in the top five in that championship. I would like to win at least three tournaments and have a top three finish in all of them. I'm looking forward to this season with Team Easton. I think it's going to be the best season that this team has had and that I will have. Thanks for all the help and support.
#7 Ethan"

⚾

When spring begins, hopes run high. This team can accomplish great things. Parents are jazzed. Boys are jazzed. The team works its way through the first tournament of the season easily. Ethan pitches in the quarterfinals against the St. Pete Stingers, one of the top teams in the state. He gives up two runs in the first inning and then settles down. He handles the Stingers the rest of the way, and Easton claws its way back. The innings rush by, and the score is tied 2-2 in the seventh inning. Ethan stays in the game, and the Stingers bring in Ryan Weber.

Weber is a tall, skinny, hard throwing righty from St. Petersburg with great control. Ethan and Weber are the same age, born within days of one another. But there the similarities end. Weber is one of the most feared pitchers in the state. He looks the part. He is elegant on the mound, flowing and athletic. After he graduates from high school he gets drafted by the Atlanta Braves and signs for 8th round money. Even as a twelve year old he was called the real thing.

Ethan is still relatively unknown. He isn't exactly clumsy anymore, but there's still work to be done getting all his body parts moving in unison. He has a very high front leg kick, and where many pitchers make their motion pretty by pointing the toe of their front leg down, Ethan's points up, heel down, making it look like he's lifting a heavy load rather than gracefully gliding to the plate.

No one on Easton has ever hit Weber well, and the boys' faces show it. Dejection. Surrender. Defeat. They're hanging their heads, and look ready to hang up their gloves. Ozzie, the first batter Weber faces, works a full count and gets a walk. He steals second, steals third. A perfect bunt and Ozzie scores. Suddenly it's over. Easton wins 3-2 and we move on to the semi-finals.

Easton faces the team that has become its archrival, the Florida Scrappers, the other half of the Sun Devils, in a rain delayed, late afternoon game. Between games Chet Lemon, the ex-Detroit Tiger outfielder who now owns the AAU franchise in Florida, comes up and tells me he saw Ethan pitch and is interested in him for his team, The Orlando Juice, when Ethan turns 16.

Something has happened to the boys from the end of the game we shouldn't have won against the Stingers to the game we have a chance of winning against the Scrappers. They move slowly, lethargically. It looks like they haven't realized they have another game, maybe two, to play. The pitcher facing them, Joey Lovecchio, is another hard throwing, tall, skinny righty. There are tall skinny hard throwing righties rising out of the grass, golems sprouting out of the clay. Everywhere we turn there's another one, an overpowering right handed pitcher. Lovecchio throws well, and our defense moves as if their feet are settling into the mud on the field. A ball goes over Nelson Gonzalez's head in left. He bobbles another ball in front of him. The infield makes errors. Ethan goes 2-3 and bats in Easton's only run, but we lose 7-1 and his hitting doesn't matter, unacknowledged in defeat. Dejection sets in. After a great start the team looks like hell in that last game. Parents are frustrated. Soaked, sweaty, hot and exhausted, we pile into our cars after numerous bleacher discussions about playing kids where they don't belong, second guessing the coaches', and I drive home perturbed, full of doubts about the course of the team. My frustration grows inside me cancerously, like a weed with no room to expand. I try to talk to Ethan about how he thought the tournament went, and while he's unhappy with the last game he's fine with the rest. I, however, am not. The loss festers inside me, and by the time we get home several hours later I'm knotted up inside.

It's been a long, hot, wet, up and down weekend. Everyone at home has gone to bed. Everyone but me. I'm stewing in front of my computer. I make one of the contemporary cardinal sins borne of frustration: I hammer out an email. In it I express both my excitement and anticipation about the coming season, and my disappointment at the way the tournament ended. Part of this comes out of my own angst and upset as a dad, listening on the way home to Ethan's frustration and disappointment with the team's effort the last game. I am focused on what went wrong, and I let that spill out electronically. I address the email to George Gonzalez and Craig Hazen. I convince myself I'm doing a good deed. I write a detailed description of why I think we lost.

67

I ask questions that sound obvious, concerned, reasonable to me. Why were players out of position? Why were certain players in the outfield when players who can field better are on the bench? If the coaches want to win this season, don't they think we should put our best foot forward, give these deserving, hard working boys the best chance to win? I am referring, of course, to George's own son Nelson, who made two errors in left field. That alone didn't cost us the game.

There's almost never one play, one player, one out, that loses games. It's a team sport, and in my heart I know that. But I've lost perspective. I want to blame someone, and so I spew. I throw all my thoughts, all my corrections, spurred on by my exaggerated need to be protective of Ethan and couched in understanding and evenhandedness, into this long email. I read it and re-read it. I wonder if I should send it or wait awhile, mull it over, get some distance and maybe modify it, edit it, delete it altogether.

Then I make cardinal sin #2: Impulsively, spontaneously, I hit the send button, regretting immediately what I've done. I realize too late that I am the lunatic who just launched a preemptive nuclear strike. Who am I? Am I the same person who focused on fairness when he coached little league? Am I a fool? An idiot? I've just sent an email blaming one kid for the team's loss. And that kid is one of the team founders' sons. I can't take it back. It's gone, sent into the stratosphere of irredeemable mistakes. I back pedal immediately. What kind of damage control can I do? Nothing tonight. I go to bed, but in the morning all hell breaks loose.

I know I have to be first on the phone, so I make the calls, first to Craig.

"George and I have already spoken," he tells me, "and we've decided to let Ethan stay on the team."

"Were you thinking about kicking him off?" I asked, my voice trembling.

"Yes, we discussed not having Ethan return, but in that case we'd would be punishing the wrong person, and we want Ethan on the team. He's a good kid." He paused. "However, you, Mr. Bornstein, need to get your act together, and you need to call George and apologize right away."

George is eminently gracious, low key and levelheaded. He never raises his voice, though he does manage to make me feel more guilty than I already do.

"David, how would you feel if you got an email like that about your son?"

Shaking on the other end of the phone, I shrivel up like a snail that realizes it's about to get stepped on.

"You need to learn from your mistakes," George tells me, "and understand something. Coaches aren't perfect, but you can assume there's some reason and thought behind what happens on the field. You need to start being positive with all the boys. You've been given a second chance because of Ethan, not because of you. Got that?"

I thank George for being such a good guy, hang up the phone and realize just how close I came in my fervor to hurting Ethan and, in hurting him, hurting our relationship. I never tell him how close he was to being kicked off the team because of me. That's my burden to bear, and I don't want him looking over his shoulder worrying about what I'll do next. There can be no next.

Lessons learned: always abide by the 24-hour email rule. If there's any doubt about sending an email, wait a full 24 hours and read it again. Everyone says it, but now I've lived with the consequences of not waiting, and the scars run deep and long. And the second lesson? Get a grip. My hold on this is a lot less firm, a lot more slippery, and doesn't happen overnight. But the impression's been made, the wounds are being licked, and I'm huddled in the back of the cave, cold and alone, but grateful, deeply grateful, that I'm still part of the tribe.

That's not my last incident of the season. I wish it were, but it's not. These lessons take a long time to really sink in. In the first game of a weekend double-header Ethan strikes out in one game and looks bad doing it. He throws his helmet towards the dugout when he walks away. I watch for a reaction from the coaches, but all Craig does is shake his head. I am furious. Furious that Ethan would display such a bad temper, be such a bad sport, and furious that the coaches aren't going to teach him a lesson. Make him sit out a game. Make him apologize to the team. Do something. But I don't see it. In between games, while everyone else eats and rests, I go over to Ethan

"Come with me," I order him.

"What's wrong? What did I do?" he asks as he hustles up beside me.

"You know what you did. You're going to run poles for your bad behavior."

I point for him to get going, and he looks at me aghast, angry at his punishment, embarrassed for being singled out. He's run once across the field and is starting his second lap when Craig sees this and stops Ethan's running. Now it's Craig's turn to take me aside

Politely but slightly exasperated, he says, "Mr. Bornstein, you're not the coach. I am. If I want to discipline Ethan for bad behavior I will, but while he's out here it's not up to you."

In other words, butt out. I take a deep breath. I realize I've overstepped my bounds once again. Kick myself in the head. Pull my head out of my ass. When will I be able to step back and let go?

⚾

We're in a tournament in Clearwater and Ethan is snoring. We always stay in the least expensive hotels. Pat has stopped traveling with us, in part because she's so uncomfortable when she does. Her back hurts from the lousy mattresses on the beds. She hates the feel of the paper-thin sheets, the cheap blankets, the ratty pillows. She can't sleep because of the noisy window air conditioners. So I spend weekends away from her and our other two children on a regular basis.

And then there's Ethan's snoring. It's 3 a.m. He sounds like a freight train. I can't sleep. I turn him over. It doesn't help. I wake him up and he mumbles "Sorry," and starts to snore again, even louder. I get up, put on a pair of flip flogs and drive around for a half hour until I find an all night drug store that sells earplugs. I must look like a zombie, a drugged out wreck when I walk in, dazed, shuffling around in my flip-flops and sweatpants, mumbling about cheap sheets and snoring boys.

It's the end of the spring and it's been a good season (personal missteps excused) for Team Easton. They've won nearly all their games. Parents have bonded. Boys have bonded. Ethan's had a great time. He's come close to meeting the goals he set for the season. He's batted fourth in the lineup most of the year, is tied for the team lead in home runs and leads the team in runs batted in, has the fourth highest batting average (.390), and is the team leader in innings pitched (37) and strikeouts (46), while throwing strikes more than 60% of the time. He's also the team leader in errors by far (19), combining misplays at first with botched balls on the mound. And in a coup of sorts, he got to pitch against Rob Haben and his old friends from Pony League.

Rob's son Robbie is the opposing pitcher. Robbie pitches a good game, but on this day Ethan does better. He hits two doubles, bats in two of Easton's four runs, and controls the boys who once were all-stars ahead of him. Easton wins 4-2, and afterwards, with grace and unreserved praise, Rob comes up to Ethan, extends his hand and then grabs him around the shoulders and tells him, "Congratulations, son. You've really become a pitcher."

The pitching mound in front of our house has begun to grow grass and anthills. One night at an Easton practice I suit up in catcher's gear to catch a bullpen for Ethan, but the low lights in the pen cast shadows that cut between him and me, and I have a hard time picking up the ball. His pitches come in hard, fast, and move so much I can barely handle them. The ball bites into my glove, leaving my left hand numb and swollen. Every time he throws a pitch I'm a little scared, nervous. The ball comes in whizzing, and it dips and dives and I'm trying to adjust. Whoa whoa! I get hit in the shin, the knee. I almost take one in the crotch, and I'm not wearing a cup. I get through, but leave bruised, mentally and physically exhausted. It's the last time I ever catch him.

We're all in Sarasota for the state AAU championship tournament, and hopes, as they always do, run high. The team is in a bracket it should win handily, and parents are already looking ahead to who we'll play in the winner's rounds.

Ethan pitches in the first game, and the team we play, a local Central Florida team we have beaten three times already this year (the last with a football game-like high score), lays down bunt after bunt, something Easton hasn't practiced. Ethan mishandles them. So does the catcher. They get in each other's way. Before anyone knows it they are losing 3-0 and never get untracked. The coaches take Ethan out and put in Alex Burgos, a better fielding pitcher, but the results are the same, and they lose the game and any chance to advance. Out of the three games Easton plays, they lose two and tie one. A miserable end to the season, but one that seems almost epidemic in nature at this tournament. Another Central Florida team, the Vipers, lose their first game 1-0 on an in the park home run, which also happens to be the only hit of the game. They are eliminated. The Tampa Crush, home of super hitters Petey and Jaimie, lose a game and go home. Most of the favored teams drop a key game, and in a tournament like this, the only way to be assured of advancing is to go undefeated, and the strange losses pile up. Only the Central Florida Scrappers, who played an enormous number of games during the season, barely winning half of them against good competition, play well, and win the tournament. Another dagger in the hearts of the parents. Another craw sticking, throat choking, take it in the gut event, but one that the boys shake off by the time they're back at the hotel and swimming in the pool.

That night, our last night in the hotel, the boys vote on where they'd like to go for a final summer tournament. The choices are Burnsville, Minnesota, for the AAU National 12-under championship, or the Cooperstown Dreams Park National Invitational 12-under tournament. I want to go to Burnsville, the biggest AAU tournament for our age bracket and the last big tournament before the boys move on to regulation size fields. The boys vote to go to Cooperstown.

Sitting and voting with them are Beau Glorious, who has agreed to travel with us to the tournament, and another boy we've also picked up, a right handed pitcher and catcher named Brian Johnson, the losing pitcher for the Vipers in the one hit loss. I am told Brian is one of the best right handed players in the state. "Better than Beau?" I ask. Wait and see, I'm told.

Pat and I go to bed, leaving parents still talking and reminiscing in the lobby about what could have been. Ethan is playing in the workout room with several of his buddies from the team. About an hour later we hear a frantic knock on our door. Please get dressed. Come quick. Ethan has been hurt. We get clothes on and dash out to the lobby. Ethan sits with George's wife, a registered nurse who has his foot wrapped in a bloody bandage. He had decided to show everyone how he could moonwalk backwards on the treadmill. One of his toes got caught between the metal edge and the moving tread and nearly got torn off. I rush him to the nearest emergency room where his toe gets stitched back to his foot. Nothing nearly as serious as we might have thought, the ER doctor assures us. It'll heal good as new. Just no baseball for a couple weeks. And by the way, he played baseball when he was younger, too. His picture is hanging up....where? In the Cooperstown Dreams Park Hall of Fame. We promise to look it up when we go there later in the summer.

For two weeks prior to departing for Cooperstown, the boys on the team attend a "boot camp" run by Jesus Perez, Ozzie's father, a one-time major league prospect at shortstop whose career was cut short by injuries. After the debacle at the state tournament, the team buys into the idea of hard training and additional practice prior to their big trip. And it's summertime, so for three to four hours a day it's like an extended baseball camp, only harder. Jesus makes the boys run. And run. And run. Ethan's least favorite thing. He complains bitterly about how much his legs hurt him every day. They run poles on the field. They jog like Marines on the sidewalks between the fields. I encourage him to stay in the middle of the pack, but inevitably he's pulling up the rear. Then they practice, with Jesus drilling them on the fundamentals. Lots of ground balls. Lots of reviewing how to back one another up, how to cover bases in different scenarios. Lots of batting practice and simulated games.

I watch all this, losing half days of work each day because I don't have time to get anywhere. Unlike me, my wife is not self-employed, and she doesn't have the luxury of working her schedule around baseball. At times like these I wish I didn't. It's an hour to my job, and an hour back. I field calls on my cell phone. I'm in the middle of developing a new piece of property, so I struggle to be a responsible businessman and a dedicated baseball dad.

"What do you mean you gave away a washer, dryer and refrigerator to sell that house? Just because I'm not there doesn't mean you can't talk to me!"

"I know I've got to make payroll. I'll be out before the end of the day."

"I never said he could use the front end loader on the golf course. He doesn't even know how to drive it!"

I dash out to Polk County and then dash back. I meet with my salespeople and subcontractors if I have to, but otherwise I'm watching practice from whatever shade I can find. It's miserably hot, and the practices, while great for the boys, great for team bonding, are not great for watching day after day. Even so, I can't tear myself away. I have things that need doing, but I don't want to miss a minute. I'm the only one there every day. I feel as ready as the players, ready for this to be over, ready to travel, ready to play ball.

CHAPTER 4
Cooperstown and Beyond

On the Cooperstown Dreams Park webpage titled, "The Dream," Lou Presutti III writes that "one day, while standing in the Cooperstown National Baseball Hall of Fame with his son and grandson, a grandfather exclaimed…"every kid in America should have the opportunity to play baseball in Cooperstown!"

It may have been the opportunity that Lou Jr. and his son, Lou Presutti III wanted to provide to the 12 year olds of America, playing ball in the idyllic, fog shrouded fields and rolling hills of historic Cooperstown. It may have also been the opportunity they saw to capitalize on a brilliant business idea. Utilizing the backdrop of the Cooperstown name and Baseball Hall of Fame, they built a 20 field complex with a small, classic stadium, a Baseball Village complete with a dining pavilion, arcade, round the clock medical and security facilities, souvenir and clothing shops, concession stands, and cabin-like bunkhouses for attending teams and their coaches to live in during their weeklong stay. They made the fences short (200') to encourage home runs and make good pitching a premium. They took the two American traditions of baseball and summer camp and wrapped them together into a package that is virtually impossible for the 12-year old baseball boy to resist. And since 1996 when they opened, it has been successful beyond their wildest field of dreams.

On their website the Presutti's tout their goal of "promoting a high caliber of play…." and "to have young players experience the purity of baseball as it was meant to be." They describe their venture as "an opportunity of a lifetime," and in fact, for many boys and their families, it is. Ethan still says it was one of the best weeks of his life. But of course it is more than that. It has also become their business opportunity of a lifetime with no real competitors in Abner Doubleday's backyard.

96 teams visit the Cooperstown Dreams Park and play on their 20 fields each week for 13 weeks during the summer: 10 weeks for 12-under teams, one week for 10-under teams, and 2 championship weeks. That's 1,248 teams in all. Each team is required to bring 11 players and two coaches, and the per person fee in 2003 (the year we went) was $745. If we assume the average team carries the minimum (Team

Easton brought 13 players and 2 coaches), that equates to $12,086,880 in fees to feed the Dream. Add to that favored vendors: Pepsi, Kodak, Campbells Soup, Tropicana, Gatorade, Sara Lee, Frito Lay, Reebok, Bank of America, Quaker Cereals, Hormel, Heinz, Sherwin Williams, Tyson Foods, Louisville Slugger, Jugs Sports (they make a popular radar gun). The website posts the names of local restaurants, shops, places to go, things to do, and touts more than 40 local business sponsors. The dollars generated could just about pay the salaries of some major league teams.

Pin trading is big every week. Teams come with their own specially designed pins, and boys spend much of their free time collecting these team pins from the other 95 teams playing during their week of competition. It has become one of the Cooperstown traditions, and younger family members get in on the action as well. My daughter and three year old son spent almost all their free time trading and collecting while we were there. And naturally, the Cooperstown Dreams Park has a chosen pin vendor, The Cooperstown Pins Company, who can "assist you in designing and producing pins for trading. As the official pin supplier of Cooperstown Dreams Park, Cooperstown Pins offers top quality pins at a reasonable price."

The Presuttis have done something masterful and typically American: they coupled the American game with American ingenuity and capitalism to make the American dream of fame and fortune come true.

We are a motley family, an odd collection of boys and parents making this pilgrimage to Cooperstown the big summer vacation. Dads are taking their sole week off to travel with their boys. Families are making this their big expenditure of the year. We are rich and poor, black, white, Hispanic. My three year old lives in his Spiderman outfit. My daughter, cornrows in her hair, tags along grudgingly. She hasn't reached the point where she's interested in either baseball or boys. And Ethan has a crowd around him: Ozzie, Mirko, Jordan Mays, all helping him fend off his plastic sword wielding little spider-brother. We caravan to Cooperstown in a row of rental vans. The park itself is beautiful, deep green fields, pennants waving in a cool breeze, a relief from the Florida heat. We walk up to the stone entrance sign and take the mandatory team and family pictures. Then we go to our weeklong rental vacation house, an ancillary Cooperstown business that benefits from the Dreams Park, which we are sharing with Brian Johnson's parents. It's a tight fit, with narrow staircases leading to the second story bedrooms outfitted with noisy window air conditioners, but we're not there much. We're either in town playing tourist, or at the ball fields watching games.

Team Easton plays in Week #4 of the 2003 summer season. We've picked a tough week to come. A number of the best teams in Florida are here as well: the Gainesville Thunder, whose star shortstop/pitcher Jacob Tillotson pitches 80+ mph, the Tampa River Dogs, a team morphed from the Tampa Crush with Petey and Jaimie, the North Florida Hurricanes, all teams that have beaten Easton handily. And there are all-star teams from North Carolina and Georgia, and other Florida teams we've heard are great, but whom we've never faced.

Easton's first game is early Sunday morning, and it's a tightly fought battle. Ozzie goes 3 for 3 and scores 3 runs, and Easton wins 4-2. My wife has made arrangements for us to spend the night at the summer house of a cousin in the Lake Region of New York, so we miss the second game. We return the following day to hear all about Josh Hazen's perfect game (often and proudly from his dad, Coach Craig), a 13-0 drubbing of the Massapequa Blue Wave from New York, a team of 11 year olds Easton run rules in 5 innings.

Ethan starts the third game Monday afternoon. He gives up a 2-run home run in the first inning, then settles down and doesn't allow another run scored through six. Unfortunately, the pitcher from the Charlotte Heat Baseball pitches a complete game, goes 2 for 3 with the two run home run, and doesn't give up a run. Ethan is relieved after the sixth, and Brian Johnson and Beau Glorious give up an additional 5 runs in the seventh. Brian comes out with a hurt shoulder which, it turns out, is a fractured growth plate. He doesn't pitch again for the tournament.

Over the next four games different boys share the spotlight. Jordan Mays and Jordan Dailey allow only 4 hits in two games, beating both opponents by a combined score of 21-0. In the other two games Easton faces tough teams from Georgia, winning one on Brian Johnson's 2 run home run, and the other off home runs from Ozzie and Rafi Gonzalez. In that game the pitcher from Georgia, Ben Atkins, is unhittable through the first four innings, and Easton is losing 2-0. In

76

an exciting 10 pitch at bat, Ethan fouls off ball after ball until he hits a line drive so hard it thumps against the right field wall. But the right fielder has his glove between wall and ball. He holds onto it for the out and gets taken out of the game with a bruised hand. After that Atkins isn't the same. The Easton bats catch up to him, and win 4-2.

Easton goes into the championship, single-elimination round seeded seventh, one of 12 teams with a 6-1 record, and as luck would have it, all the top seeded teams, all the teams that were most feared and loaded with star players, lose. The Charlotte Heat, the team that handed Easton its only loss and is undefeated, loses to another North Carolina team, the Stars, who also beat the Gainesville Thunder. The Wellington Warriors, a Florida team and one of the three undefeated teams in the tournament, lose to the Arizona Demons. The top seed, the Cherokee Reds from Georgia, beat the North Florida Hurricanes but then fall to the Coughlin Chargers from Michigan, seeded 21st, who also beat the Tampa River Dogs and make it all the way to the finals.

In the first championship round game Alex Burgos pitches Easton to a 9-2 win. Josh Hazen gets the save and Nelson Gonzalez hits a home run. In the second game Ethan starts and pitches 3.1 erratic innings but only allows one earned run. He hits two of Easton's five home runs in the game, and they go on to win 14-5. George Gonzalez tells me he had Ethan taken out early so he can pitch the semi-final game to take us into the championship. I don't like the idea. Pitching two games in one day, after your arm cools off and tightens up is asking for injury. But I'm too cowed to say anything. Ethan wants to pitch. The team needs him. And George is convincing. Ethan will just hit in the third game. He didn't throw too many pitches the previous game or all week. He'll be all right. We have a chance to go all the way, assuming we can win two more games. George believes it's riding on Ethan's arm. Who am I to say? What do I know?

Jordan Mays and Alex Burgos combine to win the third game of the day. Ozzie hits two home runs, and Easton beats the Arizona Demons 15-6. Ethan pitches five innings in the semi-final game against the North Carolina Stars, a team that has beaten The Charlotte Heat and three teams from Florida – the Miami Baseball Bandits, the Tamiami Stars, and the Gainesville Thunder – to reach the semis. Though he doesn't have much velocity he's almost unhittable with his change-up and slurve, a half-slider thrown like a football that supposedly doesn't put stress on the elbow, and I fret over every pitch.

77

It's obvious his arm is tired. He's keeping the Stars off balance with location and off-speed pitches, but he's not throwing hard, not at all, and this makes me anxious. It's not that I care about his velocity. In this case I really don't. I'm worried about his arm. He's throwing tired, and I don't have the balls to say or do anything about it. I'm torn between winning and my son's health, and I feel crappy because of it. On the other side, the pitcher for the Stars, their "star" player, throws heat – 75 mph – and looks good, until Ethan hits one of his fastballs almost a hundred feet over the fence. Suddenly the boy is complaining of a sore shoulder, and he is switched to shortstop, where he proceeds to play in short left field because the Easton hitters start hitting the ball hard, and he throws hitter after hitter out at first from the grass in the outfield. Some sore shoulder. Jordan Dailey closes the game, and Easton wins going away. They're in the championship game.

There are varying opinions regarding protecting young arms, and what the leading causes of arm and shoulder injuries in baseball players really are. What is known is that pitching is an unnatural action that places incredible forces of repeated stress on the shoulder and elbow in particular, stresses for which the arm was not constructed. For years it was thought that certain pitches were dangerous, especially if thrown too young. Don't let your kid throw a curveball before he's fifteen. Or sixteen. And sliders – never. Not until they're even older. The danger consists of both the hard snap and twisting action of the arm necessary to make these pitches work, and how easy it is to throw them wrong. When thrown correctly, little danger exists. When thrown incorrectly, or too hard, or too often, at which point mistakes occur more frequently, danger increases exponentially. Fastballs and changeups were (and still are) considered the "safe" pitches. More and more doctors and medical experts now believe injuries have more to do with volume than specific types of pitches. The more pitches hrown over extended periods of time, the greater the risk of injury. It's a simple, direct causal relationship.

Little League baseball began limiting innings pitched years ago, but this was an ineffective, backwards way to deal with the problem of overpitching youngsters, because too many pitches could still be thrown each inning. A pitch count has been in place since the Little League World Series of 2005, when players threw inordinately high numbers of pitches. Dante Bichette, Jr., a local Florida boy and the son of an ex-major league baseball player, threw 133 pitches in one game – as a twelve year old, and two-thirds of them were curveballs!

Which brings us to the topic of baseball in Florida, where many boys play two seasons a year from the time they're five or six years old. Ethan was one of those boys. He took a short break between December and January (which he always hated, saying it took his arm and eye awhile to get back in shape), and in August. The rest of the year was throwing, hitting and fielding non-stop. Because of this extreme overuse and the need to focus on one sport only if you are going to excel (as opposed to the older tradition of multi-sport athletes, in general now a product of a bygone era), more and more young baseball players are suffering serious injuries. The numbers are staggering. Torn and separated labrums. Torn ulnar collateral ligaments. Injuries that were once rare and occurred largely to professional players occur with frightening frequency to boys in middle school and high school. Tommy John surgery, named after the Los Angeles Dodgers pitcher who first had the surgery performed on his elbow, is now so common and successful some parents want it done on their young pitchers as an enhancement to their throwing, since it may (though it has not been proven to) strengthen the elbow and increase pitching velocity.

Dr. James Andrews, one of the foremost specialists in the surgical reconstruction of elbows and shoulders for baseball players, performed nine Tommy John surgeries on teenage patients from 1995-1998. From 2003 to 2008, he performed 224. He points to research that indicates pitchers who throw past the point of fatigue are 36 times more likely to need surgery than those who don't. What is fatigue, in this case? With young pitchers, who will almost always say they're all right and can pitch more, it comes down to pitch count.

The following tables were devised by the American Sports Medicine Institute (ASMI), located in Birmingham, Alabama in the same hospital as Andrews' facility, Andrews Sports Medicine. ASMI's mission is "to improve the understanding, prevention, and treatment of sports-related injuries." To that end they have evaluated the biomechanical pitching motions of more than 1500 pitchers of various ages using extreme slow motion photography to break down the minutest mechanical flaws in pitchers, and come up with the following recommendations:

1. Watch and respond to signs of fatigue. If a youth pitcher complains of fatigue or looks fatigued, let him rest from pitching and other throwing.
2. No overhead throwing of any kind for at least 2-3 months per year (4 months is preferred). No competitive baseball pitching for at least 4 months per year.
3. Follow limits for pitch counts and days rest. (Example limits are shown in the table below.)
4. Avoid pitching on multiple teams with overlapping seasons.
5. Learn good throwing mechanics as soon as possible. The first steps should be to learn, in order: 1) basic throwing, 2) fastball pitching, 3) change-up pitching.
6. Avoid using radar guns.
7. A pitcher should not also be a catcher for his team. The pitcher-catcher combination results in many throws and may increase the risk of injury.
8. If a pitcher complains of pain in his elbow or shoulder, get an evaluation from a sports medicine physician.
9. Inspire youth pitchers to have fun playing baseball and other sports. Participation and enjoyment of various physical activities will increase the youth's athleticism and interest in sports.

Example limits for number of pitches thrown in games:

Daily limits

	2010 USA Baseball Guidelines	2010 Little League Guidelines
17-18	n/a	105/day
15-16	n/a	95/day
13-14	75/game	95/day
11-12	75/game	85/day
9-10	50/game	75/day
7-8	n/a	50/day

Weekly limits

13-14	125/wk; 1000/season; 3000/yr
11-12	100/wk; 1000/season; 3000/yr
9-10	75/wk; 1000/season; 2000/yr
7-8	n/a

21-35 pitches --> 1 day rest;
36-50 pitches --> 2 days rest;
51-65 pitches --> 3 days rest
66- pitches --> 4 days rest

There had been other times when I was concerned about Ethan's arm, but nothing like this, nothing where I was consciously making a choice between his possible well-being and the success of the team. Rob Haben reminded me of an incident when Ethan was pitching and told Rob his arm was bothering him, but he wanted to keep going because if he didn't he thought I'd be mad at him. Ethan doesn't remember this and neither do I, but that doesn't mean it didn't happen, and if it did and if I ever created the impression in my son that I would be angry or disappointed because he stopped throwing due to pain or discomfort, I should have been taken to the outfield and shot and buried in a flat grave with no marker, so outfielders wouldn't trip over me in the future.

In this case, though, many of the worst possible conditions were in place. Ethan had already thrown and stopped, which meant his muscles had warmed up, expanded, cooled off, and tightened back up before he threw again. He threw too many innings and too many pitches, and even though George believed, and helped me believe, that Ethan would be all right so long as he was throwing easily and comfortably, I look back on that moment, that decision, and cringe. I can't help but think that I abdicated some of my responsibility as a father that day.

How often do we, as parents, allow our children to go through something that in our hearts we know they shouldn't? How often do we allow a small sacrifice to occur, looking back later and saying to ourselves, "I wish I hadn't. I wish I'd done something to resist-change-stop that from taking place?" How often does our child have a teacher in elementary school who has given up, who's lost the empathy so vital to their work? How many times do we insist that they take their medicine, finish their lessons, not quit what they're doing, when what they're doing is pure torture? And what they're telling us is no, and what we do is force something on them that's wrong? What if we just said the heck with it and did what we knew in our hearts was in their best interest? What if we complained to the principal that their teacher was unfeeling, bored, miserable in her position? What if we didn't succumb to public pressure and force our stage stricken child to recite in front of hundreds when what they're really thinking about is not peeing in their pants? What if we didn't put them in embarrassing situations, if we listened to them, and listened to our consciences, which are the greatest barometers of truth and well-being we have, the protective shield that all parents wear in the fight to help their children survive childhood? Would the world be different? Would the wounds of growing up go less deep, feel more superficial, be more easily healed, hold less sway over our stunted emotional futures? Would a pitcher's arm last longer? Perhaps. And perhaps not.

But as parents, all the what-ifs aside, we do know a few things for sure. We are our children's best and most important advocates. Society is set up in many ways to undermine that position. Doctors tell us how to treat our children. Teachers tell us the best way for them to learn. Administrators tell us there are no other options, that this is the way it's always been done, the way it is, the way it's going to be. But that's not always right. That may not be the case. Sometimes we, as guardians, really do know best.

And here's the other side of baseball and pitching. Let's think, for a moment, about the numbers. Not the number of pitches thrown, or the number of surgeries, but the number of dreams fulfilled. 2,534,580 children played little league across the country in 2009. In the same year Major League Baseball drafted approximately 1,500 high school and college players. Of those 1,500 players only a handful will actually ever play baseball in the major leagues. That means that today, for any given little leaguer, the odds of being drafted (not playing in the big leagues – just being drafted) are about 1,690:1. The odds of a little leaguer playing college baseball at an NCAA school (the NCAA estimates that there were 30,365 baseball players the same year) are better, about 83.5:1. And the odds that a little league ballplayer will play in high school? About 5:1. Given that the chances of any little league baseball player attaining one of the two biggest dreams of all baseball players – playing in college and the pros – is statistically negligible, that the odds against any child making it that far are staggeringly against him, one ought to ask whether it's all right for the child athlete – especially the average child athlete - to burn out their arm at an early age for the sake of a momentary fulfillment of a dream, 15 minutes of fame, a shot at the spotlight for perhaps the only time in their brief athletic career.

On top of that, it's virtually impossible to predict who will make it to the "next level," who will continue playing past puberty, girls, booze, drugs, driving, and other self-interests. There are so many reasons why a boy won't play pro ball. Few have the "five tools" commonly attributed to the best players: hitting for average, hitting for power, base running skills and speed, throwing ability, and fielding abilities. Some might argue that one great skill, say being a great hitter without the commensurate running and fielding skills, or a great pitcher who's not a great fielder, can still make it in the pros. But the strikes (and the scouts) are against him. So when you evaluate a player like Ethan, obviously slow afoot, with perhaps clutch (but not great) fielding skills, an exceptional hitter whose base running leaves a lot to be desired, would you let him pitch and pitch and enjoy those glory moments as a 12, 14, 16 year old?   Should we be telling all these children who will probably quit playing baseball by the time they're fourteen that they can't pitch that last inning to win the big game and, for the briefest of moments, be a hero to everyone – their teammates, coaches, their parents, themselves? Or would you hold him back in the hope that, against all odds, he makes it to "the show?"

For those children with exceptional ability, if we limit their play, if we tell them to play basketball in the fall (with its own injury record) or soccer (the worst of all sports for injuries) or god forbid suffer through football (it's not if you get hurt, it's when), will that inhibit their chances, later on, to play at a top level Division 1 school? And on top of that, by holding him back, by following the recommendations that a boy pitch only one season a year, play multiple sports and thus not put in the hours, the work, the extra practice to excel, might you not be holding them back and keeping them from competing at the highest levels? While other boys are hitting 300 balls a day and throwing bullpens year round with only a handful of weeks off, are you going to tell your son to let them get ahead of him while he plays basketball or tennis or some other sport in the fall that he doesn't love nearly as much, doesn't have goals set nearly so high, if they are set at all? Could the price of baseball success, of attaining the status of "college ballplayer" be Tommy John surgery or labrum surgery when their bodies break down? Is it worth it if by playing as much and as hard as they did it opens the door to one of the best universities in the country, after which they get surgically repaired? The questions are confusing, the lines gray, the answers undeterminable, undefinable. But the questions ought to be asked, by each parent for every kid, and the solution – not playing, not throwing, not participating – may not be as straightforward as we'd like to believe.

It's always hard to judge, at the moment, what our children will remember and what they won't, what will become, in later years, a great, indelible memory, and what will fade into meaninglessness. Perhaps if we knew beforehand, if we could tell that this second, this lesson we're trying to teach, this particular stroll that meant so much to me with the sun breaking through the trees and my hand on my son's shoulders as I spoke to him about abandoned dreams and unrealized hopes, about what I wanted to accomplish and who I thought I'd be, someday, would mean as much to him as we knew right then it meant to us, we would make better choices, different choices. We would know what to say when, what to strive for, what to let go. We would know that this game was a passing thought, a flickering image that no one would recall, but this one, this seemingly insignificant catch, this at bat, this offhand remark, this inconsequential decision, would be acknowledged and recalled again and again for the rest of their lives. This week at Cooperstown, I knew, was important to Ethan. He'd already said more than once he was having the best time of his life. And this was his moment. This was his heroic act.

Who was I to deny him that? Who was I to place limits on his glory, even at the risk of future success? And so I let it go. I let him go and go, and took the burdens of abandoned responsibility on myself, cutting scars that would make me wince in guilt for years and years to come. At that moment I allowed a sacrifice to take place. E would have had it no other way, but he paid for it physically, and it wouldn't be the last time, or the worst.

Though I failed to live up to it a few critical times in the future, I swore from that moment on that my biggest job as a dad, one that would solidify my role as an asshole, would be to protect Ethan's arm.

Easton beats the North Carolina Stars 11-3. In the game Ethan hits another 2 home runs, giving him four for the tournament, all on the last day, along with two wins and 8-1/3 innings pitched. Easton is in the finals against Coughlin, Michigan.

The team has invented a theme song – Coco Crisp – and they have become the darlings of Cooperstown. Their pins are the most collectible. Hordes of fans follow them and sing along and clap their hands while the boys hoot and chant. We are the Pied Piper team of the tourney, leaders of a parade of baseball teams and families that escort us back to the boys' village.

The boys and coaches retire to their bunkhouse. They've been told they have to clean up and be out right after the final game, which is scheduled for 7 p.m., two hours later and right after dinner. We go out to celebrate while the boys eat fried chicken at the Baseball Village. Then it starts to rain. It pours. The sky seems to have held its breath until this final moment of the week, but now everything is released.

Winds swirl, the evening darkens. The Village becomes a soupy mosh pit of mud and debris, and the game is delayed one, two hours. Even so, the stands at the stadium are packed with nearly 2,000 people. Seven umpires officiate the game. It is the most awesome setting these boys have ever played in. The weather breaks briefly and play starts at 9:15 p.m.

Beau Glorious, he of the great name and reputation, gets the start, and Easton takes a 7-2 lead after the first two innings. But then the skies open up again and the rain delay lasts 35 minutes. When the players return to the field they seem to have tightened up. Beau is ineffective. He walks eight. Ozzie replaces Beau, who moves to short. Beau makes three errors, and Coughlin scores 6 runs in the third.

Ethan takes himself off first base after four innings because he's having a hard time seeing the ball in the dark. Easton scores again off a home run by Brian Johnson to tie the game, but Coughlin scores twice in the fifth to win 10-8 at 12:02 a.m.

We all have an early morning plane to catch, and the boys and coaches have to be moved out of their bunkhouse that night. Several dads pitch in, and with the coaches sweep up a pile of abandoned candy, miscellaneous trash, and unclaimed dirty laundry in the center of the room, a heap that stands nearly four feet tall. Boys sort through it for the clothes they think are theirs, and the rest gets bagged and tossed. Then we take Ethan and Brian and return to our tiny vacation house for four hours of sleep. The boys collapse on a pull out sofa bed together. They are out in minutes, still wearing their muddy baseball clothes, soaked in rain and sweat, stinking, filthy, sprawled side by side.

We let them be. We pull off their cleats, their wet shreds of socks and let them sleep. Out of 96 teams Easton came in second at the end of a long day, a very long week.

$$\bigcirc$$

At all levels, baseball is political. Perhaps when a player gets to the college level that dissipates, but until then politics are played. Little League may be the worst, with overzealous parents sitting on the board of the local organization and influencing everything from who coaches to who plays on what team. But it doesn't stop there. On AAU teams there are two ways to influence peddle. The first is with the wallet. The second is with the players.

For every AAU team, two components are necessary: a willing sponsor, and a willing coach. Both take a lot of time and heat, and the motivation behind both is usually their son on the team. The money man has to be prepared to underwrite enough of the seasonal costs to make joining the team attractive to working class families. In some cases, all costs are underwritten. The Central Florida Scrappers, who played more than 50 games a season against top competition all over the United States, had all costs including travel expenses covered by one of the parents.

The coach's desire to be second-guessed, questioned, berated, and occasionally publicly humiliated sometimes stems from good will alone, but almost always stems from one other factor: seeing his kid play ball on a good team. With lineup card in hand, the coach controls the number of innings played and the number of at-bats each player receives.

The glory and the danger of daddyball is hard to resist. I fell for it when Ethan was younger, and was silently grateful that I had nothing left to offer teams as a coach after Ethan turned nine.

In the case of Team Easton, grumbling began the middle of the second season. Craig Hazen was favoring his boy Josh. Josh got too much time at third. Josh got too many innings pitching. Craig wasn't tough enough. Craig didn't have real baseball experience. Craig was getting outcoached. The truth was, Josh was right in the middle of the pack: 12 innings pitched (5th most on the team), 45 at-bats (7th most).

The perception of daddyball, that a father will favor his child over others no matter what, could be so pervasive that even when it wasn't real it felt real. Craig was a fair coach. If he didn't have the world's most astute baseball mind, he didn't lose games for the team on a regular basis either. But when the boys played poorly in the state tournament, and when they played so well at Cooperstown after two weeks of boot camp, the movement was on. Whispers began in the bleachers. Craig was being ousted. George was replacing him with his friend and ex-big league ballplayer, Jesus Perez, the father who ran Easton's boot camp, a handsome, athletic Puerto Rican ballplayer with short cropped hair, stilted English, and very specific ideas about how to run a baseball team. It was thought that this would pacify the parents, keep Ozzie on the team and attract other top players. And two new players did join the team: Brian Johnson, whose shoulder was healed, and Rasheed Mitchell, a speedy outfielder with a good bat. For the time being Josh stayed on the team, too, and after Cooperstown we looked forward to another great season with Easton.

Ethan's popularity and sense of belonging peaked the summer after Cooperstown when he became a bar mitzvah. The juxtaposition, the juggling act of sports and religion had always come hard to us, but now it merged into a symbiotic oneness of friendship, fulfillment, and joy. The invite list included his religious school class, and also his teammates, their parents and siblings, almost all of whom had never been to a bar mitzvah, or any Jewish celebration before. The theme colors for Ethan's party? Easton red and black. The party itself? Baseball, with a diamond outline taped to the dance floor, bleachers for seating, a batting cage in the corner of the room, old baseball cards strewn on the banquet tables, and servers wearing umpire uniforms. Overdone? Yes. But we were living and breathing the dream. In our minds there was no other way to go.

I'd always predicted that Ethan would be taller than me by the time he turned 13 and he was, by an inch at 5'9". And I'd always imagined myself standing with him on the bimah, looking out over the crowd gathered for Saturday morning Shabbat services to celebrate with him and us, and telling him, "Look at all these people, all your friends, here to share this special moment with you. Take it in. Breathe it in. Remember it. This is yours forever." I hadn't imagined, sitting in the back, squirming uncomfortably but happy, working hard to keep their yarmulkes on their heads, would be black and Hispanic families, the baseball family we had finally, completely joined.

At the party Ethan leads the boys on the team in a performance of Coco Crisp. The Easton parents dominate the dance floor. We end in a circle, holding hands and closing the night, and the summer, in one last, sweet outpouring of friendship.

I used the subject of Ethan's bar mitzvah as the topic for several of my weekly columns in our local Jewish newspaper, the Heritage. In one I said:

"Ethan has done it again. Pinned on his bedroom wall, between baseball trophy plaques, is a page torn out of Sports Illustrated. The picture's of one of baseball's most moving moments, when Lou Gehrig gave his farewell speech. The headline above the picture reads, "To some it's a sport. To others, a religion." When he hung it up he pointed it out to me proudly. "See?" he said. "That's me." My eyebrows curled. I thought for a moment about an appropriate response, holding my knee jerk "Judaism is your religion" in check. I knew, at that moment, it would do no good. So I smiled, bookmarked the scene, and said, "I know how important baseball is to you. Have you done your bar mitzvah study yet?"

And the week before the big day, I wrote him a letter, which I read to him at our family Shabbat dinner the Friday night before. "Dear Ethan,

A bar mitzvah is a coming of age. That doesn't mean you are "of age" yet. It means that our sages and teachers, many years ago in their deepest wisdom, recognized, as cultures have recognized for millennia, that this transitional time is truly a turning point in life. Growing up is hard. You'll feel like a little boy who needs a hug one second, a self-assured man who can't imagine asking for help the next. The only advice I can give you there is that it's always all right to ask for help and a hug. We need them both, for people don't exist in a vacuum and can't make it alone forever.

Choices you make from here on out will have great impact, not on who you become, for you will always be in a state of becoming, but on how well you travel the road of becoming. Drugs, sex, following the wrong crowd or making the right call – it's more up to you now than ever before.

So my wishes for you are simple. Be kind to yourself and others. Cut yourself some slack. Be patient. The world gets rougher as you get older. Look to your family, your community, and your traditions and teachings for strength and support. It's all there if you only ask for it."

○

From the first fall practice, I begin to see changes I can't explain, changes that make no sense after Ethan's heroics the season before. Ethan gets less and less practice time at first base. Jordan Mays, whose parents have been quietly concerned that their son was getting the short end of the stick at third base for Josh Hazen, is getting trained at first. He doesn't know the position. He doesn't have a feel for the base. He doesn't have Ethan's arm, though his is adequate. And he doesn't have Ethan's mouth, the constant chatter, the aggressive banter that keeps everyone involved. But he has quick feet and natural athleticism. I feel that gnawing sensation of constant worry in the pit of my stomach. What's going on here? Is it my son who's getting shortchanged now? Is this a plan to have two first basemen, or is it a sign of things to come?

Josh Hazen has a brief tryout, then is told he's not going to make the team. Suddenly, he and Craig are gone. I don't feel comfortable talking to Jesus. There is a language barrier. He speaks broken English, and I speak next to no Spanish. And I sense a lack of respect towards Ethan, and echoing off Ethan, towards me. With Craig, Ethan was an important cog on the team. And George had once, at a team dinner while we were on the road, pulled me aside and told me that, of all the boys on the team, he thought only two had real long-term baseball potential: Ozzie and Ethan. This kindled my fantasies more than anything else he could possibly have said. Long term potential. Did he mean college ball? The pros? Could baseball go on for Ethan forever? I had only one thought in my head at that time. Ethan had shown the ability to rise to the level of competition. He was willing to work hard enough to reach the top. He had done it in Little League, Pony League, and now on two AAU teams. My cup overflowed. The floodgates opened wide. Ethan might be bona fide. But to Jesus Ethan was another matter altogether.

Jesus builds the team around speed. He had been a quick, slick shortstop in the Yankees organization until knee injuries stalled and eventually killed his career. Now he makes Team Easton over in his image, and I begin to have doubts about where Ethan fits in.

In our first game of the fall, Ethan is bounced down to seventh in the batting order. Brian Johnson is in Ethan's four spot. I am visibly upset. I shake my head. I grumble. I do what every parent does. I gossip. I talk to other parents in the bleachers. Can you believe this? What's going on here? Ethan is being demoted? After Cooperstown he's dropped to seventh in the order? Can you explain that? Can someone explain that to me please? And Jordan Mays is at first. Who would you rather have at first, Jordan who's just started playing there, or Ethan who's been there all his life? Ethan is a mind reader, a psychic at first. Ethan may not be the fastest player out there, but he'll make the key play, the game saving catch or throw when everything's on the line. You know that. You've seen it a dozen, a million times. He'll get the runner stealing third. He'll snag the throw that's over anyone else's head. What's going on?

Word quickly gets to Jesus. Between games he takes me aside. "Seven is spot for hitters," he tells me. "For RBIs. You see what Ethan did?" I nod my head. "Very important to team. Ethan do very well there." He pats me on the back and leaves. I have to acknowledge his point. Ethan did drive in three runs in the first game, but I am not mollified. I am keeping my eyes and ears very open.

At the Johnson's recommendation, Ethan takes hitting lessons from the instructor who's taught Brian. Brian is considered one of the best right-handed hitters in the state. If Ethan's going to be bounced down in the order, we're going to do everything we can to prove Jesus wrong. At his first lesson the new guy changes Ethan's stance, where he positions his hands and the bat before he swings, how wide his feet are set. Ethan struggles with it at first, but by the end of the lesson he's catching on. BOOM BOOM BOOM. The balls are flying off the bat in the backyard cage.

Games are not, however, the same as hitting in a batting cage. Nerves are tighter. The stakes are greater. Pitchers and catchers do whatever they can to throw the hitter offstride, confuse him, think fast, throw slow, think high, throw low, look outside, throw inside. Ethan looks uncomfortable out there. His hands are flying out. He has no weight behind the ball. He misses by so much I can see the air between the bat and ball. He hits weakly. He lunges at pitches. The balls roll slowly to infielders. It is only the third week of the season, but Ethan's hitting has gone to hell, and he is suffering in baseball purgatory, unsure of his place, his value on the team.

I suffer with him. As he gets marginalized, so do I. As he sits by himself, asking himself what's wrong, so do I. I can't bring myself to participate in the bleacher chatter. Everyone else seems happy. Everyone else remains animated, watching the play behind home plate, commenting on the new aggressive base running of the team, the change in coaching philosophy. Parents shake their heads and chuckle at the way Jesus goes after the umpires, what he gets away with as he swears in Spanish. Everyone else's boys have their place, their position, an understanding of what's expected of them. Not Ethan. And so I sit on the fringe, choking on the bile of the outcast, chin in my hands, silently shaking my head in confusion and dismay. My mother comes to a game and sits beside me. "Why isn't Ethan in the game?" she asks aloud. "Shouldn't he be at first base?" Other parents look askance at her, at me, but no one says a word. They know he's been displaced, and that a grandmother has no chance of understanding this.

Every at bat now is an experiment. He chokes up. He puts his feet closer together. He puts them wider apart. He starts with his hands up higher, down lower, further back, but nothing helps. He can't get a hit if it means saving his career, his dreams, his entire future playing ball. That's how it seems to me. It's all ending here. Everything. The door is closing. The daylight is disappearing. What once, just a few months before had been promise and expectation and limitless possibility has become one grudging out after another, one hope dashed, one disappointment followed by one embarrassment. Jordan Mays has become a fixture at first. Ethan is no longer in the lineup. He's sitting by himself at the end of the bench, hoping for one moment, a swing of the bat, a single important hit that will redeem him, put him back where he belongs among his friends on the field. But it doesn't happen. He sits and waits, and when he is given the opportunity, he misses. Another weak grounder. Another pop fly or foul ball caught by the catcher. All he has left now is his pitching, and coming to terms with the new experience of being an end of the bench role player, the one the parents root for not because they are heroic, but because they are tragic, and any success at the plate would be seen as miraculous, the crippled boy who throws away his crutches and walks, a wonder worth remembering. And I continue to play the role of coward in baseball purgatory. As he sits on the bench, I bench myself. I shrink away from the team, the game. Unable to puff myself up with false pride earned not by me but by my son, unable to cheer on the other boys, to make small talk and brave this tough season out, I reduce myself to a silent shell of doubt and disbelief. I am in a daze, confused, shaking my head as if it were full of bees, muttering noiselessly about where the wrong turn was, what I could have done differently, how we came to this place, with this team we loved and poured our hearts and blood into? I should have cheered until the end. I could have stayed true to the spirit of youth, joyful in every moment of every boy's success, but I wasn't. I grew quiet and bitter and shrunk away, waiting impatiently until it was all over.

We talk. I realize I contributed to him getting screwed up as a hitter by taking him to someone who changed everything he did, everything he was as a hitter. We talk about him forgetting it all, going back to who he is, how he's comfortable and relaxed at the plate. And we talk about the team.

I tell him that it's tough to succeed when your coach doesn't believe in you.

"But I love this team," Ethan says.

"He's built it around speed," I tell him. "You don't have a place with him."

"But I'm one of the original members," he replies. "We're like family."

"Even families go their separate ways," I say. And this hurts more than anything else.

Without meaning to, I undermine the single most important foundation of faith Ethan has. Families stick together. They support each other. They hold each other up. There are ballplayers who have a different, broken concept of family. They have been taught by their parents that if they are not treated right, if they aren't batting at the top of the order or playing every inning that they shouldn't stay. They should leave and go where they'll be appreciated. It's the "star mentality." These players have the reputation, buttressed by their parents whispering in their ears that they're better than all that, better than everyone else, and deserve better accordingly, jumping ship whenever the tide changes. They bolt without warning, leaping from team to team without discernible loyalty or concern for the impact it has on others. We have seen it again and again, and these players, especially the great ones, get away with it, though their teammates look at them out of the corners of their eyes, aware that they can only be counted on for as long as they're in view. If something goes wrong, they may be gone. It's the fifth marriage, the one with all the doors and windows open, a half-commitment, and though it goes unsaid, it remains in the air. This player is only half here. He can be counted on to deliver, but only for today, maybe for tomorrow. Don't do anything to damage his ego, displace him, demote him, treat him less well than he expects or he'll be gone. And beyond that, no one places any bets.

I've tried to teach Ethan differently. I've told him when he makes a commitment to a team he abides by it no matter what. It's not a lifetime. It's not forever. It's for the terms of his verbal contract with the coach. Of course, it's been easy to do when he's been in the spotlight, when he's the one who's playing all the time, garnering the praise, getting all the attention. It's been like saying don't worry about money when you're already rich. Say that to the starving wretch hustling for change on the street corner.

But now the conflict and the pain are real. Now the temptation is to quit or suffer the quiet humiliation of the retired racehorse, standing alone in a quiet, shaded, out of the way field watching the stallions on the track that have replaced him.

Ethan doesn't want to leave Team Easton. He wants everything to go back to the way it was, but he knows, and I know, there's no going back. The team has moved in another direction, and it hasn't taken him with it. We agree, finally, that he will tell everyone he's leaving after the season.

At the beginning of the next practice I see Ethan huddle with his teammates in the outfield. It's a closed huddle, a tight huddle, an embrace. The boys have never given up on him. He is one of them.

The huddle breaks. Ethan walks towards us alone. His head is down, his shoulders slumped. This is going to be hard. I know what's coming, but none of the other parents do. Ethan approaches the benches where we're all sitting.

"I already told the guys on the team, but I wanted to be up front with all of you and tell you face to face," he begins, sighing heavily. "You've been like a second family to me, but it's time for me to move on. The Puerto Rico tournament will be the last time I play with Team Easton. I'm really going to miss you all. This has been the best time of my life." He looks like he's about to cry, choking back the tears. Then he turns and walks away, taking his place in practice behind Jordan Mays at first base.

Parents are, if not stunned, surprised, and many come over to me to shake hands or give me a hug. Many say they'll miss us, too. They'll miss Spider-Man and Big E. They wish us the best. But no one says please change your mind. No one says "we'll talk to the coach." No one says, "we'll work it out so you can stay." In the end, this kind of baseball is about nothing other than your own boy and the skin he's got in the game.

Ethan is in the lineup in a local tournament in Osceola County on another viciously hot day. He gets a chance to bat against the Tampa Crush. Parents cheer him on when he comes to the plate, cheer for him when his bat connects with the ball, a sharp grounder, and sigh, deflated as he is thrown out by the second baseman. That's the last time Ethan bats for Team Easton.

Jesus and his wife Anna plan the trip to Puerto Rico, their home, as an adventure for the boys. It promises to be a competitive baseball event and a cultural experience. For us, it turns into both with an aftertaste that was 10% relief and 90% bittersweet.

We stay in a nice oceanfront hotel with the team, and all of us – Pat and Jerica and Gabriel included - enjoy the water, the pool and Jacuzzi. We have the strangest Thanksgiving dinner ever at a local Spanish restaurant owned by some of the Perez's family. Turkey hash in a brown Spanish gravy, yellow rice and mashed sweet potatoes, and I am already thinking of home. Though we are together as a family, my wife and all three kids, we have begun to separate from the extended baseball family of Easton. We are visitors, temporary passengers aboard their ship, and our departure, everyone knows, is imminent.

Ethan gets one last chance to shine, on a field with almost no pitcher's mound, strewn with broken glass, a hulking rusty mass of a semi-abandoned stadium surrounding it. That's how all the fields we play at are maintained. There is no money for irrigation systems. The infields are all "skinned," without any grass whatsoever. The outfields are rough, bumpy, baked hard by the tropical sun, prone to bad hops and twisted ankles. No one wants to lay out to catch a ball. You might come up with glass shards in your arms and sandspurs in your legs. The Puerto Rican boys share a few old metal bats. We come to the field with each boy carrying an equipment bag that has as many bats as their entire team. Ethan gets a new bat every year. The boys we play against may not have had the chance to feel the pop and sting of new aluminum alloy bats ever. They may be swinging bats that are too big, too heavy, too light, too long, too short for them. Their gloves are worn, slick with the stains of sweat and years of use, patched and stitched back together with leather laces that don't match the original color of the glove. But they play hard, and they know the game. We're told they're a good team.

For the first time, earlier that season, Ethan has thrown over 70 mph, and right now he is bringing heat. Everything works. He keeps the ball down low. It moves. It bites. The batters don't stand a chance. He scatters three hits and Easton wins going away. For a moment it's like old times, Ethan triumphant, happy, proud, the team rallying around him. But even that moment doesn't last long. In the last game we play Brian Johnson pitches against the team that is arguably the best we face. He throws harder than Ethan, is even more impressive against tougher competition while Ethan sits on the bench, and wins a pitcher's duel 2-1. He also hits well, and in the community center where we have lunch with the opposing team and their families and on the plane ride home the game Ethan pitched is forgotten next to Brian's gem. Ethan's game is a footnote. The rest of the book no longer mentions him. He is already gone, disappeared by the time we collect our bags and say goodbye.

CHAPTER 5
The Tweens

Between Thanksgiving and New Year's Day, once word gets out that Ethan is no longer attached to Team Easton, other teams come courting. Three in particular make strong pitches: The Florida Tars, the Central Florida Scrappers, and the Winter Park Wildcats.

We attend an open practice and tryout for the Tars. They are a new, well-funded team, and make the promise to Ethan that he will be a cornerstone for them, a fixture on the mound, at first, and in the lineup. We're tempted, but there are so many uncertainties about joining a start-up, so many peculiarities, so many unknowns about the people, the dynamics, the politics. We don't commit.

Fred Mannara, the coach of the Scrappers, puts on a full court press. We know who they are and what they've accomplished. Everyone knows, Fred is quick to remind us. Two state championships. The best players. Everything underwritten by one of the parents. It sounds too good to pass up, and Ethan is sorely tempted. He wants to play for a winner. But we've heard grumblings about the Scrappers, too. There's a tightly knit power structure on the team, and you're either in or out. Fred's son James is an excellent hitter, lefthanded pitcher, first baseman and outfielder. They also have another outstanding lefty on the team, Jason Boyer, and Joe Lovecchio, the big, hard throwing righty. Where does that leave Ethan? We don't know, nor are we told anything other than that he would fit in. We bide our time.

The third team, the Wildcats, intrigues me. They are a 14-under team, so Ethan would be playing "up," with boys a year older than he for the first time ever. We are introduced to the head coach, Vic Incinelli, by his son Matthew, who had been, until recently, Ethan's pitching coach. Matthew has recommended Ethan to Vic, who knows nothing about him, or me. I found Matthew through a business associate, who knew I was looking for a new instructor when Todd Bellhorn moved to Miami. Matthew, I was told, was a college all-American at the University of North Florida and came from a very upright, conservative Christian family.

Matt was second in a line of great pitching coaches. After Todd left, Ethan worked with Matt for almost a year. He was a righthanded pitcher with brilliant high school and college careers. Though not a hard thrower, he was known for his unflappable demeanor on the mound (an emotional state Ethan needed to learn), and his pinpoint control. He could throw his changeup within inches of wherever he wanted whenever he wanted. He could move the ball inside and outside. He had taken his high school team, the Winter Park Wildcats, to their only berth ever in the state finals. He was the winningest pitcher in history at UNF, and has since been inducted into the UNF Hall of Fame. Ethan's command and understanding of pitching grew quickly under his tutelage. By the time Matt's father was asking about us, Ethan was working with another coach, Chip Gierke, the head coach of Edgewater High School. While this caused Matt's father some consternation ("Why had we left Matt? Didn't we know he was the best pitching coach in the area? Would we do the same to him and his team?") I promised him no, Ethan would live by any commitment he made for the upcoming season, and that was enough.

Vic shakes my hand firmly at lunch. I realize quickly this is an interview, not a chat. He stands just over 6 feet tall, with dark thinning hair he combs to the side, a middle-aged paunch, a quick, staccato laugh and an opinion about everything. Vic played ball in high school, and specializes in pitchers. Besides Matt, his second son Jared is a 6'5" RHP (righthanded pitcher) at UNF, and his ten year old son Evan is a pitcher-in-training.

There are no grays in Vic's world. He deals in black and white. He knows we're Jewish, and he respects that.

"Will you have a problem with prayers before games and after practices?" he asks. "I invoke Jesus' name. That's who I am."

"That's fine," I tell him, "as long as Ethan doesn't have to actively participate."

"There'll be no swearing, no chewing tobacco," he says.

"Good," I respond. "No problem there."

"And I teach baseball and behavior. I want....no....I expect my players to grow up to be good men. You can attend my Bible study classes if you want. Plus, Ethan will be my only lefty. If he's as good as Matthew says he is, he'll get to pitch. And he'll learn how to be a pitcher, not a thrower with me. I'll have to see about the rest. I don't make promises up front. I've heard Ethan swings a good bat, but that remains for me to see, especially since he'll be facing older boys."

97

He pauses for a second to let all that sink in.

"And I don't need any more yahoos on my team. I have plenty of yahoos already. How's that sound?"

Playing up. A coach who promises to be both righteous and fair. The concept appeals to me. I tell the Tars coach we'll stay in touch. I have a tough conversation with Fred Mannara, who is taken aback when I say no. How can someone say no to the Scrappers? It's like turning down a free meal. Oh well. That's a burned bridge. Ethan's playing up this spring.

With Gierke on vacation, Ethan asks Matt Incinelli for one last bullpen. Matt arranges for a young catcher to work the bullpen – Alex, or AC Carter. AC is two years younger than E, with long blonde hair, frumpy, wrinkled baseball clothes and a goofy attitude that I'd have no problem ascribing to my son, which causes me some concern. Can he handle Ethan's pitches? Is he in over his head? But he's excited about catching Ethan. Ethan, I realize, has begun to have a reputation of sorts in Central Florida, and besides, the kid's dad is here and I don't want to make an issue out of it.

AC's dad and I lean against a cinderblock wall while the boys stretch and throw. He is a few inches taller than I, with white Albert Einstein hair, a sharp, aquiline nose and an accent I can't quite place. British perhaps (it turns out he's Aussie). When I ask him what he does and his background with baseball, I find out he was once a world-ranked tennis pro (as high as 48th), and played against some of my all-time favorite players – Bjorn Borg, John McEnroe, though he never beat them. His philosophy on sports, his dry, low-key sense of humor, his world-weariness charm me immediately. Here's a dad I can hang out with. Here's someone I can talk to without worrying about editing politics or swallowing references to literature or religion. I look forward to the time when Ethan and AC play on the same high school team.

David speaks to me about his perception of baseball as it related to other sports, jaundiced as he was in favor of tennis.

"All sports," he tells me in his Aussie drawl, "have intellectual and physical components that can be rated on a 10 point scale. Let's say that 10 is the highest and 1 the lowest. Most balance the two. Take football, for example. With the exception of the quarterback, perhaps, football is a high physical low mental sport. Basketball – higher physical than mental. Golf – high mental low physical. Baseball – higher mental than physical."

I react to that. "What makes you say that?" I respond defensively. "Baseball takes extreme physical skills."

He laughs. "Have you seen all the overweight pro players? Now just think about it for a second. There's strategy. There's numerous possibilities every pitch. There's the constant pressure of failing as a hitter, and outthinking the hitter if you're a pitcher. That's all mental. Tennis, of course," he says proudly, "ranks high both physically and mentally."

And truthfully, I can't argue with his evaluations. This conversation sticks with me, and now I evaluate sports and their players on the basis of the two quotients. The great athletes raise the bar for their sport on both levels. They exceed the expected norm of the physical and mental requirements of their game, and thus excel. Ever since then I've tried to convey this to Ethan, with limited success.

⚾

While Ethan struggles to fit in with the older boys, Vic and I become friends. I don't know why, but he trusts me and I trust him. I know if he gives me his word I can count on it. He knows I'll tell him the truth. Somehow, because of that the barriers are down. He relies on me to gauge the mood and temperament of the other parents. I don't ask for anything for Ethan. I know he's getting a fair shake.

This is a different model of baseball. Vic has a deal with the coach of the local high school team, Bob King of Winter Park High. He'll train a team of boys in the district who can go to Winter Park, and he gets to use the team's name and play other high school teams of like age. In Ethan's first games with the Wildcats, he pitches in a local tournament and is the winning pitcher in one and the closer in another. Vic gives him the best pitcher award for the tournament. In the next series of games he works in relief against Lake Brantley High with the bases loaded and gets the starter out of a jam. The boys on the team aren't very receptive to a younger player coming in and stealing innings, but they grudgingly accept the fact that he can pitch. Ethan senses their lack of acceptance, and his insecurities bubble forth again. He can't keep his mouth shut about his own play. If someone else pitches well, he reminds them of how well he just threw. If someone gets a hit, he responds, "Yeah, but did you see my double in the gap?" He is pissing his teammates off right and left, and the season hasn't officially begun.

I see Vic pull him aside between games of a doubleheader. We are playing one of the best 14-under teams in Central Florida, the Olympia Bombers, and got killed the first game, the game Ethan pitched, a combination of errors (which seem to multiply like fruit flies behind him when he's on the mound) and a great hitting team. Ethan is upset, angry. Vic has his hands on Ethan's shoulders and is speaking inches from his face. I can't hear what he's saying, but I can feel the force of the words. Vic is not being gentle, but Ethan shakes his head yes in understanding.

I find out later that Vic wasn't talking to Ethan about his performance during the game, but his behavior afterwards. Ethan opened his mouth again, and spewed sour milk and bitter gruel. Coming from the youngest player on the team, this alienated and angered the other players even more. He bitched about the errors, and when another boy came into the dugout proudly talking about his base hit, Ethan's response was, "Yeah, but my ball nearly hit the fence."

Vic invokes his three cardinal rules of baseball, which he may have made up on the spot for Ethan's benefit. In words Vic hopes Ethan understands, he tells him:

1. Don't ever say anything about yourself.
2. Don't ever say anything bad about your teammates.
3. If you don't have something good to say, don't say it.

Ethan nods his head, and Vic pushes him back towards the dugout.

The next game Bronson Gagner pitches for the Wildcats. Bronson is a big boy, the biggest on the team by far. At 14 he is already 6'3" and weighs 240 lbs. Bronson plays first when Ethan pitches. He is the hardest thrower and the least flexible player on the team. He struggles bending down to touch his toes. He stands straight up when he pitches, which leads to errors when he tries to pick a runner off first and a loss of velocity on the mound. Vic works with him on this, but it comes and goes. The second game is no better than the first. The Wildcats are ten run ruled by a superior team.

Baseball rides on the back of a team. But it's also the rare sport that begins every play with a confrontation between two individuals. Hitter and pitcher, each one trying to overpower, outwit, outsmart the other. And pitching and hitting are considered two of the most difficult skills in all of sports. Pitchers, in particular, unlike any other team sport, control the game. A pitcher who throws a no-hitter almost always wins. A pitcher who's got his stuff working makes it difficult for the other team to score. The football quarterback relies on tailbacks, receivers to finish the play. He may throw a perfect pass, but it can still be dropped. One person in basketball can change the game, can make a team better, but rarely does one player win a game outright. He must have a supporting cast.

The hitter tries to pick up the spin of the ball out of the pitcher's hand. He looks for tendencies. Does the pitcher slow his front leg down when he throws a changeup? Is his arm slot different when he throws a curveball? The pitcher, meanwhile, does the same analysis of the hitter. Does the batter have a long swing? Can he get his hands around on an inside pitch? Can he be fooled by a high fastball? Can he hit an off speed pitch? The pitcher who throws "ched," fastballs that leave the hand at more than 94 mph, may be able to get away with velocity alone. The hitter with fast hands may be able to rely on the same – quick twitch muscles and good instincts.

But for the hitter and pitcher a hair below brilliant, for the 99% of all players without celestial abilities, something more is required. They not only need a set of physical attributes, but a temperament and a mental approach to the game that set them apart.

Few have those attributes. Hitters need to shrug off their failures, which are much more common than their successes. Pitchers must focus one pitch at a time, one moment at a time. It's not enough to say it's all about passion or emotional control, because some players thrive on intense emotional expression, while others rely on stoicism and restraint. It's about making the most of what you've got, about actualizing potential. And for the pitcher, this occurs pitch by pitch.

Ethan wears his emotions, pitch by pitch, out by out, hit by hit, on his shirtsleeve. What he had going for him on the Wildcats was Vic Incinelli.

During a game in Gainesville Ethan pitches and loses his cool. He doesn't execute the pitches Vic calls. He overthrows. He misses his spots. Vic walks out to the mound and reams him out. I watch Ethan shrink. He has suddenly, instantly lost inches of stature and composure. I worry that an ugly trend is beginning again. Ethan is being diminished and marginalized in front of his teammates. Vic returns to the dugout and kicks a metal bat into the waist high concrete wall that buffers the players from the playing field. BOOM! The bat clangs against the wall and ricochets off. Players duck. He is madder than I've ever seen. Ethan does no better, and is pulled at the end of a terrible inning.

But then something wondrous occurs, something beautiful I haven't seen before. In between games Vic puts his arm around Ethan's shoulders and walks him down the right field line. Now he is talking to E man to man, heart to heart. I can see it from a distance. Ethan absorbs what Vic says. Vic gestures, speaks animatedly, and Ethan is not cowed, not depressed, not shrinking away. He is learning. He walks back to the dugout and he's ok. Vic walks back and he's ok. I know this is different, an example for me, for the first time, of how tough love can really work. Vic is tough during the games, but teaching, kind, compassionate afterwards. I don't believe this means he is soft, or says anything other than the truth – his truth - but Ethan believes Vic is invested in him and cares about him. What an incredible epiphany, that the love of a coach, a second father to many of these boys (occasionally the first good father), can be so grounding and reassuring, even after a serious tongue lashing. Of course, it also helps that Vic is the best pitching coach Ethan has ever had in game situations. He calls games that accentuate a pitcher's strengths. He recognizes hitters' weaknesses and exploits them. He mixes up pitches and teaches boys how to think about pitching, not just how to go out and throw. It is a whole different ballgame with Vic in charge.

The Wildcats, a team of local neighborhood boys being groomed for high school baseball, play against all-star teams drawn from across the state, and time and again are overmatched by bigger, stronger, faster, more highly skilled players. The Wildcats shortstop, Kyle McLanahan, is a great point guard. The center fielder, Bryan King, is a great running back. The pitching corps are all in training, from the underaged Ethan to the oversized Bronson to a group of part timers who primarily played other positions – outfielders Matt Toelke and

Josh Bastian and Jay Moroff, second baseman Jared Keck, third baseman Will Harris, and McLanahan. But Vic is a molder and a modeler of behavior, and his hope is that, as a team, they will come together by the end of the season, and as a team they will learn.

For the first time E is learning how to behave, not as a star or a pariah, but as a team member. He has to earn his place with the older boys – in all aspects of the game – and he has to win their acceptance and approval after a widely acknowledged rough start. None of this would have been possible if he hadn't had the humbling experience of warming the bench his last season with Easton. Now all it takes is a look from Vic for Ethan to shut up. During prayer sessions E hangs his head respectfully, but refrains from saying anything. When Ethan is on the mound, scuffing the clay and showing visible frustration as the team makes error after error behind him, Vic can call time, strut up to him and ream him out.

"What on earth are you doing out here?" he asks. "Get your act together, get yourself under control, throw the next pitch properly or you will be out of the game. Understand?

And Ethan can hear him, because he knows that Vic cares about him. No hidden agendas, no favoritism, no doubt about his feelings or support. Vic is sincerely committed to every boy on his team, and every boy knows it. So do I.

The team suffers its first casualties early in the season. Two catchers quit to play on other teams. One informs Vic. The other leaves without a word. Both were unhappy with their playing time, and rather than compete, they quit.

Bronson's father Ralph has begun a whispering campaign about the team. He and Vic are friends, but he also thinks Vic isn't giving Bronson a fair shake. He wants Bronson in more games at first. He wants Bronson in more key games pitching. What he doesn't get is that Bronson can't hit or bend over at first. How do you say that to a father? When he speaks to me I nod my head, and when Vic asks me the mood of the team, I tell him, without revealing anything, that he needs to have a chat with Ralph.

We drive to Atlanta to play a series of games. I give a ride to another boy on the team, Ramses Wallace, the brother of Rasheed who played for Team Easton. Ethan's in the passenger seat in the front next to me. Rams is chilling in the back. Just as we're making our way into the heavy traffic of the city a car next to me starts honking furiously and my car begins to shake. We are rattling out of control at 70 mph. I don't know how, but I swerve the car through three lanes of traffic and stop in the far right median. One of my back tires has shredded and I was driving on the rim. Our first game is that evening, and Ethan is scheduled to pitch. I call for a tow truck. An hour passes. Two hours. Finally the truck arrives mid-afternoon, and tows us to, of all places, Hank Aaron's car dealership. The boys think this is great, hanging out at a car dealership owned by the home run king. This is proof to them that baseball rules. I call Vic and let him know it's going to be close.

"Vic, I'm not sure we'll make it to the game on time," I say.

"You know I have Ethan penciled in to start," Vic tells me.

"I know." I'm panicking inside, but there's little I can do.

They inspect the car, put on a new tire and we drive to the game as the dealership closes and the sun sets. We arrive at the ballfields while the team is warming up. Ethan dashes out of the car, glove in hand. Vic is yelling for him, motioning him over to the bullpen. He stretches out his arm and throws for ten minutes, then runs out to the field.

Ethan throws a great game, using his changeup and two seam, moving the ball in and out on the batters, and Vic jokes that we should get in accidents more often. He picks off two runners at first, and Bronson misses another two pick offs when he can't get down low enough to catch the throw. The Wildcats win going away. It's the only game they win that weekend.

In a local end of season tournament the team sets a new record in futility, making ten errors behind Ethan while he pitches. Balls go through legs, bounce off gloves. Throws fly errantly around the infield. Outfielders miss routine fly balls. Ethan watches helplessly, as do the parents in the stands. Four errors are made the first inning. There's nothing anyone can do but shrug it off. You can't even laugh. It's too dismal, too humiliating. Ethan tells me later he feels like an error magnet. Whenever he's on the mound errors are attracted to him. The Wildcats get run ruled again in five brief innings. Afterwards the boys, parents, and Vic huddle together to discuss how to conclude the season. We can either go to the AAU National Championship Tournament in Sarasota, or The Road To Omaha, a special tournament Vic's teams have played at in Omaha, Nebraska during the College World Series. Everyone opts for Omaha.

☺

We arrive to a grey, chilly, wet Omaha. The fields are, to everyone's surprise and chagrin, black clay, and short. The mounds are 54' from home plate, not 60'6". The bases are 80' apart, not 90', so plays happen faster, have to be made more quickly. These are all adjustments for which the Wildcats are completely unprepared. The parents drive off to outlet stores to buy cheap sweaters and ponchos. The players stay inside the hotel and play cards and watch TV instead of playing catch or batting games in the parking lot. The grounds are wet, the fields muddy. It's a whole new ballgame for Florida boys.

We are staying in the same hotel that houses the University of Miami baseball team that has made it to the College World Series. In the lobby are tables laden with Miami baseball cards, souvenir key chains and trinkets, baseball caps, shirts and jerseys. The college players are all great with our 14 year olds (and 13 year old Ethan, who is enamored with the tall, strong, smiling young men in sharp green and orange uniforms). They sign autographs, joke around, enjoy a bit of small talk with the young Florida players.

Amazingly, we win our first game. Bryan Hill hits a home run that goes so far the pitcher on the opposing team watches it until it disappears over the fence, then over the grassy berms beyond the fence. He shakes his head. The ball must have traveled more than 400 feet.

For entertainment we go as a team to one of the College World Series baseball games: LSU vs. Miami. Omaha is awash in baseball, as it is every year at this time. The main street around historic Rosenblatt Stadium, where all the games take place, are a college student's party playground. Pavilions with team merchandise. Tents with burgers and hot dogs and lots of beer. Hawkers selling tickets to games. Pretty girls in short shorts and college boys in dirty t-shirts and worn cut off jeans line the sidewalks three deep. Moving through the hordes with young boys in tow is a challenge, but we wend our way to the long, winding line up to the stadium. Our tickets are the least expensive seats in the distant outfield. We are surrounded by students. LSU students. Drunk LSU students. Drunk rowdy LSU students. They throw food. They pour beer on one another. They shout profanities at the players, the crowds, anyone within earshot. This is not Christian Vic's cup of tea. One of our parents, Vinny Dassaro, who like his son is built like a 250 pound basketball, nearly gets into a fight with an LSU student a row ahead of us who is particularly obnoxious. Of course, we're cheering for Miami, the team from our hotel and our home state. This doesn't endear us to the ranks (and rank) LSU fans who surround us. Miami goes on to win that game 9-5, but we weren't in attendance. Vic pulled us all out before Vinny or any other of our parents could land punches on the drunks in the row ahead of us. Miami loses its next two games to Cal-State Fullerton and South Carolina and is eliminated from the tournament. We return to the hotel after one of our games to find the lobby empty, the tables gone, the memorabilia missing as if it were never there.

⚾

In the second game the Wildcats face the most highly touted 14 year old pitcher in Illinois. He throws hard, in the low 80s, and with the shorter distance from the mound his pitches are overpowering. The boys on the team swing at air. They are behind every pitch. It looks like he pitches in fast motion, or our boys are swinging in molasses. We can actually hear the ball thump into the catcher's mitt before the hitter's swing is complete. THWUMP WHOOSH. THWUMP WHOOSH. It goes on like this through four innings. We are visitors, so they will have the last at bat.

But they're not hitting us either. They're winning, but barely. The score is 2-0. There's a two hour time limit on these games, and we're coming up on it. In the fifth inning our first batter walks, and Ethan is up next. He hits a squishy, squibbly ground ball that the shortstop misplays. Runners on first and third. It's our first runner in scoring position all day. A wild pitch, and the run scores. 2-1. Ethan is stranded on base. We don't score again that inning.

As the team runs onto the field Vic pulls Ethan aside. "Are you ok to pitch?" Ethan tells him yes. "Ethan," Vic says, "Listen to me closely. We're almost out of time. We need three outs in five minutes so we can get back on the field before time expires. Got that?"

Ethan responds with a "Yessir" and trots quickly to the mound. Then the almost impossible happens. Working quickly, Ethan gets the other team to do exactly what he wants. Nine pitches. Three strikeouts. Five minutes. We're back up to bat.

Ethan is up first, and he hits a bomb, the first hit into the outfield off the pitcher all game. He hits the ball down the left field line over the left fielder's head. It one hops to the fence, and Ethan is on second. The truth is, Ethan was probably lucky to get his bat on the ball. His swing was late, and he connected with the very end of the bat. The next batter up, Kyle McLanahan, lays down a bunt. The opposing team is slow to react. Ethan is safe on third, Kyle on first. A wild pitch, and Ethan scores. The game is tied and Kyle is on third. More wild pitches. A walk. A single. The Wildcats are up by two. They're one-half inning plus one game away from moving into the championship round.

Ethan is not quite as sharp in the bottom of the seventh. It takes him eleven pitches to retire the side. The next day Kyle pitches and wins with an assortment of junk and side arm foolery, and we're in the semifinals against a tough Missouri team.

The next day is again gray, blustery, with a cool mist in the air and highs in the 50s. Ethan starts the Missouri game and controls the big hitting team through five innings. He's only thrown 60 pitches. They can't hit his changeup. The Wildcats are ahead 5-0. In the sixth inning he tires visibly. The changeup starts to turn the wrong way. He has now thrown 86 pitches and they've scored three runs. I am getting nervous, but I trust Vic. He knows that Ethan is tired, too. Vic calls time during the inning and walks out to the mound. He wants to save Bronson for the championship game. He asks Will Harris if he can pitch and Will, averting his eyes, says no, it's too cold, he's not warmed up enough to throw. Vic asks Ethan if he's got one more inning in him, and of course Ethan says yes.

Unfortunately, he doesn't. He gets one out, but on the 22nd pitch of the inning, with two runners on base, the big hitter for the Missouri team crushes a ball and sends it way over the left field fence, across the street behind the fence, hopping into the yard of the people whose house sits beyond the street, the fence, and the field. They win 6-5. Game over. Tournament over. Ethan has thrown 108 pitches. Vic tells me later he realizes he made a mistake and shouldn't have let Ethan go so long, but he had nowhere else to go.

Ethan's tired. His arm hangs limply at his side. It's not hurting, just exhausted. He has nothing left. Some of the boys on the team are upset that we lost, that Ethan gave up that last home run, but Ethan's not. He knows he gave everything he had, and he's smiling and relaxed, taking it easy in the hotel pool and hot tub. His arm's dead, but he also knows it was the last time he'll pitch until the fall.

I, on the other hand, am full of fret and regret. I am left wondering, once again, what I should have done. I had been pacing all during the sixth inning when Ethan's pitch count began to grow and he started to struggle. Vic saw this and knew I was concerned, but told me not to worry. Ethan hadn't thrown much all tournament. He'd be all right. And he was all right. And Ethan threw too many pitches.

◯

During the next week Vic confides in me.

"I'm not sure I'm going to coach again in the fall," he says. "There are too many problems with parents. Too many kids who lack the commitment to me that I give to them. Sometimes I just don't think I can go through all this again."

Vic doesn't believe in picking up kids from other teams to bolster his lineup for tournaments, eliminating playing time for his own players. He doesn't believe in cutting or replacing players who have been loyal to him and the team. If you're on his team, you're on his team. He carries the same players from season to season. Ideally that means his teams become better over time. But the defections, the quitters, the whispers behind closed doors have taken their toll.

With that uncertainty, and with Vic's knowledge, Ethan and I go shopping for another team. We land on the Florida Tars, the most talented group of boys Ethan has ever played with. The two coaches, Randy Snodgrass and Ralph Albano, both have college and minor league experience. The team boasts four pitchers who, at age 14, throw 80 mph or more: Ethan, who has just touched 80; Joe Lovecchio, the tall, hard throwing righthander from the Scrappers; Brian Johnson, who now, after multiple injuries and teams, plays shortstop and throws in the mid-80s; and rubber-armed Mike McDonald, whose snappy, slingshot arm delivery has balls touching 88. Another player, Nick Franklin, is a soft-throwing junk ball pitcher who throws a high percentage of strikes from a variety of arm positions (Nick later goes on to be a first round draft pick of the Seattle Mariners, plays shortstop and throws in the low 90s). The team is fully funded by two baseball dads – Hank Varnell, an executive for Sysco Products, and Alan

Rainey, recently provided a large severance package from the biggest timeshare resort company in Central Florida. Their sons, Henry and Greg, play prominent positions on the team. So does Ralph's son Nick, the starting second baseman. They've put the team together. They've hired the coaches. And even though they are unquestionably the controlling forces, grumbling begins almost immediately. The ugly spectre of daddyball rears its head and won't go away. The fall season ends in controversy, one into which I'm sucked. The team, arguably one of the most talented in the state, if not the country, goes nowhere. No chemistry. No great wins. No big tournament victories. I get calls from other parents who are disgruntled by the playing time Hank and Ralph's sons receive. I am lobbied to join a group who threaten to leave unless there are new coaches. Both Hank and Alan talk to me, as I'm sure they talk to many other parents. The team stays together. Ralph and Randy are let go. They hire Shane Gierke, the son of the Edgewater High School baseball coach, Chip Gierke. As part of the deal we get the use of the Edgewater baseball fields during the weekend. But like any deal that's too good to be true, this one has its hidden side.

ⓓ

As it turns out, one of the assets and the curses of the "travel ball" system is that the best players become commodities. When a boy plays high school baseball, he has nowhere to play but at the school (and for the baseball coach) in which he is districted. Since schools are delineated by established boundaries, where you live determines who you play for, much like little league. In high school, if you're lucky you get a good coach. If you're not, you don't. In travel ball if you're not happy with your coach, or your playing time, or the position you're playing, or the other boys on the team, or a myriad of other self-determined issues, you can pack up and leave, or you can live out your team commitment (something I've always told Ethan he has to do), and then leave. The best players thus become valuable possessions, to be coddled, sucked up to, wooed, and pacified. So do their parents, whose high expectations of what their children deserve as well as the high talent level they believe their children have, are often so inflated as to be unapproachable.

I was not immune to this. I believed that Ethan deserved lots of playing time, lots of innings pitched, lots of at bats. I believed he was one of the best. My own hubris and pride tainted my perception. My only saving grace was that I was loyal. I wouldn't threaten to quit or leave, unlike other parents who quit at the drop of a hat, convincing their sons that their saleability as a product meant more than living up to their word, that because they could influence others by threatening to quit and play elsewhere, they should. Some parents had already developed the reputation of "team hoppers," jumping from team to team in mid-season if they weren't satisfied that their boy was getting precisely what they thought he deserved. But there's conflict even in this moral lesson. Do you teach your child to tough it out in a bad situation if you've given your word, teaching them to place a high value on personal commitment, or do you use the power you have to change that situation, making a move that is better for them, that will subject them to less anguish and greater opportunity for success? Parents can justify either, though it often came down to a simple case of ego. Some parents just couldn't stand for their child not to be in the limelight, to be the star, and while they rarely admitted it to themselves, that was the cause of their leap to another team, and perhaps, the leap by bad example into the pit of self-absorbed, attention sponging bad behavior.

Coaches for these teams also suffer the consequences of the system. Just like in the big leagues, if a talented team didn't perform up to expectations, the coaches bore the brunt of the blame, not the players. Randy and Ralph both knew baseball. Randy was a great motivator if not a brilliant strategist or pitching coach (even though he pitched in college). They were both easygoing men who were accessible, talked to the parents and cared about the boys on their team. They also had a reputation for being too soft, too easy on the boys during practice, and coached under the yolk of satisfying petty parents and the team organizers with sons on the team. Sadly, at any time there is doubt about a father's son, and there is room to question why the boy is playing, the gossip and questions fly. Ralph took the heat here. Nick was a good second baseman with a weak arm and not much of a bat. He later grew to become not only an excellent infielder with an innate ability to get the clutch hit, but an outstanding student as well. But because Nick played, Ralph got shafted. Enter Shane Gierke. Young, hotheaded, uncommunicative, Shane Gierke.

Shane, it is widely perceived by team parents, has a crush on one of the team mothers, whose son, the replacement for the departed Nick Albano, is getting inordinate time at second base despite having a weak arm and not much of a bat. He's replaced Nick 1 with Nick 2.

Shane's impatient, prone to temper tantrums, and he and I quickly butt heads.

I am now the team asshole. I have walked, not once, but twice into the dugout to tell Shane Ethan is done pitching. He's told me to stay out of the dugout, off the field, that he'll kick both me and E off the team if I do it again. But I don't care anymore. I'm not going to risk further abuse, further damage to Ethan's arm over meaningless games. When he's thrown enough pitches, he's thrown enough. He's through. Done. No more two games in a day. No more hundred pitches. In my head that number is 80. Sometimes, because of game situations, Ethan exceeds it by a few, but Shane knows now that Ethan has a limited pitch count, and he despises me for it.

The boys on the team aren't taking too well to me, either. I hear them imitate my shouts, my comments. "Eee-than!" they mimic in a deep voice, then laugh as they walk away. Ethan laughs too, but I can see the mixture of anger and anguish on his face when he does – anger at me, I assume, not his teammates, anguish over the embarrassment I've put him through, the taunting I receive that he believes I deserve. It doesn't matter what I say anymore, or whether other parents do the same. Joey's father comments on every pitch, every move Joey makes, but he doesn't have the reputation I now wear like a scarlet letter. I can yell out, "Good pitch!" and applaud, and they mimic me. They like E, and think it's the best joke on him and me, unaware of how it hurts, how it festers under my skin. Don't I have the right that other parents have, to praise my son on the field, to let out a moan under my breath when he walks a batter or strikes out? Or have I given up that right at this point because of past transgressions? I wear the capital letter A, asshole, all the time.

⟊

Ethan pitches against a Michigan team, the same boys who beat Easton in the Cooperstown finals, and beats them 7-4. It is a moral victory for E. After he has pitched five innings he is put on first base, where he promptly gets spiked by one of the Michigan players. The cut doesn't need stitches, but he has a bloody wound to sport for his victory, and a purple scar on his thigh to live with forever. His left hand gets stepped on during a weekend tournament, and two knuckles fracture. He continues playing, even though his fingers are so swollen they look like little sausages.

The season ends with Ethan pitching against Team Easton in the state championship tournament. The winner advances into the championship round. Ethan is so hopped up he tries too hard. He wants to show his old teammates what they lost when he left. He overthrows, forsaking control for velocity, and they hammer him. The first baseman who replaced him hits a double. Ozzie gets a hit. Mirko gets a hit. Three runs in the first inning. Another run in the second. He is taken out for another pitcher, who controls Easton, but the Tars lose once again. The talented team with a plethora of arms isn't worth a footnote in the AAU record books.

CHAPTER 6
Preppie

Lefthanded pitcher Frank Viola won the Most Valuable Player Award in the 1987 World Series with the Minnesota Twins. The next year he went 24-7 for the Twins and won the Cy Young Award as the best pitcher in the American League. When we met Viola, he was the head baseball coach at Lake Highland Preparatory School where his son played baseball, one daughter was a nationally ranked diver and another daughter played volleyball. Ethan was excited to attend Lake Highland to work under a renowned coach like Viola, but we quickly learned, by his own admission, that he didn't know how to coach or teach pitchers. He didn't start pitching until late in his teens, and was one of those players who could do everything right, but couldn't describe how or what he was doing.

Viola is a big man with a big mustache and a pronounced New York accent. Affable, quick to smile and quick with an opinion, we hoped, after Ethan's stellar sixth grade year playing for the high school middle team, that Frank would move Ethan up to the junior varsity team, but that's not what happened. At the first mandatory team meeting of the year, attended by both parents and players, Frank laid down the law. He wanted a 100% commitment to Lake Highland's baseball program. No interference from travel ball. No playing for other teams. It was all Lake Highland or nothing. At the same time we found out that he wanted Ethan to play another year on the middle school team, a hodge podge, now, of seventh and eighth graders of varying degrees of skill and experience. I realized, quickly, that we were right back where we'd been in little league – held back, in my opinion, to a lower level of play and competition than was necessary for Ethan to grow as a player. We talked about the choice – middle school ball or the Tars, and Ethan chose the Tars.

That may have been the beginning of the end for Ethan's first high school baseball experience. Once again, I was moving Ethan down a path that I thought was in his best interest, but left a trail of controversy in its wake. There's no way to know now how much that decision tainted us in the eyes of the coaches, but where we thought we were following the dictates of the baseball program by not playing for them, it may have undermined Ethan long term.

We were at the very cusp of a major change in baseball philosophy. In the past, high school ball in the spring had been paramount....king....the first big goal every ballplayer wished to achieve....a mandatory achievement for a player to play in college. The face of high school baseball, its preeminence and power, was changing rapidly. We were watching high school ball move from prestige to irrelevance, and were caught in the maelstrom of change.

High school coaches, who work for a pittance, don't like to think they're irrelevant, and it used to be they weren't. They wrote the recommendations that got players into college. They were the father figures who shaped young men and women. They were the models of behavior for young athletes. They were the first real experts, the acknowledged authorities in their field.

In baseball, that all began to change in the late nineties and continues to evolve today. Suddenly players realized the highest level of competition wasn't in high school, where teams were made up of players from districted regions, but on travel teams where players from all over the state tried out. Premier teams in Central Florida would attract players from as far away as Tallahassee and Jacksonville. The best and largest organizations like the East Cobb Astros actually had families who relocated to Atlanta for the sole purpose of having their sons play ball with them. Other teams would house boys for the summer from anywhere in the country. It was, literally, a whole new ballgame.

At the same time parents and players alike were taking a closer look at the coaches of high school teams. Some, like Viola, had real baseball experience and lengthy, irrefutably impressive resumés. Others came with few credentials and even less experience. They hopped from high school sport to sport, and the only real knowledge they had came, not from college or pro ball, or years working under established coaches, but from their own high school experience, or books, or college clinics. They sometimes came armed with less know-how than the high school players they coached, who had been playing under various coaches and instructors for a decade or more.

When Ethan tried out for the Lake Highland team as an eighth grader, unbeknownst to us he started with one mark against him. He had rejected them the year before. Now he is placed on the junior varsity team, and is warned, once again, that his commitment must be 100% to his school, not his club team. He is playing for the Florida

Tars and doesn't want to give them up, so we come up with what we think is the perfect compromise. He makes the high school team his priority. Whenever he is supposed to pitch for Lake Highland, he will, and he won't pitch for the Tars. If games conflict, he'll play for the high school. When there are no conflicts, he'll do both. Other boys at Lake Highland are doing the same. None of them, however, are pitchers, which places an extra strain on the arm and an additional dilemma on scheduling.

Everything works fine until one weekend when the Tars, in a minor tournament, advance to the semi-finals against the Windermere Wildcats, a local team with several very good baseball prospects and another ballplayer from Lake Highland. Ethan throws 84 pitches and wins. We have been told his next pitching assignment for Lake Highland was Thursday night, so he has plenty of time to recover. We also discover that the father of the Windermere player from Lake Highland reports Ethan's pitching to the junior varsity coaches. Then his pitching gets changed to Tuesday, and we panic. There's no way he'll be ready to throw again by then.

As luck, or karma, or coincidence would have it, Ethan gets sick on Monday. Maybe it was the heat, or the exhaustion from the weekend, but he starts running a fever Monday night and can't go to school the next day. We are equally relieved and realize we've dodged a bullet, one we won't allow to occur again.

It's the Thursday after Ethan got sick and missed his start. Ethan is scheduled to close against Eustis High School, a bigger school than Lake Highland. His grandmother is visiting from Scarsdale, New York, and we're all excited to drive out to the country ball field and watch him throw. Four innings pass. Five. Six. The game remains close, the teams separated by a single run, and the Lake Highland pitcher, who has thrown a great game, is tiring. The Lake Highland junior varsity coach calls time, walks to the mound, takes the ball from the pitcher, and brings in someone else. Ethan doesn't know why. He remains on the bench, ready to throw. The coach doesn't say a word to him. Ethan has no idea why he didn't go in after warming up. Another left handed pitcher/first baseman quits the team due to lack of playing time. And that's the way the season plays out.

For the next eight games Ethan shows up to every practice, works hard, keeps his mouth shut, and doesn't get in a single game. He sits. He stews. He waits for his name to be called. Finally, frustrated and grasping little, with my encouragement he asks the coach why he hasn't played the second half of the season. The response, with Viola's support: They know that Ethan missed a pitching assignment on a Tuesday because he chose to pitch instead for the Florida Tars. They saw it online, posted on the Tars website. That went against his commitment to his high school team, and so he was benched for the remainder of the season. But the coaches never said a word to him or told him anything.

Ethan is dumbfounded. "Coach, I'm sorry but I was sick that day," he says. "I pitched the weekend before for the Tars, but I never once missed pitching for you because of my AAU team."

The coach doesn't believe him, or me. And the truth is, while he would have been available to play, pitching would have been the worst thing for Ethan that Tuesday. In lieu of that, he lost half a season, and at the end of that school year, Lake Highland lost him. Looking forward to a higher level of competition, and because of the breakdown in communication between player and coaches, Ethan transfers to Winter Park High School, a public school with nearly 4,000 students, and a baseball coach who is virtually a local legend, has been at the school for nearly 25 years and who has a reputation for being a pitcher's coach – Bob King.

As we leave we are asked by the school to list the reasons for our departure. We cite the quality of the education at Winter Park, a highly rated high school, the higher level of competition at a school that size, and the issue with the Lake Highland coaches. I detail this lack of communication in a letter to the dean of the middle school, and find out, in the process, that a handful of other junior varsity players also played on AAU teams during the season. The junior varsity coach is not brought back. This could have been for any reasons, both his own personal or the school's decision, but we are never privy to the process. A year later Viola is also dismissed as head coach. He goes on to become a TV commentator for baseball games, and a colorful figure on local sports talk shows. Ethan goes on to the first goal he's worked so hard to achieve, the first benchmark for all baseball players – high school ball.

CHAPTER 7
High Ball

On August 5, 2008, 15 year old Nate Winters of Winter Park, Florida fell off the Super Air Nautique ski boat his older brother Zach was driving. The boat had turned sharply, and Nate was thrown into the lake. When he tried to swim back to the boat, he realized he couldn't kick with either his right or left leg. The boat's motor had chewed him up. His left leg was torn apart from mid-thigh to mid-calf. His left foot was intact, but barely attached. His right foot was split apart, his Achilles tendon severed, and he had multiple cuts from his thighs to his chest.

While a friend on the boat called 911, Zach made a tourniquet from ski rope to stop the remaining blood from spurting out of Nate's torn legs. Everyone on the boat thought he would die before they reached shore, before he could be loaded onto an emergency helicopter, before he could be operated on at the hospital.

Nate lost 80% of the blood in his body, and somehow, miraculously survived. His left leg was amputated above the knee. He had nine surgeries in the first ten days after the accident.

"The night that Nate got injured," his father, Dr. Tom Winters, an orthopedic surgeon said, "over 100 people showed up to the hospital." Nate had played the season before as one of five freshman on the Winter Park High School varsity baseball team. Ethan was the first baseball player to show up at the hospital. "It's something I'll never forget, Ethan showing up first," Dr. Winters said later. "We had a really nice chat."

For about fifteen minutes Ethan and Dr. Winters talked baseball. Dr. Winters told Ethan that Nate had always looked up to him, that deep down he knew Ethan was really a good kid and that he'd talk to Coach King and tell him that the team was going to need his leadership that year. As more and more people poured into the hospital waiting area to hear news about Nate, Bob King, the head baseball coach at Winter Park, showed up. He went up to every baseball player on the team and said hello and shook their hands.

Everyone except Ethan. He wouldn't look him in the eye. Ethan tried to catch his attention, and King walked right by without

117

saying a word or acknowledging him at all.

A year later, amidst much fanfare and media coverage, Nate pitched again for Winter Park High School. He was featured in an ESPN special, was on the cover of local magazines and was the subject of several columns in the Orlando Sentinel. He and his family met with the Pope. Bob King called what he accomplished "an unbelievable, unforgettable lifetime experience." Through the course of his recovery and rehabilitation, King visited the Winters home regularly, almost daily. A once strained relationship with Dr. Winters became a close friendship. And through it all, King never once recognized Ethan's existence – Ethan who had helped the high school win its last district championship.

How this came about, how this relationship ended so bitterly, how it got to the point where, in the most desperate, extreme circumstance a coach couldn't bring himself to show a momentary kindness to a player, is the story of Ethan's time as a high school baseball player. It is a stunning sequence of misunderstandings, miscommunications, and mishandled affairs by all concerned. No one came out unscathed, and no one was beyond criticism or reproach. The person who paid the most was Ethan.

For many years a unique institution, separated from the main campus, the 9th grade center at Winter Park High School is a mosh pit of awkward, self-absorbed, bombastic, hormonally challenged, insecure 15 year olds, coming together for the first time. It's a mix of two primary feeder schools, private school students who want to try public school for the first time, and a handful of long distance transfers. There, for a year, the ninth graders become top dogs, kings and queens of their turf. Scared of sex and curious about it. Flirtatious and shy. There is no one older. There is no one younger. It's just same age boys and girls in a new environment, meeting one another and establishing new cliques, new territories, new hierarchies of popularity and isolation during one of the most trying times of teenagerhood.

The most obvious group is the athletes. They also interface the most with the older students at the main campus, because they shuttle over to the main campus in the afternoon on school buses and work out and play with the tenth through twelfth graders. Along with a few others, Ethan came in with a reputation. Because of his time with Incinelli, he'd already played with many of the boys on the Winter Park team, some of whom still held him in disdain because of both his mouth and his ability, and some of whom accepted him for what he could do, and these looked forward to having him on the team.

During the fall many parents comment that this might be a group of boys who could one day challenge for the state championship. Under Incinelli's volunteer coaching the team plays gritty, competitive baseball. Besides Ethan there were three other quality ninth grade pitchers: Chad Modomo, a stocky right hander who, when he kept the ball down low was virtually unhittable, Kyle Gonzalez, a 220 pound linebacker and straight A student projected to someday have a 90+ mph fastball, and Ryan Lamkin, a right handed version of Ethan. Matt Toelke, a hard throwing tenth grader, and Hugh Hart, another tenth grader with a big curve ball, rounded out the rotation. And the team was loaded with athletes, boys who could run fast, throw far, who looked the part and played the game, boys with quick hands, light feet, boys with fire in their eyes and a desire to excel at this level and compete at the next.

Bob King walks back and forth from the small cinderblock equipment shed to the field, pausing behind the backstop to watch the junior varsity tryouts. He's heard a lot about this group of players, too. The boys are throwing the ball around the infield. Ethan is at first base with the first group, and they toss the ball around fluidly, confidently, quickly.

My eagerness overcomes me. I go over to the coach and introduce myself. "Coach King," I say, "I'm David Bornstein. They look good, don't they?"

"Oh," he says, smiling, revealing all his teeth, "you're Bornstein's dad. I was warned about you."

I'm taken aback, flustered. I don't know what to say, so I reply, "What do you mean?"

"Viola called me when you left," he tells me. "He said your boy can hit as well as pitch."

"Warned about what?" I ask, but I don't get an answer. I can't tell whether he heard me or not. His back is turned to me. He's close to the fence, watching the action on the field. The assistant coaches hit fungoes to the infielders, who simulate outs at first, double plays, and King is totally absorbed. I sit back down in the bleachers with the other parents who have come out to watch. Did he mean warned about you in you two? Me and Ethan? Or just me? I don't know whether to pursue the conversation or not, but I understand that I've been warned as well.

☉

Ethan is getting more…teenagerly? Difficult? Ornery? Ninth graders can attend the high school homecoming party at the Hard Rock Live at Universal Studios Theme Park, and Ethan has been invited to go with a group of his friends in a stretch limousine. I discover a bottle of tequila is missing. He admits, later on and after much questioning, to having taken it to impress his friends. He wants to be out later on weekend nights. He chafes at the idea of a curfew of any sort. I'm glad we have the law on our side. We tell him he has to be home by eleven. His sixteen year old buddies can't drive past then.

He's also developed a set of hand signals for me to obey during games. It's a difficult combination, because he can ignore every sound, every shout, every belch and insult thrown his way, but if I sigh too deeply he hears it like I'm screaming at him. It was as if I shouted his name to get his attention while he blotted everyone and everything else out. And then he does something even more blatant, more obvious to everyone. He stops what he's doing on the mound, in the batter's box, stares and me and gives me a signal.

So he hears me groan when he swings at a bad pitch and he turns around, glaring at me, and runs his thumb and finger over his lips. "Zip it!" Or he's pitching and I can't help but notice that everything's going high and outside to righties. "Your arm's dragging!" I shout out, and he takes his index finger and draws a line across his throat. I look up at him and shrug benevolently, with a stupid grin on my face. He does it again, cutting his throat with his finger. "CUT IT OUT!" his gesture silently screams. Everyone looks over at me, and now I raise my eyebrows in embarrassment, half-smile, and slink away to the farthest corner inside myself I can find.

Ethan's finger across his throat means more than just shut up. We're so tied together, so tightly knit after years of travel, years of practice and pain, that this is his first effort – clumsy, over the top, extreme – to start cutting the cords. He's at an age where he needs to sever the connection, and yet his choice of symbols is far more fitting than he knows, for he's cutting his own neck to get what he wants. "If

120

you don't back off I will die," he implies. "I am prepared to END IT ALL if you don't cut it out." His message is overblown, overwrought, full of teen angst, hatred, total disregard. And at the same time all he hears is me. He directs all his attention towards the one person he's trying to separate from – his dad. And I'm fighting it with all my heart. I'm not shutting up, though I try for minutes, sometimes tens of minutes at a time.

He's telling me, loud and clear in his silent gestures, his symbolic suicide, that he needs to go his own way, to take control of his own life, of what's most important to him – his baseball - and that I have to let him. And letting go is hard, especially after the investment I've put into him. Not just the time, or the money, or the sweat equity, but all the emotional investment of watching him succeed and knowing, in part, it's because of me that it's happened. That's what he's asking me to give up. He's telling me that now and forevermore, it's about him, not me. His dream. His accomplishments. His successes to bask in, his failures to deal with, and the results of his work are borne of his commitment, not mine. That's hard for me, and, I imagine, any parent to bear.

For some, I suppose, the act of letting go isn't that difficult. They were never holding on in the first place, or else they made a vow early on to kick their little ducklings out of the nest and watch them float downstream. Off you go. On your own. Send me a quack when you get where you're going.

I was not one of those. I never had a dad who played catch, and I wanted to make sure my children knew I was there. I wanted to be the dad who caught everything. And in being there so steadfastly, so solidly, I felt like I might vanish, like a puff of smoke in the wind, if I were to suddenly become uninvolved. I might not be part of their lives anymore. That's where I was now. The scary part is, of course, that in cutting the throat it's the child who must suffer the real pain. Parents have already been through the loss of childhood, the special strength and loneliness that comes from separating from parents once. Children experience that loss daily for years. I watched Ethan in the early stages of cutting away. I saw the bitterness grow in him as he refused to ask for our help because he was convinced it was the only way for him to be strong, and I wanted desperately to reach out and save him, to offer him the exact help he refused to take, only to watch him draw his finger across his throat. Ethan may have been 15, but I knew he still needed me more than he wanted to admit. He still needed an adult to sit next to him when he drove. He still wanted his mom to hug him when he needed it, but he wanted her to know without his asking. He still wanted me to be there, but to be there silently, ambiguously, invisibly present and ready at a moment's notice to toss him a safety net, though he'd never be the one to call out for it. He'd rather fall and break a bone.

And it was painful for me, painful to the point of being impossibly hard. I was being asked to say goodbye for good to something I'd helped create. I was his enabler, his benefactor, the genie who made his wishes come true. Now I was being shown the veritable bottle of my own limitations. I was being shown the door, told where to go by my 15 year old son. And I knew it was the right thing, the only thing to do. Ethan was the one pitching, hitting, performing, not me. Of course I knew that, but high school was the time to finally accept it.

At the time Bob King was entering his 22nd year coaching baseball at Winter Park High School. King's tenure had been nothing short of a model of consistency. In those 22 years his teams posted one season in which they lost more games than they won, and he was approaching his 500th win as head coach. He had a reputation as a coach who played the game by the books and followed the odds. He liked small ball. He liked moving runners into scoring position with a sacrifice bunt. He'd always give up the out to get the runner to second. He hated walks. He appreciated the beauty of a low scoring game.

King is a short, thin, wiry man with glasses perched on a gaunt face stretched by years in the Florida sun. When he smiles he bares his teeth in an expression that could as easily be a grimace or a warning growl. He's had heart problems, shoulder problems, and even though he can hit fungoes like a machine that knock infielders back on their heels he no longer throws batting practice. He always wears shorts and a floppy safari hat. He is organized and thorough. In fact, he brags about the fact that he has kept a record of every practice he has ever held. He can tell you the cloud cover, how hard the wind was blowing and the drills done on March 15, 1989, or any day practice was held during his entire tenure at Winter Park. On the days practice wasn't held he could tell you whether or not it was raining, or the other reason it might have been called off. Games he coaches have historically been low scoring affairs. It sounds like the perfect opportunity for a competitive pitcher.

King was a middle infielder in high school in New York, and a utility infielder at St. Frances College. After four years in the Navy, he got his MS degree from Nova Southeastern University in Health Education, and taught at Richmond Heights Elementary, Evans High and Glenridge Junior/Middle School, where he coached boys basketball for 18 years. His teams had won 8 district championships, three regional championships, and been to the state final four twice, coming in second place once, in 1998 when Matt Incinelli was the number one pitcher. He has never won a state championship.

King has always prided himself on what he calls "brutal honesty," code for saying anything under the guise of objective truth without regard for anyone else's feelings or well-being. He likes to say he just tells it like it is. This is a common old school coaching philosophy, the belief that the coach, in a position that is at once unassailable, objective, and all-knowing, can help his student athletes by letting them know exactly where they stand on the team, their real strengths and shortcomings, not those opinions to which their biased and overly invested parents cling. It's also an excuse for not worrying about the effects of what one says, about speaking without consideration for how much hurt could be inflicted, how low someone could feel when the message gets delivered. It lets the sender off the hook in the name of honesty, but brutal honesty, painful honesty, honesty without compassion.

Think of all the times, all the lines people use to say whatever they want without repercussion or concern it may have on the receiver. They start by saying they're just being straightforward. They're telling it like it is. They call it the way they see it. All these catch phrases are code for "brutal honesty," for compassionless comments that don't allow room for discussion or debate. They're all ways of saying, "I know the truth and there's no rebutting what I tell you." They're all vehicles designed to cut off second opinions, to put the receiver in their place. How often does someone say, "I'm going to tell you like it is," and then say something nice, something complimentary, something caring? Rarely. Is it wrong for your guard to go up when someone prefaces their conversation with the simple justification that they're just being straightforward? Brutally honest? Absolutely not. Put up your shield and prepare to get battered. Brutal honesty is just a way to hurt someone under the guise of constructive criticism, and then walk away without guilt or consequence.

When E came into the program Coach King had his own concerns to deal with. His son Stephen, a nationally ranked shortstop, having already signed with Louisiana State University, one of the most prestigious Division 1 baseball programs in the country, was preparing both for his senior year on the baseball team and the professional draft in June. Stephen looked like the picture perfect, prototypical baseball player: 6'2", lean, long-legged, a chiseled body, square chin and sandy blonde hair. He could throw 92 mph off the mound, hit with power, and run like a jackrabbit on steroids. The pro scouts were drooling over him. After years of living on a teacher's salary, the idea that his son would soon command a six or seven figure signing bonus after the draft was foremost on King's mind, and for that matter, on everyone else's as well. The baseball program at the high school revolved around Stephen that year. He was only the fifth player in King's time at Winter Park who was going to a Division 1 school to play baseball. And few, if any players had the draft potential that swirled around him all year long. There were a handful of professional scouts at every game, taking notes, evaluating his every movement, his batting, his demeanor at short. With Stephen and three lefthanded starters, the Winter Park Varsity team is expected to be one of the better teams in Central Florida.

Varsity doesn't need another lefthander out of the gates, especially a ninth grade lefthander. That's fine. Ethan's become best friends with Chris Quintero, who joined Team Easton when Ethan left. Chris was a real stud for Easton, pitching, playing outfield and infield, but he stopped growing at 5'8", and now has settled into the outfield. Ethan doesn't mind hanging on junior varsity at all. It takes any pressure or focus off him and puts it back on the game.

Controversy's already begun. During tryouts Anthony Morin, who played shortstop and pitched for Incinelli, gets cut. Admittedly, he had a bad tryout, but it's more than just a kid not getting an opportunity. It's about a boy's well-being. He lives with his grandmother. They don't have much in their lives except the hope that he will get a scholarship to play baseball somewhere. Otherwise, they don't have the money for him to go to college. He gets cut anyway.

Another boy, one of Incinelli's catchers, quits. Rumor has it he likes to party more than play. A third boy gets cut when he is blamed for defecating in the ball field urinal. He staunchly denies it. He is one of the fastest players on the team, an athletic kid with lots of potential. His parents are devastated. The father goes to talk to the coaches, to no avail. Just like that, three players who were expected to make the team quit the sport.

Meanwhile, Ethan begins the season hot and cold. His pitching is on the money, but he presses with his hitting, goes 0 for 3 in the first game, and downhill from there. Bob Lutz, the coach of the junior varsity team, bumps Ethan down in the batting order, then takes him out of the lineup almost altogether. In the first half of the season, while he is undefeated as a pitcher with an ERA under 2.00, as a hitter he is 0 for 11 in ten games. With few times up at the plate, there's not much chance of him working out of whatever slump he's in.

We are working on some kinks in the backyard. Hitting kinks. I have erected a big net, and E and I go out with a regular batting tee, a horseshoe shaped tee to hone his swing, and a bucket of fifty balls. I sit on the bucket as I set the balls on the various tees and do "soft toss" with him. He starts off by missing everything. He hits the top of the ball, and the ball goes into the dirt. He hits underneath the ball, and it pops up slowly into the top of the net. He knocks over the tee. He breaks one of the tees on the horseshoe when he hits it with the bat. He slams the bat into the ground and is about to swear when I raise my finger, and he stifles himself and instead shouts out "Argh!" He slams the bat into the ground again and wants to slam it into a tree, when I say, "Eee-than!" more sternly and he stops, catches his breath, and returns to the tee.

I've noticed a few things. The truth is, I'm not sure what exactly his problem is, but I know his swing doesn't look right. I can't pinpoint the precise difference between this and his normal swing, but I know something's off. Maybe it's his stance. We widen the distance between his feet, then shorten it until he feels comfortable. Maybe it's where his hands are when he begins to swing. Not far enough back. Not high enough. I wonder if it's the little hitch when he triggers his swing, or if he's pulling his head, or striding too far forward. But I know there are way too many possibilities for him to try them all in one backyard BP, so we focus on a few. "Keep your hands inside the ball!" He chops the ball into the ground, shouts "Jeez!" and is about to hit the ground again with the bat when I shout at him to stop.

"You're not doing what I tell you. You're throwing your hands out. Just keep them in…"

"Shut up, dad! " he yells.

"No, you shut up," I tell him. "Just calm down and do what I'm telling you."

"You don't know what you're talking about."

"I know what you're doing wrong."

"You're not my coach. You can't tell me what to do," he shouts, and begins to stomp off.

I have a ball in my hand. "Get back here right now. You stop right there," I holler.

"I'm outta here," he says.

I'm boiling. He's not listening to me. He's disobeying. He's not doing the simplest thing. All I want is for him to stop, calm down, and reset. Take a deep breath. Start over. Listen to me and think about what I'm saying. I don't realize I need to follow the same advice myself. Instead he turns his back to me, which infuriates me further. Suddenly the ball is no longer in my hand. I've flung it at him, hard. I gasp when it hits him in the shin.

"Ow!" he screams. "What the fuck did you do that for?"

"I'm sorry," I say hurriedly, guiltily. "Are you ok? Are you hurt?" I can't believe I just threw a baseball at my son from five feet away. Thank god it hit him in the leg, not his head or shoulder or elbow. Thank god it didn't break any bones, or hit him in the eye. I could be arrested for that. Maybe I should be.

"Of course it hurts. Gaww, dad."

"I'm sorry. I'm really sorry," I keep saying over and over. "I just lost it."

Everything stops. He breathes. I breathe. The decibels disappear. The tension vanishes. We both feel small, like we're taking up very little space. He sets a ball on the tee, picks up his bat and gets ready to swing.

"Come on," he says. "Let's finish up."

It's questionable how much Lutz really knows about baseball. While he coached both baseball and football at Boone High School for 16 years, and has been the JV coach at Winter Park for five years, his real passion is golf, and he is the Boys Golf Coach at Winter Park. He stands at third base when the team is up to bat and refuses to have anyone coach first. Coaching alone, he is limited in what he can do. During practices the boys run through a set of daily drills, and Lutz's job consists of making sure the boys move from hitting station to hitting station. But there's no instruction, no corrections, no advice. No one oversees what the boys do, so if their swing is wrong, they swing wrong all practice long. They ingrain bad habits as well as good. They take fielding practice, but no one says anything or changes anything. It's just hit fungoes, throw to first. Hit fungoes, make the double play. There's no teaching the fundamentals, no practicing more complicated plays – pickoff moves, suicide squeezes, situational plays that might come up in a tight game. It seems the coaches just assume the players know these things or they wouldn't be playing high school ball.

There are also no bullpens. Pitchers don't practice throwing off a mound from 60' during the week. They throw batting practice from 40', which teaches them how to throw softly right down the middle of the plate. None of the pitchers on the team improve during the year. Some backslide. Ethan gets private pitching lessons, but clandestinely. King doesn't want his players, even the JVers, learning from anyone but him, which makes matters difficult when this coach with a reputation as a pitching guru doesn't teach pitching. On the other hand, when King hears about Ethan's limited at-bats he intervenes, and Ethan suddenly finds himself back in the top of the order and the second half of the season he goes 14 for 28, to finish with a .333 batting average.

⚾

Ethan is pitching against University High School in a tight game. It's the sixth inning, and Winter Park is leading 2-1. He's pitched the whole game, and the leadoff runner has just reached first on an infield error. Ethan gets ready to throw the next pitch when Lutz walks to the mound.

"Watch the kid on first," Lutz tells Ethan, "He's fast, and you have a really slow leg kick. Mix things up so he can't steal. Got it?"

Ethan nods his head. Lutz walks back to the dugout and Ethan starts from the stretch. He throws a first pitch strike, and the boy at first steals second. Lutz walks back to the mound.

"What did I tell you?" Lutz glares at Ethan. "Don't you listen? Now the tying run's on second. Just....get the batter."

"Yessir," Ethan mutters, his arms crossed over his chest. I can see, from the bleachers, how pissed off he is, though I don't know at that moment what's going on. It's as if I've zoomed in on him, and can feel the tension in his chest, how tightly he's gripping the ball, how his fingernails are digging into the stitches, how angry he is. He strikes the batter out with the next two pitches. After each pitch he stares straight ahead. He refuses to look anywhere but at the catcher. Two outs later, the runner remains at second. Inning over. Ethan pitches a complete game, and Winter Park wins. He doesn't say a word on the drive home, doesn't tell me until later that evening what pissed him off so much. If Lutz had walked to the mound one more time he would have had to come out of the game, and what if he really needed to come out to the mound? What if he needed to talk to the infielders, or go over a pitch sequence he wanted? What then?

I have been mostly quiet this year. There's no one responsible for Ethan's bad start hitting other than Ethan. He put too much pressure on himself, and tightened up. There's nothing to say about his pitching. He's been given the nickname E-Nasty when he's on the mound. As King had been warned about us, we were warned about Lutz - his lack of knowledge, his focus on minutiae. "Shirts tucked in at all times" seems more important than key hits, mental focus, or hitting the cut off. But while he is, at best, a non-factor during the season, a quirky disciplinarian and a borderline uncommunicative coach, he doesn't do anything that's particularly destructive or humiliating either.

So we live with him, and he with us. At season's end Ethan is the only player Lutz recommends be pulled up to varsity. He makes it a point to come up to me after Ethan's last game with the JV to tell me that Ethan was the only boy who deserved it. It's the most he's spoken to me all season long.

There's a month left in the season when Ethan is moved up. Ethan is told he won't hit, but he'll be given opportunities to see if he's ready to pitch at this new level. This is the first time I'm watching the Varsity play, and Stephen King in particular. Rumors have been flying about Stephen, and it's not surprising given the fact that his dad's the head coach and his mom's the official team scorekeeper. I watch game after game in which he hits towering fly balls as he swings for the fences only to be caught and go 0 for 3, but his batting average hovers constantly around .350. I see him make three errors in one game (two on one play) He overthrows the ball to first on a ground ball. Then a few moments later he bobbles a ground ball and, while staring at it the runner on third breaks for home and he overthrows the catcher to allow the runner to score. He is credited with no errors for the game. I watch as pitchers throw batting practice for him alone while pro scouts stand in attendance. Even so, he is unquestionably a talent worthy of LSU and probably a high draft pick. He's fast, strong, athletic, the hope and culmination of his father's dreams, and the focus of everything that goes on at the field, much to the chagrin and annoyance of many parents.

Ethan hopes things will be different on Varsity, but practices, at least, are exactly the same, only the throws are quicker, the hitters bigger. There are still no bullpens, no corrections, little teaching. King likes to talk about his pitchers developing a rhythm, and that's about as far as it goes. Having rhythm is better than not having rhythm. But what is rhythm? How does one get rhythm, and what do you do if you get out of rhythm or lose your rhythm? These questions remain mysteries. All the pitchers continue to throw batting practice from 40 feet, right down the middle of the plate, all to develop rhythm. What it develops is pitchers who throw right down the middle of the plate.

Ethan is on the mound for the first time as a varsity pitcher. The team is playing Colonial High School, a poor, mostly black school that has been rumored to be in line for demolition for years. Their baseball team is as poor as the school. Many of the players didn't start baseball until they reached high school age. It's just a sport to them, something to do after football and basketball. They share equipment, and their uniforms, the ballfield, the catcher's gear, all show signs of long use and disrepair. It reminds me of the fields in Puerto Rico. We sit baking in the sun on exposed, rickety aluminum bleachers. I am alone on the first rung of the bleachers. None of the parents know me as anything more than the year's curiosity. I am the father of the JV pitcher who just got pulled up. Some of the parents wonder what it is that Ethan can do to help the team. Some are resentful that late in the season he will take innings away from their son. Ethan has supplanted one boy in particular – Zach Winters – who has pitched well if not spectacularly in limited appearances. With Ethan on the team Zach does not get into another game the rest of the year. It is the sixth inning. Winter Park is winning 6-0, but the score should be much worse than it is. This is a team to ten run rule. Every time Stephen King has gotten up to back, he has tried to hit home runs, and instead has hit sky high fly balls that are easy outs. He is 0-3.

Tall, skinny Ethan stands scratching the mound like a rooster, making himself a home with the varsity. He throws his first pitch and the boy at the plate shuts his eyes and swings. It's an amazing swing. I see him shut his eyes, throw his bat out and he connects, hitting a blooper over the first baseman's head for a single. Ethan kicks the clay furiously. He turns around and mutters something to the air. "Oh boy," I think to myself. "He's pissed off. Not good. Not a good way to start." The other parents have a variety of expressions on their faces. Bemused. Confused. Hostile. They don't know what this kid is doing playing up. Ethan turns around to face the next batter, and suddenly, angrily, wheels towards first and picks the poor kid off. He strikes out the next two batters and stomps off the field, still upset that he gave up a hit with his first varsity pitch. Another pitcher finishes the game. But Ethan has broken in with the most transparent showing possible, revealing at once his skills, his volatility, his emotional strengths and weaknesses in ten short minutes.

It is the third game of the district championship, the first set of games on the way to the state championship tournament. To move on a team must win districts, then regionals and state. If Winter Park wins the next game they are undisputed district champs for the first time in five years. Ethan gets the start. He is pitching against Edgewater High School, the team coached by his current pitching coach, Chip Gierke.

Gierke has been an outstanding, compassionate pitching instructor. A past pitcher for Florida Southern who blew his arm out, Gierke walks with a limp and looks like the grizzled bulldog in Looney Tunes cartoons. During lessons he claps when Ethan throws a good pitch. He shakes his head and smiles when Ethan's been on for an entire lesson. Standing behind Ethan he barks out pitches. "Fastball!" "Curveball!" "Fastball high and away!" "Backdoor curveball!" "Now bust him in!" Gierke knows everything about Ethan. He knows how Ethan's pitches move, what he likes to throw when. He knows Ethan's arm slot, and can tell whether he's on or off quickly, more quickly than me or anyone else.

What I don't know is how much Gierke has told his players. What Gierke doesn't know is that Coach King has come up with a great game plan. The Edgewater hitters are free swingers. Ethan is to throw everything tailing away to right-handers – two-seam fastballs and changeups. When they catch on he'll bust them with a four-seamer inside. To date Ethan has not had a run scored against him in three Varsity outings. But this is big. This is pressure. There are hundreds of people watching, including coaches from some of the top showcase teams in Central Florida – the Orlando Scorpions and the Central Florida Renegades. Ethan wants to play for one of them, but he doesn't know if they're interested.

In the first inning of the game Stephen King hits a routine infield ground ball and races down the first base line, stepping hard on first. Something jams in his leg. He calls time out, limps off the ballfield. This is not good. Our starting shortstop and three-hole hitter is out just as the game's begun. King shifts players around. He takes a sophomore catcher/utility player, Ben Adams, who hasn't played all year except in spot situations, and puts him at second. He moves the starting second baseman, Nick Adams (no relation) over to shortstop. The game continues.

The plan works to perfection. Batter after batter, pitches are flailed at, missed, swung at early, chopped down into the ground. Ball after ball is hit to short and second for easy outs. Through three innings, Ethan has thrown a one-hitter, and that batter is stranded at first. In the third the Winter Park centerfielder, Colin Sterba, makes a beautiful, difficult diving catch of a line drive, a shot that would have gone to the fence if he hadn't stabbed it out of the air. We've gotten used to Colin's heroics. He's made plays like this all year, has batted .450, and has received no interest from any major colleges. King is not known for promoting his players, though he's done a masterful job packaging and marketing his son. "If boys would only follow my system they could get results like Stephen," he's been known to say.

I am pacing back and forth between my family, who sit in the bleachers on the first base side, and behind home plate where I have a better view of Ethan's pitches. He's throwing in the low 80s, but what keeps the hitters off balance is his location and ball movement. People are patting me on the back. Parents are telling me what a great job he's doing. I'm nervous with every pitch, ready for the world to cave in, for Ethan to tire, for the hitters to catch on and catch up to him. But it doesn't happen. Winter Park hits the ball, and finds itself sitting on a 5-0 lead in the fourth. Matt Gerber and George Martin from the Scorpions tell me they want Ethan on the team, that he's earned a spot with what he's shown tonight. Amazingly, rather than falling apart, it seems that the world is falling into place.

In the fifth inning Ethan shows the first cracks. After getting the first two outs, he gives up a hit and a walk. With runners on first and second, he is taken out and replaced by the fourth lefty King has used in the tournament, Jose Nunez, who was the number one pitcher for the high school until injury cost him most of his senior year. Jose closes out the game without any problems. Winter Park is district champ, and in every picture taken that moment Ethan is smiling as brightly as the lights on the field, holding the district trophy, leaning into his teammates, leaping into the mad dog pile on the pitcher's mound.

The crowd clears after many hugs. My back and hands ache from all the heartfelt hand slaps and high fives. On the way out Chip Gierke finds me, shakes my hand and Ethan's. "I don't like losing, but I couldn't be happier for Ethan. He pitched a great game," he tells me. Bob King spots me just before he gets on the school bus with the team. "You must be very proud," he says.

For a few moments Ethan and I stand together outside the bus before he boards it with the rest of the team. Ethan looks over at his coach, who has just gotten on the bus, like he's about to follow the Messiah to the Promised Land. "Coach King is God! He really gets me," Ethan tells me with all the unbounded exuberance and enthusiasm of youthful inexperience. "He called a great game!"

Later that night the team gathers at the varsity players' favorite after-game hangout, the local Wing House. Bob King is at the far end of a long table, sitting with parents he'd come to know over the recent seasons. We sit distantly opposite him, alone at a small table watching the festivities. We don't know the parents yet, or feel comfortable enough to fully participate, so we ride the euphoria of Ethan's performance as this new chapter in his baseball life begins. Pat and I sit and have a beer and smile across the tables at the coach and his friends, and he smiles back. E-Nasty has started his varsity career with his first big win.

◯

The Orlando Sentinel's John Ritter wrote that "Winter Park freshman Ethan Bornstein and senior Jose Nunez combined to toss a two-hitter and Timmy Williams went 4-for-4 to lead Winter Park to a 5-0 win over Edgewater in the Class 6A, District 4 championship Friday night, securing home field advantage in the first round of the state playoffs.

"Bornstein, a recent call-up from junior varsity, went 4-2/3 innings and allowed only two hits.

"The pitchers were amazing," said Winter Park Coach Bob King. "Bornstein did an outstanding job for us."

"But when the Eagles put two men on for the first time in the fifth inning, King called upon Nunez to avoid any damage. The lefty coaxed his first batter into a groundout and didn't allow a hit for the next two innings to preserve the win."

Ethan is one of the three pitchers for Winter Park named to the All-Tournament Team. In the three games the team gives up no runs. They move on to single elimination in the regionals against arch rival Lake Brantley, a perennial baseball powerhouse with a great junior lefthanded pitcher who will start the game, Johnny Gast.

Gast is virtually unhittable. With excellent control and a dirty pickoff move, he keeps the ball low, throws a hard slider and a 92 mph fastball. He already has a scholarship in hand to Florida State and is projected to be a first round draft pick the following year. He has struck out as many as 17 hitters in a 7-inning game. Gast plays for the Scorpions in the summer and fall. He has never lost to Winter Park.

Stephen King is out for the duration of the season with a sprained knee. His father isn't taking any chances with the draft approaching, and rightly so. They're looking at a payday that far eclipses what the coach would make in fifteen years, even with his $2,000 annual stipend for his baseball duties.

Winter Park starts Kaz, a senior who was converted from being a good hitting first baseman to a lefthanded pitcher who worked his way into the number one spot on the team when Jose got hurt. Kaz is a mid-80s lefty who doesn't make mistakes. He pitches well, but Lake

Brantley is still able to score two runs. In the late innings Brantley is ahead 2-1. Then, in the sixth inning, Winter Park runners reach second and third with one out. A routine ground ball is hit to third. The runner on third breaks for the plate, and the freshman third baseman throws the ball over the head of the catcher. The score is tied 2-2 with runners still on second and third. Sophomore Steve Garvey is up to bat. Steve, who has been a powerful if erratic hitter all year, decides this time he's going to battle. He fights off pitch after pitch - good sliders that bite the corner of the plate, bad pitches that he's lucky to foul off, until he hits one off the handle of his bat over second base. Winter Park leads 3-2. The team erupts. Gast turns away from the plate and kicks the dirt on the mound. He gets out of the inning without another run scoring, but Kaz pitches a complete game and the team moves on to face Deland at Stetson University's stadium.

Deland has two outstanding pitchers. The first, Michael Main, set a goal when he was a sophomore to hit 100 mph with his fastball. He's come close, touching 99. Main has suffered from arm and shoulder injuries. His mechanics are less than perfect, and that, combined with being overthrown and overused by his coach, has led to several setbacks in his high school career. Tonight, however, he's in center field, and Matt Collins is on the mound. Collins is also a student of Gierke's, a tall, skinny right hander who lives in the upper 80s and touches the low 90s. He keeps the Winter Park batters off balance all night. Winter Park has started Ryan Wolfe, going with the same rotation that got them through districts. Wolfe is a tall, unpredictable lefty. He can throw hard. He can throw not so hard. He can hit his spots. He can be wild and all over the place. Tonight, he doesn't make it through the second inning. Jose follows him, and fares somewhat better. Even so, the score is 7-4 through five, with Deland in the lead. When Jose tires in the bottom of the sixth with runners on first and second with one out, King puts Ethan in.

This is totally unexpected. It's one thing for my kid to start a game, to have the control as well as the pressure in his hands, but here, now, in single elimination, to put him in where a mistake blows the game open and he goes from hometown hero to fresh meat in a few short days - that unnerves me. Ethan looks stiff walking out to the mound. He's had enough rest, so I imagine it's the weight of the game that bears down on him, or the stress, hunching him over and making him look small and unsure. His warmup pitches don't have the same fluid motion they did when he pitched against Edgewater. His breaking balls bounce in the dirt, he cuts his arm across his body and his fastballs tail far outside. He throws his first pitch high, and the batter lays off. 1-0. The next pitch is a changeup, and the batter hits a weak grounder to short. It's a ready made double play ball, which the two Adams turn without problem. Ethan is out of the inning in two pitches.

The top of the seventh, though, has no heroics. Winter Park is able to get runners on first and second, but the rally dies there. With the third out, a routine fly ball, the season ends. Ethan doesn't have to take the mound again. King later tells me, "I would have let him go the rest of the game. He could have done it."

Disappointed in the loss, Ethan is nonetheless excited about the team's prospects. "I can't wait to pitch for Coach," he tells me. "It's going to be a great year."

That summer Stephen King is drafted in the third round by the Washington Nationals, and signs for $750,000. Shane Brown, the team's starting catcher, walks on at the University of Central Florida without a scholarship. He later blossoms into UCF's leading hitter and is drafted by the Yankees. Nick Adams goes on to be a student/athlete at Mercer University. Three senior heroes of the tournament – Kaz, who won two games pitching, Colin Sterba, who made play after outstanding play in center field, and left fielder Timmy Williams, who hit the snot out of the ball all season long – remain unrecruited and their baseball careers end for all practical purposes with the Deland game. Like so many high school athletes, these boys who played with abandon and enthusiasm, were done at the end of the season, forced to move on whether they were prepared to or not.

$\mathcal{D}$

Since the end of the state tournament, three showcase teams have offered Ethan automatic spots on their rosters: the Scorpions, the Renegades, and the Orlando Baseball Academy. Only the Orlando Juice, run by former major leaguer Chet Lemon, hasn't stepped forward. Gierke recommends the Scorpions to us. He has a friendly relationship with George Martin, the coach of the 16-under Scorpions team. Martin is a low level scout for the Atlanta Braves, and Gierke promises us we can't go wrong with the Scorpions. We are getting regular, almost daily calls from Bob Pincus, the owner and organizer of the Renegades. "If you want to be da besht you have to play with da besht," Pincus tells us in his thick New York accent, and this line quickly becomes the theme of the summer. The Renegades and Scorpions are arch-rivals, and the owners of each organization couldn't be more different though their Yankee backgrounds are similar. Sal Lombardo, the founder and head coach of the Scorpions, is low-key and thoughtful, careful with the words he chooses and clear when he speaks, short and stocky, who somehow despite his body is more flexible than the teenagers he coaches (he can almost do a split and can touch his head to his toes) and once was a 90 mph pitcher. He and Gierke are known as the pre-eminent pitching instructors in Central Florida. Pincus is hotheaded, loudmouthed, argumentative, and when we tell him Ethan is joining the Scorpions, he virtually foams at the mouth on the other end of the phone. He tells us we're stupid. We're making the biggest mistake of our lives. We're going to be losers, not winners. In the first game we see him he gets tossed out by the umpires for throwing a fit at home plate, kicking dirt over the plate a la Billy Martin and looking for all the world like a bantam rooster trying to make an impression on a hen twice his size.

More than 50 boys have been invited to try out for the Scorpions 16-under team, and if Ethan is an example of the norm, many have already been promised spots, leaving only a few holes open in the roster for outstanding performances during tryouts. The team reeks of talent. Ethan now stands 6 feet tall, and he is average size among these giant teens. The tallest boy, a right handed pitcher from Lake Brantley named Greg Larson, also plays basketball. He should. He's 6'8". Another boy, Sean Olenek, is a 6'5" outfielder from Trinity Preparatory School. Sean hits a home run off Ethan during tryouts, a screaming line drive that is still rising as it clears the fence. Ethan looks over at me and sighs deeply. I know what that means. We're both glad his spot is locked up.

There is only one tournament of any significance for boys this age. They're still too young to be seriously scouted by colleges or the pros, so the summer revolves around the Junior Olympic Tournament sponsored by USA Baseball in Jupiter, Florida. Eighteen boys from the east coast and eighteen boys from the west coast will be selected from the thousands who participate on the more than 140 teams. Of those, the final team will be whittled down to eighteen participants who will represent the United States in the Junior Olympic Tournament in Venezuela at the end of August. It's more than an honor. It's instant recognition. It's one of the best lines these boys can put on their baseball resumés, and the competition to make the team is beyond fierce. It's cutthroat.

Pat and I decide to tag team the tournament. It lasts eight days, and neither of us can afford to be away from home and work for that long. We plan it so we're both there for the first two days, then Pat takes over for two, I follow for two, and she returns with our other children for the final weekend games. During this time there will be one night when Ethan gets left on his own with the coaches. We have it all set up for them to watch him during that time, but it still makes us a little nervous. That's how convoluted our schedule has become. When Pat complains about baseball overwhelming of our lives, I can't really argue. There is a level of insanity at play.

The saving grace of the week turns out to be the hotel. We're staying at a Holiday Inn. We have two connecting rooms. The kids is normal sized. Ours is huge, large enough, for some reason, to set up a dining room table, and there are Tempur-Pedic mattresses on the beds. I've never slept on a memory foam mattress before, and fall instantly in love. For the first time ever, I sleep well at a baseball tournament. After years of suffering through Hooters Inns with paper thin sheets that tear when you turn over, La Quinta Inns with roaring window air conditioners, $49/night no-name hotels that kept me up at night with their haunting, indecipherable scratching noises, bubbling pipes, and the 3 a.m. parties in the parking lots outside our windows complete with breaking bottles, shining headlights and police sirens, this hotel with comfortable beds near shopping and the beach is a blessing.

The games begin disastrously. The Scorpions lose a laugher to a mediocre team 16-14. Pitching, defense, teamwork - all are nonexistent. Though the boys come back at the end, they are immediately thrust into the bottom of their bracket, and the only way to move on now is to win out.

Which they do. Ethan starts one game and closes a second. Martin is not known for watching how much his pitchers throw, and he relies on a few arms which tire as the week progresses. Some of the boys, like Greg Larson who already throws in the 90s, are a year too old to make the Junior Olympic team, but they're looking for boys who can pitch, hit and play a position, so Ethan is on their radar screen – if he can throw hard enough to make an impression.

Pat and I pass each other somewhere on I-95, she heading north, me south. We have left Ethan alone in our big, oversized room with strict instructions. We're letting two boys who would otherwise be sleeping together in a double bed in a room with one of their parents use our extra room while we're shuttling back and forth. But no one else is allowed in. No big team gatherings. No card games. No late nights. We think we can trust Ethan alone for one night.

When I'm about an hour away from the hotel I get a call on my cell phone. "Dad, are you sitting down?" It's Ethan. This is how he always starts a conversation when he's done something he fears will knock me off my feet.

"Of course I'm sitting down. I'm driving. What did you do?"

"We had a little accident here, Dad. The coaches are in the room with me. They want to talk to you and me when you get here."

"What happened?"

"I sort of pushed someone through the wall in our room."

Against our orders boys from the team had flooded into our room to play poker. Ethan swears they just found out he was staying alone and barged in. Maybe, maybe not. They brought in tables and had multiple games going on. Things got a little rowdy, and the boys started having pillow fights, jumping on each other, and wrestling on the bed. Concerned that the situation was getting out of hand and that he would be held responsible, Ethan shouted for everyone to stop. He was ignored with laughter and continued roughhousing. He grabbed an aluminum bat and slammed it on the ground to get their attention. "Cut it out now!" he shouted. Steve Garvey, a Winter Park Wildcat who'd made the team, grabbed Ethan from behind. Steve thought Ethan was losing it, threatening the boys with the bat and got him in a bear hug to stop him. Ethan tried to break free and backed Steve into a wall in the room, leaving a body sized crater in the drywall. That's what I come back to. A room with the imprint of a body in the wall.

Coaches sitting like judges behind one of the card tables. Ethan and Steve with their heads hung low, the accused waiting for their sentences to be passed.

Matt Gerber takes the lead. The young assistant coach, he has great rapport with the boys, and wasn't that far removed from his own college days of poker, beer, and cheap cigars. While both boys are held responsible, the majority of the blame falls on Ethan, who opened up the room, lost his cool, grabbed the bat, and flung Steve into the wall. Both are put on probation and told another episode like this would get them kicked off the team. Both are held responsible for the damages (though Steve and his family have no ability to pay). Like a dog with his tail between his legs, Ethan apologizes to me a dozen, maybe a hundred times that day. If not for the $1,000 we have to pay the hotel for repairs (half of which Ethan works off over the remainder of the summer), it would have seemed like a teenage blip, a laugher of a story rather than a portent of things to come.

This is the last tournament of the summer for Ethan. The Scorpions 16-under team makes it all the way to the quarterfinals. Ethan starts that game, and representatives for the Junior Olympics selection committee are there to watch, but Ethan is running on fumes. His arm is tired. His body moves slowly. He has nothing left in the tank, and tops out at 78. After an inning the scouts move on. I see this and know what it means. Bye bye bid to the Junior Olympics. It was nice knowing you.

Ethan doesn't pitch well the first few innings, and the team from West Palm Beach tags him for four runs. He settles down, using his off-speed pitches since his fastball is big and fat and slow, and he manages to keep them off balance through four. Then he is taken out and the team goes on to lose. We have a family vacation to look forward to, and the Scorpions move on to several other tournaments in July.

During one of these, George Martin loses his cool and his coaching position on the team. He likes to tell dirty jokes without regard for the boys' ages. He fails to edit what comes out of his mouth. Then he blows up during a game in which, every parent reports, the officiating blatantly favored the home team with whom the umpires were friendly and familiar. Martin tells the Scorpions pitcher, Matt Toelke, the closer on the team and a teammate of Ethan's at Winter Park, to hit the next batter. Toelke obeys his coach, albeit a bit too obviously, and both he and Martin are thrown out. The parents and benches erupt. The game almost gets called early because of the mass disruption. But somehow it concludes, and so does Martin's tenure with the Scorpions. Matt Gerber, the young coach who played for the Scorps throughout his high school career, takes over and moves up with the older boys as they begin to get showcased for college.

We hear about all of this second hand, and at that point our thoughts have already turned to the spring, and our unbounded, unblemished hopes for a great official start to Ethan's time on his varsity baseball team.

CHAPTER 8
Sophomoric Season

As naïve as Pat and I were about baseball in general, from the politics of Little League to the intensity of the AAU circuit, we had no clue whatsoever about the unrestricted power and authority wielded by high school coaches. A head coach in high school, typically, gets paid an additional annual stipend of a few thousand dollars to spend an inordinate amount of time every afternoon during their sport's season coaching young athletes. Add about 25 2-1/2 hour games on top of that, with hour long warm-ups, talks and either bus rides or tidying the field after games, and a baseball coach who makes an extra $2,500/year is actually getting paid about $7.50/hour to coach – minimum wage. For that low wage coaches get the satisfaction of being rulers of small fiefdoms – the playing field. Their servants are the players whom they hand pick. Their authority is vested by the school administration that, for unknown reasons, treats these coaches differently than other teachers. The same treatment that athletes commonly receive would get a regular teacher fired. They belittle. They chastise. They berate. They humiliate. All in the name of sportsmanship. It is an accepted part of Americana, a cultural phenomenon of poor behavior that we tell our kids to suck up and deal with.

Now many of you will be turned off by my unwillingness to blindly accept these standard coaching practices, but I have to ask you why, when we try to teach our children not to use bad language, to show respect, to have good manners, is it all right for coaches to scream in those same children's faces using every unfiltered word that comes into their minds? Why is it all right for a coach of teenagers to denigrate those young people at a time when they are the most insecure?

I venture to say that the Central Florida area, as productive as anyplace in the country when it comes to providing colleges and professional sports with athletes, is typical in the quality of its high school coaching which, in general, is low. Many coaches have limited experience in the sport they coach. Many more have even less experience in the art of coaching, not teams, but individuals who come together for the purpose of becoming a team.

Coaches coach for different reasons. For some the money, though meager, is enough to get them to spend a ridiculous number of hours barking instructions and leading practices. For others there is a true joy found in still being part of a game they love, in teaching young people, in helping their wards make the successful transition to young men and women, helping them reach their potential and fulfill the dream of lettering in high school. For others it is pure ego. They rule. Their word is undisputed. They decide who stays, who goes, who plays, who plays where and how much. They control the strategy of the game. They dictate the terms. An effective coach on the high school level can win games for his team. He can also lose them. But ultimately, power resides with him, and that can be intoxicating.

Of course, power comes at a cost. I cannot imagine the toll it takes on coaches when they cut players. Every year these same coaches who wield such authority take enormous beatings from irate parents who just can't come to terms with their kid being cut, whether deservedly so or not. They grapple with the pain (occasionally) and guilt (perhaps) of cutting good kids who just can't play at the high school level. They make good decisions and bad decisions. They tell some kids it's time to call it quits when it is, and they force others to quit when they shouldn't.

Because of all this, many parents fear what coaches can do to their children. For many, high school coaches are like an almighty boss, to be both feared and respected. They believe there must be a reason for them to be there. They must know more, be more experienced. They must have the kids' interests at heart. They are unquestioned by school administrations as long as their sports ship runs smoothly and consistently. And of course, this is the last chance for many kids to play ball, their final hurrah before heading off to college. They want it, and they want it badly.

The flip side of fear and intimidation is respect and admiration, and coaches, especially for boys, I think, inhabit the enviable role of father substitute. While this can be a positive or negative role, at its best it comes at a time when teenage boys are poised in direct opposition to their fathers, blanketly, knee-jerk rejecting most if not all of the advice, the rules, the examples posed by their parents as they struggle with self-identity and their own roles as independent individuals while still dependent and tied at the hips to mom and dad.

The coach, on the other hand, occupies a natural position of wisdom and authority without the burdens of years of saying no, years of battles, years of judgments and disappointments. The high school coach comes in fresh, the undisputed leader, acknowledged expert and sage of his proscribed realm. He is there to nurture and protect his tribe – his team of teenage boys. They huddle in a circle around him and listen to his wise words. They have been taught for years not to argue with their coach. They have been taught to be polite, to address him as "Coach" or "Sir." He holds the ultimate power of doling out positions and playing time. He can just as easily give them the opportunity to be a hero, or cut their throats. At his best the coach is kind, compassionate, understanding. He sincerely cares for his wards, and does what he can to teach, to soothe raw nerves, to take on the burden of blame when appropriate, and to help them understand their own culpability and responsibility wrapped within the concept of team, that one person does not cause a loss, but that winning and losing are both shared endeavors.

It used to be a given that a college needed a high school coach's recommendation to recruit a student/athlete. Now, with the advent of showcase sports, this is less so, but there is still the perception, some of it founded, that the opinion of the high school coach can have a serious deleterious effect on the future of an athlete. For those who are good enough to play in college and beyond, this is a serious matter. A bad high school coach, or a coach who has it in for a kid, can damage or completely derail a future in sports. For the student who knows that he is only good enough to play in high school, or has no desire to continue after he graduates, this is the one chance to gain a little prestige, a back thumping, chest expanding pride in representing his or her school in sports. Challenging a coach, then, is almost unheard of, and the power of the coach, their ability to impact a student-athlete's future, is almost unprecedented. Unless the coach does something extreme, something extraordinary like hitting a student or making such a public spectacle that the school principal has no choice but to fire him, he is safely entrenched for as long as he posts a reasonable record and keeps his program within budget, out of controversy and in the headlines only as it relates to wins.

Bob King had a clean, if not a spotless record. He coached the current principal of the school, Bill Gordon, in one of his first years as head baseball coach. He almost never had a losing season. He didn't swear. He had a reputation as a great strategist and a pitcher's coach, traits we'd seen in action during the previous year's district championship game. Once, a few years prior to Ethan, there had been some problems with boys being kicked off the team for smoking pot. We had heard grumblings from parents who complained that King had bent, even changed longstanding rules to coddle his son Stephen. Besides the questions of padding statistics and being named Most Valuable Player every year, there were the Stephen Rules, the Before Stephen: "No wearing batting gloves," the During Stephen: "You can wear batting gloves (Stephen liked batting gloves) to the After Stephen: "No wearing batting gloves!" "You can't tape your wrists." "Sure you can tape your wrists." "No taping wrists!" "No one is allowed to play travel ball." "Go ahead and play travel ball." "I hate travel ball. No one plays travel ball if they want to play for Winter Park." He preached the importance and value of good nutrition (who can argue with that?) and during his son's time on the team always had a cooler loaded with snacks – peanut butter sandwiches, chocolate covered strawberries, candy bars - for Stephen and the other players, but once Stephen was gone food was no longer allowed in the dugout. And now Stephen was off to rookie ball in the Washington Nationals organization, and we hoped and expected a return to normalcy.

$$ \textcircled{D} $$

It has been an interesting fall. The Scorpions weren't sure if they were going to field a 16-under team, so while in limbo Ethan signed up to play for a team Gierke was coaching, Orlando Baseball Academy. He pitches a few games for the OBA, then the Scorpions, realizing they may lose some of their loyal players to other organizations, put a team together and Ethan rejoins them immediately. Several of his Winter Park teammates are on the Scorpions team, helped, no doubt, by Matt Gerber's graduation from and allegiance to Winter Park. The pitcher Matt Toelke, the catcher Matt Tralka and utility infielder and outfielder Steve Garvey all play. It's a sign of the talent on the Winter Park team.

The fall is a time of informal games and hard workouts. The boys have regular weightlifting and conditioning in the afternoons at Winter Park, and oftentimes games afterwards. Throwing and hitting are not conducive to same time weightlifting, but the fact that the players can barely swing their bats or throw a ball doesn't deter King.

He's done it this way for years, as do many coaches at the high school and college level. It's hard, but not unusual for there to be hard workouts, practices, and scrimmages the same day in college. In high school, when practices are not allowed during the fall, it's all about strength and speed work and a light game schedule. Bob King's official teaching position at Winter Park is as a physical education instructor. He runs the weight room, a huge, well-stocked room the size of a small auditorium crammed with cardio and weightlifting equipment. It is not only his baby, his pride and joy, but the largest facility of its kind in the county, and the envy of almost every high school coach.

Ethan has taken it upon himself to double up on the workouts. He's been working hard both to get in better shape, and to increase his pitching velocity, the one area where, as a lefty, he's good but not outstanding. Many boys are now throwing harder, faster than he. For years I was pleased, even impressed with the steady progress of his fastball velocity. It crept upward 3-4 mph every year. No great leaps, no incredible jumps that would put him in the 90s and onto the national radar screens, but it was consistent, and thus safe improvement.

Lately, however, he seems to have plateaued, and he and I are both worried that he might be topping out somewhere in the mid-80s. There are programs – long toss, plyometrics, band work, stretching, weighted balls and medicine balls – that promise increases of 5 mph or more during a season of work, and this is what Ethan is shooting for. Even Bob King has a throwing program that he says shows great results – if the player truly commits to it.

I find a trainer who specializes in working with pitchers to improve their pitching speed and at the same time get them in better shape to limit injuries. To date, as far as I know, Ethan has been blessed by being relatively injury free. There had been the time he hyper-extended his elbow in Pony League, and he occasionally complained of a "dead arm" during the early stages of spring, but he'd never broken a bone or fractured a growth plate, torn anything in his elbow or shoulder. I want to avoid that at all costs, and at the same time help him become more of a complete package – a power pitcher who throws four pitches with command.

Twice a week I drive Ethan after school on days he doesn't have weightlifting to do the extra band work, core work, plyometrics and shoulder strengthening with Mike Bradley, the young assistant head coach at Winter Springs High School. Bradley had molded an outstanding pitching staff at Winter Springs, and comes highly recommended by Gierke. Coming from a family of wealth, he coaches for the sheer pleasure of it and as a way to stay connected to baseball. He works Ethan hard, but never to the point of breakdown. I groan as I watch Ethan bend backwards, holding small medicine balls overhead and behind his back, only to snap them forward to gain acceleration, velocity in his release, thrust and power in his legs. I escape in my air conditioned car while he sweats out reps with weighted balls and throws off ramps for balance and explosiveness. Bradley has him shift his arm slot to more of an overhead position to gain some speed, and I think nothing of it at the time, but the change is significant, and not for the good. Even so, Ethan is in great shape, feeling stronger than ever and ready for an improved, dominating spring season.

Ⓓ

It is New Years Eve, December 31, 2006. Trying, wanting desperately to be cool parents while at the same time keeping our oldest and somewhat wild boy home and safe for the night, we make an offer to him. He can have up to eight friends over to the house for a small New Years party. Whoever he wants. They can stay as late as they want. We'll even get a little beer for them. Pat and I argue over this. I want to buy a case so they can have a good time. Pat wants to limit it to one to two beers per teen. They are, after all, underage and we will be responsible for them. It goes without saying that anyone who drinks will spend the night at our house. There will be no wandering off, no driving. Keys will be confiscated and returned in the morning. We compromise on two six-packs, no more than two beers apiece, and we'll stay home as watchdogs. One of our daughter's best friends, Lauren, a bright, extroverted, overly mature redhead is spending the night, too. We'll stay up with the younger kids, play cards and watch the ball fall in Times Square on TV, then go to bed shortly after midnight. Ethan can have his friends stay out on the patio as long as they want. We have it all under control.

Or so we think. For thirty minutes Pat and I sit on the couch in our living room with Jerica and Lauren when the first group of high schoolers appear. Then the second group. Now there are about 40 kids on our long back porch and the number grows as the minutes pass. Lauren is giggling. Jerica looks over at us, but Pat is confused and I'm dumbfounded. I don't know what's going on. It hasn't hit me yet that we've become a destination for a New Years Eve high school

145

rager. This isn't possible, I think. There's been some mistake. We only bought two six-packs. Ethan only invited 8 of his friends. I can't believe this is happening and we're right here, in the living room staring out our back glass doors. This isn't even a party house with parents gone. We haven't gone anywhere, and they're busting in from all over. We're frozen in place, trying to comprehend the situation, unable to move, uncertain what to do while both side doors to our patio have sprung leaks and the floodgates have opened. Teenagers pour in until there's no more room on the back porch. It's wall-to-wall. The noise level rises like a cacophony of crows, and someone turns on a ghetto blaster. Two boys are standing on our ping pong table with bottles of tequila in their hands. A drunk girl stumbles into our bathroom, throws up and clogs the toilet, which overflows. Toilet water pours into our kitchen. I try to take a head count but get lost when I hit 100, and I haven't gotten through half the crowd. The back patio doors haven't shut. The street in front of our house is clogged to capacity. Cars can't get through anymore. Suddenly, my brain wakes up. "David, we have to do something," Pat tells me. I go outside and start to yell. "Everyone out!" I yell. "Now!"

Over my voice I hear the sound of a police siren.

As soon as the crowd hears that, they bolt. Hundreds of kids, running in every direction, through bushes, neighbors' yards, running without focus, without looking or knowing where they're going, just running to get away from the cops. One policeman stands in the street, checking kids for booze before he lets them pull away. The other officer walks into our house and asks for us.

"You know you could be arrested for what's happened here," he tells me in a low-key voice.

"I know, officer. I don't know what happened. I was just breaking it up when you came in. My son was supposed to just have a few friends over when things got out of hand."

"Where is your son?" he asks. I point him towards Ethan, who moments before had been laughing and shouting along with hundreds of other revelers, and now sits on our back steps with his head in his hands. He knows he's screwed.

"Son, do you realize what just happened here? You put all these friends of yours in danger. And your parents could go to jail for having underage drinkers in their house." He pushes a case of beer to the side.

Empty bottles are strewn around the patio. Bottles of vodka, tequila, cheap rum litter the back porch. All Ethan can say, without lifting his head or making eye contact with anyone, is "Yessir. Yessir. I'm sorry, sir."

The house has cleared out. Only a few of Ethan's friends remain. We ask them to stick around and help clean up. Pat is mopping up the kitchen. I pick up bottles, trash, while Ethan, in his most guilty guise, stumbles around saying so that I can hear it, "I don't know what happened. I didn't even know half these kids. I don't get it."

Walking around the house we find stashes of beer hidden in bushes all around the house. We find them for days. We load the dryer with wet towels, unclog the toilet, have Ethan and his friends haul the garbage bags full of empties into the garage. I can tell his buddies are chomping at the bit to leave. They have other parties to hit. They don't say anything but their plaintive eyes say it all. They're waiting for me to dismiss them, and I look around, assess the damage, and tell them to go ahead and get out of here. They vanish while I'm turning around.

We go to bed thinking that this was just a party that got out of hand, that one of Ethan's friends must have called another friend who called another, and from there it progressed exponentially to the mess we encountered. But the next morning, when I wake, an email waits for me from someone who knew better, someone who wanted me to know.

"Check Ethan's Myspace page," is all it says, and there, for the world to see, are bulletins Ethan sent out during the days leading up to New Years Eve. A bulletin on Myspace goes out to everyone who has connected with the sender. There is no limiting, no editing. It is a universal appeal. Ethan's bulletins said, "The rager's on at my house for New Years. Bring everyone you know and don't know." A second: "Don't miss out." And a third: "It's happening tonight."

That changes everything. Realizing that we've been set up, fooled, used, we home jail Ethan. No questions asked. No limit to his term. No going out. No friends over. No more Myspace or social life or freedom or use of a car until we feel he has learned a lesson. He is grounded for the semester. It is as harsh a discipline as we can come up with. A new light is shed on our son who wants desperately to bask in the light of high school popularity, and will do almost anything to achieve it. It is one of the reasons success in baseball is so important to him. He came into high school with the reputation of being "the baseball guy." He got his first headlines as a ninth grader. Now is his

147

time to prove he's cool, a partier, someone who deserves the limelight. And he's willing to do almost anything to solidify his popularity, including screwing us over.

○

I realize that Ethan needs serious tracking. It is early February, and he has been grounded for nearly a month. We get a message on our answering machine from Orange County Public Schools. I call Pat over. "Listen to this," I tell her. A computer voice says, "This is to inform you that Ethan Bornstein was absent yesterday. If this is an excused absence please send in a note to the attendance office when he returns to class. Thank you."

Ethan knows that an automatic tracking system has been installed by the school system, and that every time he or his sister or brother are absent we get a phone call. He also knows (at least I think he knows) that if he skips school his absence is noted and he will be caught. He told us the previous morning that he was going in to school early to meet with a teacher, an action we applauded and encouraged. Then the message on the answering machine. When he comes home that afternoon we confront him.

"Yeah, I skipped," he says. "I was so stressed and depressed from being grounded that I went and played golf in the morning at the Pines (an executive golf course just down the street from the high school.)"

I am confused. "Ethan, explain this to me. You got so depressed from being grounded that you skipped school to play golf."

"Yessir."

"Even though that's exactly what being grounded is supposed to keep you from doing."

"Yessir."

"Even though you had to know you'd be caught."

"I hadn't exactly thought of it that way."

"So you skip school because you're depressed about being grounded for misbehavior."

"I guess so."

He doesn't think about the consequences. He doesn't acknowledge that he'll get caught and make the situation worse. All he can think about is, "I'm stressed. I need to play golf." His brain simply shuts down. Didn't he realize this would end badly? His response: No. I never thought about it.

I go down to the Winter Park Pines and speak to the manager. He posts a sign behind his desk informing everyone who works there that Ethan is not allowed to play the course until further notice. The grounding continues.

D

One of the by-products of living the jock's life, one that we as parents hadn't considered, has been a sense of entitlement for Ethan, and a reinforcement of values many would consider less than desirable. Ethan grew up in a system that instantly rewarded accomplishments and decried failure. When he got a good hit, he was praised. The peanuts gallery cheered. When he struck out he could always hear my audible groan. When he pitched a great game the back slaps and handshakes rained down upon him, filling him with instant gratification. And when he lost a game for his team, he could choose to either shrug it off or shoulder the blame, but either way it was all about him.

When he was growing up the real estate business in Florida was good. We were well off, and denied him next to nothing. New, expensive gloves, bats, sliders, cleats, batting tees, nets, training devices, strengthening and conditioning equipment, hitting and pitching lessons, paid time in batting cages. We sacrificed our schedules, our weekends, our family life and husband and wife time together to be with him on the road.

All this combined to make him feel like the center of the universe, and he was. Our family revolved around him, and he absorbed the attention, in the process losing any understanding about limits and not getting everything you want. If he wanted it, he expected to get it, and that's as far as his black and white, see the action and damn the consequences mind worked. As time went on and he moved into his teen years, all these tendencies, these behaviors that I helped create by giving him a gilded, spoiled childhood came more and more to the surface. If anything went wrong in his life we heard the same litany again and again:

"This is my senior year and all I want to do is hang out with my friends and have a good time."

"I've had such a hard time and now that I'm (a junior, a senior, home for the summer) I just want to hang out with my friends and have a good time."

"Since I've been injured no one pays any attention to me. I mean, my teammates are nice and all, but I can't do any of the fun things with them like travel, so….all I want is to hang out with my friends and have a good time."

"Ever since you punished me I've been stuck home alone, bored out of my mind, and the stress has gotten to me so much…. all I want is to hang out with my friends and have a good time."

Which also entailed blowing off family, responsibilities, and anything that might interfere with or jeopardize his fun. If there was a roadblock, he skipped over it. If he'd made a promise to do something or be somewhere and he got a better invitation, his previous obligations, the commitments he'd made, disappeared as if they never existed.

Add to this the values taught, not at home, not by coaches, but by the players Ethan grew up with. His friends, who hopped from team to team disregarding their commitments and always putting themselves first. Shallow misogyny that encouraged women to be viewed as sex toys (this was often promoted by young women as well, who wanted nothing more than to have sex with a jock), gay-bashing, insensitivity to players and individuals less gifted than they, and a world that focused solely on their accomplishments as players, not human beings, all encouraged and amplified the worst of Ethan's behaviors. We tried to combat these negative values with talk at home, by modeling compassion and understanding, by promoting simple ideals like being open minded, open to new experiences and different people, but we were minnows in a sea of ballers, and as often as not I got sucked into the old patterns of praise and disappointment based solely on play, not on his person.

What do we do, as parents, when we see our children involved in something they love, something they're good at, maybe great at, while at the same time we are witness to its negative aspects, its dark side, its abuses and egocentric cores? Do we deny them what they love, what they aspire to, what may lead them to recognition and excellence, turning them into something that runs against the grain of who you hoped they'd become? Baseball, perhaps all sports, has this dark and light side. The temptation of fame. The sheer beauty of instant gratification. The gloom of defeat, seductive in its own dark, deep, impenetrable ways. The ugliness of narcissism, egotism, and condescension.

Sometimes life at home just isn't enough. Sometimes setting an example of honesty, positive relationships, open communication, just doesn't cut it. Sometimes all that registers is that the world gets set aside so that the star gets to play. Sometimes the priorities are not how you live, but what you do, and what you do is sacrifice everything of importance – faith, family, fortune – for the sake of the fleeting, elusive dream of our children's success. In this case, playing baseball. All the things we're told to do, taught to do by every parenting book on the market fade away against the slim chance, the hope of our children realizing an unreachable dream, and the bright lights outside the protective walls of home attract our insecure, indulgent, gratification seeking, fame seeking, glory tasting children like doomed, blind moths.

Baseball is a game of incredible stability interlaced with subtle, constant change. From the initial steps a child takes hitting the ball off a Tee in T-ball, to coach pitch to kid pitch, to the tiny fields with short base paths and pitching mounds you can almost stretch out and reach and anthills in the unmowed outfield that has no fences so that well hit balls roll forever and ever, to the ever increasing distance to the fences – 180 feet, 240 feet, 300 feet – some stretching up 20, 30 feet to the sky to make home runs more rare, to pitching mounds that are 60'6" and base paths that form a perfect 90' diamond, to the tall, muscled young men with sideburns and the hints of beards and mustaches who suddenly are playing the game at a different level and speed where the ball is thrown on a long fast line and hit faster than the eye can follow and fielded with a grace and beauty and ease that transcends the grass and clay they glide over, everything grows and changes. And along the way, at every beginning step, the boys go back to being small, ever so small, while the older boys always look big, throw the ball harder, faster, farther.

Then, for the briefest of seasons, you are the big. You are the hard throwing, long ball hitting envy of the youngsters behind you. In a way, it's like never growing up and always growing up, going from little to big and back to little, back into childhood and then bursting through until you're back on top. And each step of the way the parent watches this with you, intimidated as the field grows larger and the child appears small once again, crowing with prideful self-satisfaction when the field shrinks and the boy is big and strong once again.

151

And now he's here. One of them. He's a big on varsity. There are no more steps. No more major changes. Sure, the game gets quicker in college, the bodies bigger and stronger, even moreso in the pros. But it's all about increments now. The dimensions have firmed. The game is what it is. The field of dreams has finally stopped shifting. It has solidified, everything fits, from the size of the players to the speed of the pitches to the strength of the hitters, it's all there, all present in an approximation of its final form.

The Winter Park baseball field is charming and classic – 325 feet to the corners, 375 feet to deep center field, with a scoreboard that works for the most part and a perfectly sloped mound and a manicured, laser leveled infield that Bob King makes sure plays straight and true, with few bad hops or obvious blemishes. With my construction connections I pay to have a load of the same rich orange clay used by the Detroit Tigers spring training fields in Winter Haven brought in and the pitching mound glows orange as a Florida sunset. It's one of the little perks I bring along with my son.

For the first time, when I fully expected boys to cling to this great opportunity more desperately, more tightly than ever before, attrition sets in. Players I expected to see don't show. Anthony Morin, the smooth shortstop who had a terrible tryout in ninth grade and was cut, doesn't come out again. He's chosen football. Kyle Gonzalez, the big, smart, hard thrower, has given up on baseball too and focused on being a two-way football player. Ryan Lamkin, Ethan's right-handed alter-ego, just quits. We hear he woke up one morning, and that was that. No motivation for high school sports. Kyle McLanahan is now the star point guard on the basketball team, and little brother Bryce has chosen football. All in all, a dozen players from Ethan's exceptional ninth grade class have opted for football, basketball, lacrosse, or out of sports altogether. It's almost unfathomable, but there it is. The incoming varsity class is a shell of what it was.

The first day of tryouts King handpicks the first group of boys to take the field. They are his expected starters, and they whip the ball around the infield like pros, faster, faster around the horn without dropping the ball or making an errant throw. It's designed to intimidate the handful of players who have come to try out but don't really have a chance. For the most part, the team has been pre-selected. Everyone knows who will make it. There are a couple spots open, a couple positions in doubt. The only questions are a few boys on the bubble who might start either on varsity or JV.

Ethan stands tall in that group at first base. He knows the position, looks comfortable with the feel of the base, moves up, back, holds runners on, makes the correct throw without thought or hesitation. After all, he's been playing there now since he turned six. He should know how to play.

It quickly becomes apparent that another boy may be tough competition at first. Keith Merkel also plays a great outfield, and I think, naturally, that's the way the season will fall out, with Ethan planted at first and Keith behind him in right. But for now they're sharing time at first base, and there's an intensity and friendly struggle going on between the two. As I sit and watch (and I'm sitting and watching every day during tryouts), the fielding appears virtually even. They spar toe-to-toe, snaring tough grounders, stabbing balls backhanded, making the routine plays. When one misses, so does the other. When one makes a great play, the other comes up with one, too. If you could meld the two you might have the ideal first baseman. Keith's an inch taller than Ethan, and is the better athlete. He has better footwork, more range, and can make the outstanding, running backwards, leaping over the fence play where Ethan still stumbles backwards and trips over himself, oftentimes landing on his rear end. Ethan makes all the routine plays, and has the ability to come up with the clutch play, the great throw under pressure. Ethan will get the runner at third, at home. He has the stronger arm and by far the bigger bat. In my estimation it's a dead heat, so why not keep both these outstanding players on the field as much as possible? But when the dust settles, it's clear that King likes Keith at first and Ethan's bat. This rankles me, but I keep my mouth shut. Coach's decision, and though I disagree there's nothing to say or do. More and more as tryouts progress, Keith gets the lion's share of time at first and Ethan gets mop-up, and Ethan hits and hits and hits while Keith fights for a place in the batting order.

When Coach King posts the varsity lineup on the side of the concession building, no real surprises leap out at us. Ethan's name is there, and he has gone from being the fourth lefty on the team to the only lefty. As such, and given his success the previous year, he looks like the designated number one pitcher, even though he's only a sophomore. The other pitchers on the team include three seniors - Randall Thompson, making his first varsity team, Andrew McHenry, an up and down mid-80s righty who loves to surf as much as play baseball, and Steve Ortman, a 5'7" right handed Jewish pitcher who gets more velocity out of his pitches than his size should allow (the team has a rarity – a short Jewish righty and a tall Jewish lefty); Matt Toelke, now a junior, and Chad Modomo, the stocky sophomore righty who starts the season on the disabled list with a cyst in his rear end. Randall is perhaps the biggest question mark on the pitching staff. He's had good enough stuff to play varsity for several years. He's strong, athletic, has touched the low 90s with his fastball, and when it's on his slider bites the corners and becomes almost unhittable. He could easily be the number one pitcher on the team. But he's cocky, arrogant, full of attitude and has never been on King's good side, so he's been vanquished to extra years in JV hell. Ethan's buddy Chris Quintero (Q) is the third sophomore who makes varsity this year.

Where there was high hope, Ethan comes home after the first week complaining of boredom. Pat and I both grow concerned. When Ethan gets bored he turns off and tunes out, and for this to occur so early makes our antenna go up. There's an inherent problem with high level athletes who have received years of private instruction and sports at the high school level. In many instances the boys and girls who have gotten used to playing at such high levels on travel teams and showcase teams and have had private instructors and trainers to fine tune their mechanics and get them in top shape come into high school programs that don't (and can't) function at the same high levels.

As much time as Ethan spent on the ball field with the Winter Park program (often four hours a day, six days a week in season), he never threw a bullpen during his entire time on the team. This always puzzled me, since every college and professional team in existence has a pitching coach who has his pitchers throw regular bullpens. But Bob King didn't believe in this. Pitchers never worked on their mechanics with a pitching instructor.. When college coaches were informed that Winter Park threw no bullpens, to a person they were stymied, disbelieving. They thought it was a joke. No bullpens? How do your pitchers get better? We had no answer.

To loosen up for hitting, King has the boys stand in a circle and hold their bats in front of their faces, twitching them left, right, forwards, backwards like off-kilter grandfather clocks, then swing them around their heads, but they rarely, if ever, take actual swings in the batting cages before games.

Once the varsity team is selected, Coach King makes it clear that outside instruction is not allowed. So what is lacking in his baseball program can not be compensated for with additional help. This includes batting lessons as well, so hitters suffer along with the pitchers. On the one hand, this made complete sense. It's hard, if not impossible, to get different directions from different coaches at the same time. On the other hand, when instruction is lacking in one area and disallowed in all others, it's tough to get better, or even maintain a level of performance. That is the case at Winter Park.

Even at the varsity level, where we hoped to discover a more advanced level of coaching, I see (and Ethan and other boys experience) a set in stone program of hitting drills, fielding routines, and batting practice that goes unchanged throughout spring training and then the season. Boys take swings in the batting cages, but not many, and with no instruction, so when they do something wrong they do it wrong over and over. Pitchers learn how to throw with rhythm – without ever working on the more difficult "feel" pitches – curve balls, changeups, and sliders.

Coach King, I begin to realize, is a master of logical illogic. There is no doubt he knows what he is talking about. He's been coaching baseball for a quarter century. He goes to some of the best baseball clinics in the country on an annual basis. He studies nutrition, sports training, baseball strategy. His teams have winning records almost every year. He's won lots of district championships. When he speaks about baseball, everything he says is true. It just isn't the whole truth, and thus is more difficult to decipher. In fact, it took me years to realize this.

When he says pitchers need to pitch with balance and rhythm, he's right. But that's the tip of the iceberg. They also need regular tuneups with their pitches, and they need to throw all their pitches regularly so they develop both confidence and command. When this doesn't happen, they get worse. Hitters need corrections, and they need to be treated as individuals. Almost every hitter has their own swing, their own stance. When it works, it works, and when it doesn't, it needs correcting. The smallest fault in a hitter's swing, his stance, his hands, the position of his bat, turning the bat over too early, swinging up, his timing, any of these in any combination can throw a good hitter into a slump. I knew that. I'd seen it time and again with Ethan. But the boys here go through the same drills and are taught to swing the same way with coaches who rarely, if ever speak or intervene to instruct. I watch it from the stands all season long, and never understand it.

Coach King can dissect a hitter's swing and expose a weakness. He'd done this against Edgewater the season before when Ethan pitched in the district championship. And he told me that when he saw a pitch a hitter couldn't hit he'd have his pitcher throw it again and again until the hitter showed that he could hit it. On the surface, this again makes sense. Why not throw pitches that hitters can't hit? But as I watch his pitching staff more and more, something isn't quite right. A pitcher with a good changeup throws lots of changeups. A pitcher with a good slider throws lots of sliders.

Against a poorly coached, bad hitting team, this is effective. But against a team with good hitters and a smart coach who sees the pattern emerge, it's bad. Very very bad. Hitters come to expect certain pitches, and foul them off, foul them off, wait for balls to be thrown, wait for the changeup that hangs a little too much, that misses its spot, and then tee off. Changeups become slow fastballs.

Curveballs become walks. The effectiveness of mixing up pitches, fooling the batter, minimizing the number of pitches a pitcher throws and maximizing a pitcher's arsenal, is lost. Pitchers throw more pitches. Mistake pitches become hits and walks with greater frequency.

Pitching, after all, is a head game. The batter tries to figure out what the pitcher is going to throw. The pitcher tries to fool the hitter with changes in speed, spin, location, break. He goes inside. He goes outside. He throws 90 and 76. He goes up and down. Everyone knows this, and while, on the surface it makes sense that you throw the unhittable pitch, what doesn't make sense it to try to do it again and again, turning the unhittable pitch into the well hit ball.

I listen to Ethan's frustration, and discount it. I hear him say they do the same thing over and over again in practices, and I assume that's what you do to become a better ballplayer. I give Coach King the benefit of the doubt. After all, he's been at it for a long time, and must know what he's doing. He makes it all sound so sensible, so right. I tell Ethan to suck it up and get with the program, and something good will come out of it.

What I failed to realize, what I didn't comprehend then, or for another two years, is that sometimes the mix of coach and player just doesn't work. Ethan was a kid who pushed limits and rebelled against authority figures he didn't respect. When you earned his respect, as his private instructors and many of his coaches had, from Bellhorn to Incinelli to Gierke to Lombardo and Gerber, he turned into a no-nonsense, yessir nosir, good soldier who'd take a bullet or jump off a

156

cliff for you. But if a chink in that armor of respect appeared, he questioned everything, dismissed much, and became an arrogant, independent agent. Years later Bob King told us that Ethan "did whatever he wanted" during practices. When he said it I didn't believe him, but he was right. Ethan did grow disobedient, but he did it because he didn't believe in the system and was trying to get something more out of his baseball. Was he still wrong in his disobedience? Yes, but not entirely. The truth was obfuscated by the system.

Bob King, on the other hand was the ultimate autocrat. He had a system and expected it to be followed. He believed 100% in what he did and said, even if, upon further investigation, it didn't make sense. He had records of everything he'd ever done as a coach. He had a huge workout room that he'd masterminded. He did his research. He studied. And he believed in himself so completely there was no room for change or other points of view. Everything about Ethan was diametrically opposed to this. Ethan who left a trail of trash behind him wherever he went. Ethan who struggled to follow two rules in a row. Ethan whose loud, incessant chatter during a game was music to his teammates ears but must have driven the controlling King nuts. If we had seen this early on, Ethan never would have played for him.

King would tell stories about the brilliant pitching career of Matt Incinelli. Matt, who was the consummate humble, quiet ballplayer who led by example, who pitched with mastery and complete control, who was always polite and never disrespectful, was the perfect player for King's program. King preached the value of the peanut butter sandwich as the perfect meal for the athlete who needed protein and energy, and he told his players countless times how he made sure his son Stephen ate right and exercised right. And Stephen was a testament to the perfectly constructed baseball athlete. But while this served to support King's beliefs, it failed to account for individual differences, for the tolerance levels of different players, for the quirks of different temperaments, different attitudes and outlooks. And Ethan was a boxful of quirks and attitudes, none of which were malicious, but all of which were a handful. It slowly became apparent, too slowly, too late, that this was a match made in hell.

⒥

Ethan gets the first start of the year against Olympia High School. I can see his nervousness when he walks to the mound. He's

157

gripping the ball too tightly, spinning it around in his hand in a worrisome sort of way. Ethan has a tendency to try too hard, to do too much in these situations, to take it all on himself, and that's what happens. The first eight pitches he throws are all balls, all over the place. He can't settle down. He has no rhythm. He looks awkward, clumsy, like he's heaving the ball instead of pitching. Coach King goes to the mound with runners on first and second, no outs. He tells Ethan if he can't pitch to get off his fucking mound, and leaves. Ethan gets the next batter to hit a grounder to second, but Steve Garvey makes an error and the bases are loaded. He then strikes out the next two batters and gets another ground ball to get out of the inning, though he's already thrown a lot of pitches. The team goes on to win the game 3-2, with Ethan getting a no decision.

As the first half of the season progresses it's Randall, not Ethan who emerges as the top pitcher on the team. Randall exploits his chance on varsity. He throws harder than any other pitcher. He's nastier than E-Nasty. Midway through the season Ethan is 2-1, but Randall continues to throw with a fierce competitiveness, and he gets the start against Boone, one of Winter Park's arch-rivals and the team favored to win districts and go far in the state tournament. Boone is loaded with Division 1 prospects, but they're facing an overachieving Winter Park team with a 6-3 record and Randall on the mound.

This is a game I wish I saw, but I didn't. My father-in-law was in town, and I get regular updates via cell phone about the game while we're out to dinner, drinking a nice bottle of wine with my cell phone vibrating constantly on the table. The Boone players can't hit Randall. I am told he is "imposing his will" on them, and that's how Randall works, like a pit bull, competing with every pitch, a bundle of courage, sweat and anger stuffed into a hardball. Inning by inning, the reports keep coming in. He's hanging in there. They score. We score. Winter Park is up. Ethan hits the ball hard and long but has nothing to show for it. It's the other players on the team who manufacture runs this game, and I'm sitting at a table listening to my wife and father-in-law catch up on family in DC and how he's coping in the Treasury Department during the Bush administration while I keep watching for my phone to vibrate, jerking towards it each time I think it's going to buzz. I'm twisting my hands under the table, imagining being at the game and having to satisfy myself with tiny hints of the action. Randall throws a complete game, a dominating game, and Winter Park wins 10-4. It's a victory the team couldn't have counted on at the beginning of the season. Now they're 7-3 and break into the Orlando Sentinel's Top Six list of area baseball teams. With spring break upon them, the boys start vacation feeling great about the upcoming second half of the season.

There are no special tournaments scheduled during spring break. There is only one game against a team from Canada at the Walt Disney World Resort's baseball fields. Coach King schedules mandatory workouts during the break, and runs the boys hard – or at least hard for them. King doesn't think he's making them work hard at all, just keeping them in shape, but the boys are grumbling, and Randall, thinking he is showing leadership, appoints himself spokesperson and talks to King about lightening up and letting them rest. King dismisses Randall's complaint/request, and Randall goes from anointed to outcast.

Ethan pitches against the Canada team, striking out ten, walking four, and Winter Park wins easily, if lethargically to ring in the second half. It doesn't start well. From 8-3 the team drops its next four games. Ethan and Randall both lose their starts. It's Ethan's hitting that has actually come on more than his pitching. While Colin Sterba leads the team with a .400 batting average, Ethan hovers around .380 all season, and doesn't have a bad hitting game.

Against Edgewater Ethan goes 3 for 3, spraying the ball to all fields and getting hits on three different pitches. Coach Gierke tells me later that he considers Ethan the toughest out in Central Florida, a nice thing to say whether it's true or not.

Even with Ethan's hitting, the team loses the game, and Coach King calls a meeting afterwards in left field. From the bleachers I watch his animated gestures as he speaks. He is visibly upset with, I assume, the lackluster performance recently on the field. The boys raise their hands in unison at one point, and when I ask Ethan later what transpired, he tells me that King asked everyone to vote on whether or not they were tired and thought he had been working them too hard. Everyone raises his hand yes except for Chris Quintero. King sees this, and Chris immediately becomes the little player who could, the player who was willing to stand up to peer pressure and vote what he truly believed. What really happened was that Chris wasn't paying attention when everyone raised his hand. He spaced out, but he landed in a space occupied solely by King's favorites, and he stayed there for the duration of the season.

We throw a 14th birthday celebration for our daughter Jerica, inviting 50 boys and girls from her class at Lake Highland Prep over for an evening pool party. We tell Ethan it's all right for him to invite a few friends over (no MySpace bulletins this time), and of course he chooses his teammates from the baseball team: Dennis Park, the senior third baseman, Ben Adams, the junior catcher, Colin Sterba, the outstanding senior center fielder, and Randall. I join them as they huddle together in a small circle on the porch above the patio, making fun of the younger kids, drinking sodas, eating burgers and talking about how the season's gone so far.

Things get out of hand quickly, not with the ballplayers, but with my daughter's friends. They're standing on the porch railing above the pool, leaping across the pool deck into the water, throwing sponge footballs and water soaked pool toys at one another. Pretty soon the Winter Park players get into it with them. It starts as simple heckling about the quality of the baseball teams, but it deteriorates into a strained competition, with boys from Lake Highland tossing the waterlogged toys at the Winter Park ballplayers, and the Winter Park players heaving the toys back at the Lake Highland kids, some of who play baseball. Randall gets hit in the back of the head twice. He keeps his anger barely restrained, and he shouts out to the kids in the pool, "Anyone hits me again I'm coming after them." The Winter Park players yell "Duck!" as a water filled sponge football whizzes by Randall's head.

"You!" he hollers at one of the boys in the pool, Skip Kovar, a tall, skinny pitcher and one of the best players on Lake Highland's JV team. Skip gets out of the pool and Randall confronts him. He backs Skip up against a wall and puts his hand around Skip's throat. Randall is 18. Skip is 14. Randall is muscular, menacing, red-faced. Skip is scared to death. I'm standing right behind Randall, and I'm frozen in place. Do I let this go? Is it just an empty threat, a game? Will Randall back off? The younger kids are watching. The Winter Park ballplayers, Ethan included, are howling with laughter. They think it's the funniest thing they've ever seen, but I can see the fear in Skip's eyes, the naked terror as he waits to get choked or beat up. I still don't move, for 15, 30 seconds, and Randall isn't moving either. "You threw that at me?" he hollers. "You nearly hit me in the face?" Skip shakes his head no, no, he didn't do it. Finally, I react. I put my hand on the back of Randall's shoulder and say, "Randall, that's enough," and he lets go. Skip drops against the wall, and the ballplayers as a group decide to leave. The party has grown noticeably quiet, and I stand there in place, feeling cowardly and awkward, the lone adult watching the events occur, so unsure what to do that I know I let it go on far too long, so long that a younger, weaker boy was manhandled and frightened. Why didn't I intervene right away? I thought about it, but I didn't. I was torn between the safety of a boy and the partisanship I felt towards Ethan's baseball buddies, and that, I know, was the wrong choice. I'm the adult. I'm the one responsible for maintaining control, but at that moment I didn't feel adult at all. I felt uncertain, hesitant, anxious, and I held back. Doing nothing was the wrong thing to do.

The ballplayers, with Ethan in tow, disappear into the night. They think Randall was hysterical. I sit back, my heart pounding, berating myself for the 30 seconds I delayed. I don't allow myself to think about what would have happened if I'd done nothing at all. The party gears up again, the noise increases, and Skip goes back to enjoying himself. Thank God for the short-term memories of teens.

Ethan pitches against Timber Creek, and he's not sharp. Something's happened to him this season. While he's not bad, he's not the starter King envisioned. Perhaps his arm slot is off a bit, coming more over the top than the ¾ slot that was his natural location. Perhaps he feels the pressure, or is just out of sorts, but he hasn't had the command he had last year. King is getting on him about his high leg kick and his inability to hold runners on first. King doesn't like Ethan's pickoff move either (though they don't ever practice it), and Ethan is not allowed to use it to hold runners close to the base. Timber Creek is hitting Ethan, and King grows more and more visibly agitated. Watching him from the bleachers I can see the tension in his body grow, the lines in his face tighten. He calls time and walks to the mound. The infield walks towards him but he motions them all away. That's odd. Normally when he goes to the mound the infield comes together and though he talks to the pitcher he also delivers the message to everyone. This time is different. This time he tells everyone to back off. It's him and Ethan, alone. I can't hear what he says, but it doesn't look good. Ethan's shoulders slump. He looks like he's been slapped in the face. King is on a rant. He goes on and on. The words are jumbled and I can't make them out, but by the expressions on the infielders faces, and the look of the mom on the field who acts as team photographer, I know it's bad. King leaves, and Ethan prepares to pitch again, but now it's really different. Every pitch he throws is from the slide step. He loses velocity as he drives to the plate without lifting his front leg more than six inches off the ground, and he gets hit again, worse than before. One hit. Two hits. King takes him out. Winter Park loses.

I ask Ethan what was going on, and he tells me that Coach King yelled at him, asking what the fuck he was doing out there, and told him that if he threw another pitch that wasn't from the slide step he'd pull him out of the game, because his move to home plate was so slow anyone could steal on him. Other players told me after the game they'd never heard King go off on a player like that, and that he'd been "dropping the F bomb" all over the place. Parents come up to me in the Timber Creek parking lot and tell me they think I ought to speak with Coach King, but I don't want to cause problems. I've had enough of that in my past already, and I just want to get through the season, which crawls to a merciful, losing end. Bob Kidd, a senior reserve outfielder, quits because he didn't start the game on senior day (King says there's no school tradition about starting seniors, just about playing them during that game), and Steve Garvey quits just before tournament play. He is told he won't start in the tournament because he was late to a practice. He throws his jersey down in the locker room and walks away, never stepping foot on the baseball field again.

The team makes the district playoffs, hovering just over .500, and the first game is against Apopka. Randall's velocity has dropped, and he's been in the doghouse ever since his talk with Coach King, so King picks Ethan to start the game, stating that he thinks Ethan gives the team the best chance to win. Ethan and Chris Quintero drive together to the game and get lost on the way. They barely make it in time, and Ethan dashes onto the field carrying buckets of balls for the team's infield practice. I see him talking to King before he goes, and I can tell it's another difficult conversation. Later Ethan tells me that he told King that he wasn't sure about pitching against Apopka because it was such a tough crowd, to which King responded with a reprimand: "If you don't want to be a pitcher and just want to hit we can do that," and sent him off to warm up.

Ethan starts off slowly, his pattern all season. Apopka scores four runs on him in the first, all unearned, as Randall makes two errors at second base in place of Garvey, and errors are also made at short and in right field. Winter Park comes back and scores in the second, but Ethan gives up 2 more runs and is replaced by Andy McHenry, who pitches solidly, gets through the third inning. Then something strange, something I've never seen before happens. I am sitting nearest to the Winter Park dugout, on the far right side of the bleachers when Coach King grabs Ethan by the jersey and, with his face inches from Ethan's, spits out, "You've heard of kids coming back from the dead. That's what you're going to do," and pushes Ethan back onto the field to pitch again. This time, shaken and unprepared, after watching McHenry pitch well, Ethan struggles and gets pulled for the last time. Since he wasn't the starter, McHenry can't pitch again, and no one left for Winter Park shows any signs of life. The team goes on to lose 16-9, with King sitting on the Apopka bench with his arms crossed in front of him from the midway point of the game to its conclusion. Parents stare at him, aghast. What's he doing over there? Why isn't he sitting with our boys? He's abandoned us. It appears that he wants nothing to do with his team in this baseball debacle. He tells the Winter Park principal that he sat there because his stomach was upset and he needed to be near the bathroom, but the general consensus among parents was that he was sick to his stomach at the way the boys played, and walked out on the team.

Before the end of school Ethan sits down with Coach King to talk about summer ball. King wants every boy to play only for the Winter Park summer squad, but Ethan has already made a commitment to the Orlando Scorpions. Ethan tells Bob he is willing to play for the Wildcats, too. He would just have to limit his pitching so he doesn't get hurt. Bob's response? "You're deserting your team, and if you get hurt I'll have no problem replacing you with a freshman. When you and your parents ask for a letter of recommendation for college the only thing I'll be able to write is that you're uncoachable."

Wow, I think. That's harsh. But I discount it and attribute it to Coach King's overzealous commitment to his baseball program, and hope it will disappear along with the long summer rains.

The truth is, the Scorpions play at a much higher level against better competition, but King has gone back to his pre-Stephen philosophy, and once again hates showcase ball and what it's done to high school baseball. If one looks closely at his reasoning, it's not completely ill-founded.

Just as AAU baseball sprouted wings and took off during Ethan's early playing years in direct competition with Little League, growing from a few elite teams to thousands of teams across the country, so too showcase baseball suddenly went from a few select teams and a couple key tournaments to a huge enterprise that eclipsed spring baseball, rendering it, if not meaningless, then almost irrelevant.

In the past, in what could be described as the All-American heyday of high school sports, boys played football in the fall, basketball in the winter, and baseball in the spring. It wasn't about lettering in high school. It was about whether or not you were a two, three, or four sport athlete. The real stud of the school was the quarterback in football, the high scorer in basketball, and the best pitcher on the baseball team all rolled into one complete package. The preeminence of high school was never in question. All the hype, the prestige, the reputations and the rumor mills were built on the revolving seasons of high school sports, and the coaches of those sports were held in the highest regard. They controlled the destinies of their student/athletes. The stars they touted, the players they highlighted, the recommendations they gave paved the way to college scholarships. Boys were recruited on the basis of their high school stats, their performance for their high school team. Scouts from colleges and the pros could be seen watching the top prospects during spring ball, taking notes in their leather writing pads, holding their radar guns, chewing gum and talking with one another in their secret confederacy of power and knowledge in the front rows of bleachers during games. Parents watched them without interfering, whispering amongst themselves in hushed tones. "Did you see how many scouts were at the game?" "Why do you think they all started scribbling when Joe Money was in the batter's box?" "Were they watching Joe or Sandy Slick on the mound?"

And then showcase ball happened, largely under the auspices of Perfect Game, an organization that describes itself in the following manner:

"Perfect Game USA produces the very highest national level individual player showcases and team tournaments all over the United States. The PG Database is the largest of its kind anywhere in baseball. At any given time there will be nearly 100,000 high school players being followed via the database.

"In the past seven years 5,293 players who attended Perfect Game events have been selected/drafted by Major League clubs. In 2002 Perfect Game broke the record for all organizations for the most participants drafted with 364 Draft picks. In 2003 Perfect Game again broke the record when 409 PG participants were drafted by MLB Clubs. In 2004 Perfect Game once again broke the record when 533 PG participants were drafted by MLB Clubs. In 2005 Perfect Game again broke the record with 823 PG participants were drafted by MLB Clubs. The record fell again in 2006 when 952 PG participants were drafted by MLB Clubs. The record was set once again in 2007 when 1,054 PG participants were selected in the 2007 MLB draft. And for the seventh straight year Perfect Game shattered its own record when an astounding 1,164 PG participants were selected in the 2008 MLB draft. This accounts for over 77% of the entire draft! It has been estimated that by year 2009 over half of all the players on Major League rosters will have attended Perfect Game events.

"People sometimes think that Perfect Game is only for those prospects that are going into professional baseball. The number of Perfect Game participants who play at the college level is much, much larger than the draft totals. Many of the top college programs in the country have nearly all former PG participants on their rosters. Perfect Game also has many players who are continuing their baseball careers at Junior Colleges and other Small Colleges.

"Our job is to identify talented players, not to develop them, draft them or recruit them. That is why we use the term "attended PG events" rather than "PG Player". We don't deserve any credit for the vast majority of talented players who attend our events and go on to get College Scholarships or become draft picks. The credit should go to the many coaches, teams, teammates, instructors, parents and most of all, to the individual players themselves. Many of these players play in excellent summer and fall programs. Without those programs PG would miss a lot of talented players."

What is most interesting here is not the number of players who attend Perfect Game tournaments who subsequently are drafted. Nor is it the attempt by Perfect Game to deflect credit to the players and coaches. It is the reference to "excellent summer and fall programs." What happened to spring baseball? Where did the excellent high school programs go? Did they all disappear, or were they replaced by the Perfect Game juggernaut? The answer is that high school ball still exists, of course, but it has been diminished and minimalized in importance with the rise of the massive showcase tournaments.

While pro scouts still attend high school games in the spring to see top prospects play (and they can; it fits into their schedule, and they normally are targeting a single player to watch on a team), college coaches don't have the same luxury. Their season begins in February, the same time high school baseball gets underway. With limited budgets for scouting and travel, why should they waste their time at a high school game where there might only be two or three prospective players for them, when they can go to the World Wood Bat Championship Tournament every July in East Cobb, Georgia, and during a period of two weeks witness thousands of top high school players compete within a few miles of each other? In 2010 the Perfect Game WWBC attracted 216 17-under teams. If each team averages 15 players (and that's a low number) that's 3,240 of the top 16 and 17 year old players in the country. What high school, in fact what state can compete with that? That's why there are almost no college scouts at high school games anymore. They wait for summer, when showcase season, and their scouting frenzy begins.

On top of that, Perfect Game ranks the top 1,500 players in each age bracket. This controversial, highly desirable rating begins during the summer after a player's tenth grade, and follows them as they advance to college or the pros. Though it is almost impossible to calculate exactly how many boys across the United States play baseball for their high school team, if there were only 50 teams in each state, and if each team carried 20 players, then there would be 50,000 boys playing high school baseball every spring. To be ranked among the top 500 players by Perfect Game means that you are perceived to be in the top 1% of all players in the nation.

When Bob King reacted to Ethan's desire to play summer ball for the Scorpions, he reacted, in part, not out of jealousy or unwarranted animosity, but out of a bitterness caused by the very meaning of his 25 years of coaching being sucked out by showcase tournaments while he stood on the sidelines, waving at his best players as the sun set on his own professional relevance.

〇

One month shy of his 17th birthday, Ethan and his mom travel up to Atlanta to participate in his first World Wood Bat Championship Tournament at East Cobb. Pat and I are splitting this tournament. She's there chaperoning Ethan the first four days. I'm there the second four, and we'll overlap and see each other for a half hour at the Atlanta International Airport where she'll hand me keys to the rental car and update me on directions and accommodations.

It's a strange, bittersweet handoff. I don't like seeing her once in eight days for 30 minutes over a cup of coffee surrounded by strangers while seated in the uncomfortable plastic chairs at the airport. I feel exposed and anxious, wanting intimacy, to hold her hands for a moment, sneak a kiss, to catch up on what seems like a year's worth of news, while hundreds of innocuous faces walk past. She warns me about the beyond cheap extended living hotel the team is staying at, the lumpy mattresses, terribly thin sheets and blankets, that no one cleans the rooms, the noisy window air conditioners, the lack of a pool or amenities of any sort, and the kind of disreputable clientele you would read about in a Dashiell Hammett novel. During the time we're there police arrest a couple for drug trafficking, there's a shooting and another man and woman get hauled away for drunk and disorderly conduct in the hallway outside our room.

At the same time I'm thinking, "Let me get out to the ballfield, where ETHAN IS PITCHING THE GAME OF HIS LIFE! Rewind for a moment.

〇

Something amazing happens the moment the high school season ends and Scorpion summer ball begins. Ethan becomes a different player. He pitches with confidence. His percentage of strikes to balls increases. He works more quickly, and with each outing becomes more and more effective. His high school season was marked by inconsistency, sporadic good pitching followed by walks and loss of control. He appeared to pitch burdened, with an excess of fear strapped to his back, but now he is free of all burdens and pitching again for the fun of it. And he is pitching and hitting both.

We travel to Cincinnati for a tournament on hard black clay fields and eat chili and watch Dan Harang battle C.C. Sabathia in a low scoring pitcher's duel in an inter-league game at Cincinnati's All-American ballpark. We visit the great Cincinnati Zoo and Ethan wins a game for the Scorpions in a tournament marred by erratic hitting and fielding.

The Scorpions play more than a high school season's worth of games in a month, traveling all over the state, playing against junior college teams, travel teams from up north, college summer league wood bat teams, and bit by bit, Ethan solidifies his spot. Not as the stud, or the best, or the leader, but as a component of a talented machine. He has a place, a role, and plays like it.

By the time he traveled to East Cobb he'd worked his way up in the Scorpions lineup to become the number four starter on a team where he was one of the youngest players. He was hitting fine, but during showcase tournaments the players being actively recruited had to be seen, and Ethan was still too young to even talk to college coaches, much less be concerned about playing time.

When I walked into the Orlando International Airport to board my flight to Atlanta, Ethan was pitching against a team from Connecticut that led our bracket. The only team to advance out of a bracket into the championship segment of the tournament was the bracket winner, and Connecticut was undefeated while the Scorpions had already lost a close, low scoring game. Connecticut could win or tie, but the Scorpions had to win to advance, and Ethan had found his groove in front of more than 50 college scouts.

Pat reported to me while I waited to board that in the first inning Ethan had been tentative, giving up a single, walking a batter and then giving up a run on an error. His coach, Matt Gerber, walked to the mound and chewed him out, but this was a different kind of chewing out than he had received during the spring. This time it came from someone who Ethan knew cared about him. Gerb was pissed off that Ethan wasn't pitching as well as he could, and this was a game the Scorps couldn't afford to lose. Ethan settled down.

When I left the ground it was the fifth inning and Ethan had struck out eight with no more walks and had allowed no other runs. His changeup was unhittable. His two-seam fastball had so much movement the Connecticut batters were being embarrassed when they swung. The Scorpions were winning 8-1. What happened next goes down in the laurels of Scorpions history.

After the fifth inning Ethan had only thrown 64 pitches. Coach Gerber turned to Ethan and asked, "Can you come back and pitch again on two days rest if I take you out now?"

"Yessir," Ethan said. With the game in his back pocket, Gerber took Ethan out and put another lefty on the mound.

Who couldn't throw a strike. After four runs score he is replaced by another pitcher, a righthander this time, who also proceeds to walk batter after batter. With a few timely hits thrown in the team from Connecticut is finally retired in the top of the seventh inning after plating eight runs, and they lead by one. The Scorpions manage to score once in the bottom of the seventh and tie the game as time expires. Ethan gets a no-decision, and the tie sends them into the losers bracket.

There is more second-guessing, more parental consternation than I have ever seen or heard at the end of this game. While it's true that Ethan was sailing along and in all likelihood would have continued to do so, there was no reason to believe that no other pitcher from the Scorpions would be able to throw the ball across the plate. The Scorpions catcher, Ben McMahon, swears that it wasn't the pitchers' faults, that they were throwing as well as Ethan, but that for some reason the umpire suddenly tightened the strike zone when Ethan departed.

Parents moan that the coaches should have left Ethan in the game, that the most important thing to do at that point in time was to win, not save pitching. But who knew? With a seven run lead who would have thought a team loaded with all-star caliber pitching wouldn't be able to snuff out any rally? The biggest reason to move on to the winner's bracket in a tournament like this (besides the sheer joy of winning) is for the boys to receive greater exposure by playing more games in front of more scouts. Now, with a demotion to the losers bracket, they are given only two more games to play, neither of which will garner much attention.

One of the most common complaints one hears at almost all high school level baseball games is the blatant, obvious biases of umpires calling the games. Umpires, in the minds of many parents, are always on one side or the other. They don't call it fair. Their strike zone is better for one team, worse for the other. They want to see a certain team win. They play favorites. They have a vendetta. The coach pissed them off during the game. The close calls always go one way. The Scorpion coaches, the catcher and pitchers all swear that happened in the tie game that sent them into the losers bracket. And there are cases when an umpire has called games for a high school coach for so long, has seen certain boys so often, that he may have a subtle bias, a modest (occasionally an extreme) partiality for one over the other. After all, he gets selected by the coach of the home team, paid by the home team. Why not favor the home team? There are times when there are make up calls, when an umpire blows one call and evens it up later. And sometimes a coach really does piss an umpire off enough to cause the calls to go the other way. Matt Gerber swears that's what happened this game.

But the truth is, this rarely occurs. Umpires with agendas don't get jobs. They get ostracized. As easy as it is to blame an umpire for missed calls that seem to always go the opposite way, it is equally easy to remember that they, like us, are human and make mistakes. And they have no real reason, no overwhelming motivation to help one team win, another lose. More often than not blaming the umpire is the easy way to deflect responsibility off the shoulders of coaches and players and onto an unseen, silent foe who vanishes when the game ends without benefit of explanation or rebuttal. And to this day I wonder why Ethan got strikes called his way and no other pitcher did, and what would have motivated the umpire behind the plate to suddenly change the way he called strikes at the end of the game, why he would help a team from Connecticut to the detriment of a group of boys from Central Florida? It just didn't make any sense.

I call Coach King after the game to tell him how well Ethan threw. "Coach," I say. "Ethan had a great game today. Tons of colleges saw him. He was living 85 with a great changeup and curveball," I tell the coach. "Ten strikeouts and only one unearned run. He can't wait for next year."

King sounds surprised by my call, but he is open and jovial nonetheless, and tells me he's looking forward to it as well. "That's nice," he says. "Don't let that travel team hurt his arm."

Hurt him? They're the best thing that's ever happened to him. But I say nothing other than have a good day and we'll stay in touch. Good move. Keep the coach in the loop. Let him know how the summer's progressing, how well Ethan's doing. It all bodes well for the future, I say to myself with smug self-satisfaction. I am doing everything right to set Ethan up for his important junior year.

⚾

That night a group of boys on the team go out and get drunk. Someone has a car. Someone else has a fake I.D. I find out that Ethan has been in the room with them, but thank God, for once he's used his head and left early without getting caught up in the partying. Our second baseman passes out on the bed. Other boys get sloppy drunk, but we don't know about this until the next day when the team plays its second to last game of the tournament, the first game in the losers bracket against a team from California. As parents we all wonder why they look so lethargic. It's as if they're moving in molasses, in slow motion with heavy limbs and clumsy feet. They make unusual errors in the field, dropping balls that are virtually handed to them, botching simple double plays, making routine fly balls look like the most difficult catches ever. The coaches know what's going on. They stand with their arms crossed over their chests, muttering to one another, frowning, not speaking, watching the terrible play.

At the end of the game they motion for the team to follow them, and on an adjacent field they make the boys run. And run. And run in the heat, in the sun, until one by one they fall on their hands and knees and puke in the outfield. Those who were drinking go down first. A few of the better athletes make it all the way through, though they're exhausted by the ordeal. The coaches don't say a word, but everyone knows the why's and the who's. Why they're running. Who's responsible. There are no smiles, no pats on the back as they hobble off the field. Ethan goes down like everyone else. There are no great heroics here, no miraculous story about how my boy was one of the last to fall. The only tale to be told is that he didn't stop, didn't give up early, kept pushing through, not better than but like everyone else. And that's something he couldn't have done even a year ago.

I ask Coach Gerber later why he didn't just kick the boys who were drinking off the team, send them home for the summer. It's what I would have done. They broke the law, embarrassed the organization, disregarded the most basic rules of conduct. And his response was telling with a generosity that I had not considered. "These are good boys with college scouts looking at them," he told me. "They make one stupid mistake. Am I going to ruin their futures because of that? If I send them home everyone knows. They don't get scholarships. Maybe their baseball is done. If I punish them it's between them and me and the team."

That night over burgers at Dave and Buster's, Vic Caban, the assistant coach and a past ballplayer for the University of North Florida, hands out team awards. Vic is short, thin, wiry, with an ever ready smile that encompasses his whole face. He's all about being positive and having a good time. He has this to say about the first award of the night: "At the beginning of the summer we didn't know if this kid would even make it through. Every time we ran he was puking on the first lap. We didn't know if he had the mental toughness to succeed at this level. But he's proved us wrong. He's toughened up and hung in there with all you older guys. So we're giving the first ever Testicular Fortitude Award to Ethan Bornstein."

Ethan rises to laughter and applause. His award is an old purple Scorpions sock stuffed with other old socks and two tennis balls. Ethan carries his purple penis sock back to his table, where it is passed around to bursts of laughter. He's more proud of this award than any medal he's ever won.

The next day, at a distant field at an obscure high school in North Atlanta, the Scorpions finish play. They throw several pitchers who still have innings left and need to be seen by scouts, and at the end of the game Ethan gets the last inning. Now, for the first time there are college scouts out to watch him throw. Miami, Florida, LSU, all have their recruiting coaches there, not to watch Ethan exclusively, but he's made it onto their radar screens. I go up to Cliff Godwin, the young, square jawed, crew cut hitting coach for LSU. I've seen him at other games and I notice him tracking Ethan. "Coach," I say as I walk up, "that's my boy on the mound. What do you think?"

"What grade is he going into?" Godwin asks.

"Eleventh," I tell him.

"Goodbye," he says, "can't talk," and walks away. The Scorpions coaches see this and quickly get on me on two counts. First, I'm overstepping my bounds and doing their job. They're the ones who work the recruitment of players. That's the purpose of the showcase program. And second, did I know that I could be breaking NCAA rules by talking to a coach with a player who is not yet old enough to be recruited? Naïve as I am to the recruiting process, I had no idea, and much as I want to brag about my boy and show him off to the assembled coaching elite, I bite my tongue, stay seated and let them watch without my intervention. What they see, that day, is a tall, long legged lefty who works fast, without hesitating between pitches, and for the first time touches 88. They've got to be impressed, I think, though I have no idea whether they are or not.

Something else happens at that game. Ethan gets invited to the end of the season AFLAC All-American Tournament in San Diego. Where the tournament has always been designed in the past for the top 100 incoming high school seniors in the country to show off their talents to pro and college scouts, for the first time they're having a mini-showcase for incoming juniors, and Ethan gets one of the last invitations. It's an unexpected honor that the Scorpion coaches make happen, and at summer's end we fly to San Diego. We visit the San Diego Zoo and watch seals sun bathe at La Jolla. Ethan holds his own pitching and hitting against the best of the best - a solid conclusion to his coming out season.

CHAPTER 9
Junior

At the end of summer I take Bob King out to lunch. We spend the better part of an hour reviewing the past season (though we avoid any direct talk about his incidents with Ethan), speaking about the upcoming one, and laying out our expectations. He is, I discover, both insightful and direct. I mention how thin the team is in pitching. "I know," he says. "We're going to need a lot of innings out of Ethan and Modomo." I talk about the batting order, and he reviews the strengths and weaknesses of every hitter on the team, including some incoming freshman who I have yet to see play, one of whom, Dante Bichette Jr., the son of ex-major leaguer Dante Bichette, is one of the most highly touted players in Central Florida. I can't argue with a single point he makes. Everything I've thought about the Winter Park players I've watched, he articulates. "Ethan is one of the most important players on the team," he says. "He owns first base this year and will be in every inning of every game." It's more than a promise. It's a given. He tells me he wants Ethan to be a leader on the team, that he has high expectations for him. We leave all smiles, shake hands, in full cooperation with one another.

At the end of the previous school year my wife and I had a similar meeting with Coach King. At it we discussed some of the situations that occurred during the season, and Bob listened openly.

"Ethan might appear tough on the outside," my wife told him, "but inside he's really a softie in need of positive reinforcement. The way to get through to him is with support, constructive criticism, and understanding."

Bob seemed to get it. He nodded appreciatively, promised he'd modify his approach with Ethan, that he'd be more positive in the upcoming season, and told us how grateful he was that we came in, because the information parents gave him about their children helped his coaching immensely.

Ethan, meanwhile, wanted nothing more to do with King or the Winter Park program. He could only think about King cussing him out on the mound, grabbing his jersey and tossing him back in the Apopka game, ending the season bitterly, angrily, as if he were some cast-off debris that had already been jettisoned by the coach. He was ready to transfer to Edgewater High School and play under Chip Gierke, but Pat and I would have nothing to do with that. We insisted he stay at Winter Park, by far the better academic school, where his friends and teammates were, and not jump ship just because of a few hard times with his coach, which we were sure we'd ironed out. We were righteous in our belief that balancing academics and athletics was a priority, even though Ethan's full focus, his energy and resolve were all about baseball.

"Coach Gierke knows me," Ethan said. "He likes me. Please," he almost begged. "I know it'll work out. Just let me go to Edgewater. King has it in for me. I swear it's gonna be bad. I can tell."

I wasn't listening. Besides issues of eligibility and recruitment violations, there were ethical issues I clung to with a near religious fervor. "Are you kidding me?" I told him. "You want to transfer just to play for Gierke and give up going to the best high school in the area? You don't bail during hard times. When you make a commitment you follow through," I insisted. "You don't hop from team to team just because it's not the perfect situation for you." Smug. Certain. Wrong. I should have seen the patterns, the pitfalls in his way, but I wanted to believe the best, and I blinded myself to what was coming, choosing the path of rapprochement instead of listening to Ethan's fears, cutting his losses and moving on.

$$\mathcal{D}$$

We often hear the role of coaches compared to that of parents, that coaches are "father figures," "disciplinarians," "role models" – exactly what parents are supposed to be. As parents we model behavior for our children so that they emulate our best, hide our worst behind closed doors, and understand that when we act poorly we are sad, sorry, mistaken. The best parents, like the best coaches, are imperfect creatures in an imperfect world, trying to impart positive values and help children grow into strong, independent adults who can make decisions based on sound judgments and reasonably astute assessments of their actions and the subsequent consequences. My parenting philosophy has always been to minimize the damage we inevitably do to our children. It's not about perfection. It's not about doing everything right. It's not if we mess them up; it's about how little we mess them up, and then layer upon that good experiences, love and the knowledge that we'll be there no matter what.

Parents, like coaches, don't need a license to raise their children, though perhaps in both cases that would be a good idea. We want to be loving, fair, compassionate. We use words like patience, kindness, enthusiasm, sincerity, concern, empathy, to describe ourselves at our best. We try to teach them the core values of honesty, integrity, responsibility, and respect for themselves and others. And we work to set our children free, to prepare us and them for the day when they no longer need to listen to us as often, as directly, as completely, when we trust them to make their own decisions with full faith that more times than not they will be the right decisions, when we can no longer be their "coaches in life" and turn them over to life itself so that the lessons they learn and experiences they live through are their own, not filtered or manufactured or interpreted by us.

Isn't that the role of the best coaches as well? We teach our sports-immersed children to treat their coaches with the utmost respect, to place their coaches on pedestals because they know more than us, because they are the new teachers, the experts, the best role models. We give them the power of parents to guide and shape our children, and we reinforce this by telling our children that these father-like, Moses-like figures will lead them to the promised land so long as they watch, learn, listen, and do what they're told.

So isn't it incumbent upon us as parents to make sure the fit works, the leadership is appropriate, the coach is the kind of person we wish we were? When we evaluate who we are turning our children over to for half their waking hours half of every year, shouldn't we make the decision based not only on what school district they happen to be in, but on what situation is the best for them, which marriage of parts works?

Ethan suffered with the disadvantages of being our first child and an athlete to parents who had no experience in the world of athletics. We had no idea how to cope with a child who was severely attention deficit, and I had no clue how powerful the magnetism of stardom would be for me, how enamored I would be with a child who was everything I wasn't, but wished I were.

By the time Ethan entered high school he had been through coaches who ranged from lenient to strict, organized to scattered, stoic to emotional, strong willed to passive, positively supportive to negatively critical. We thought we had witnessed the range of possibilities, but we had not dealt with, nor did we understand, the power of the long-entrenched high school coach, and we did not take the time or even think about the need to assess the personality match between Ethan, our sweet, talented, helter-skelter mass of chaos and confusion, and Bob King, the methodical, organized, opinionated, judgmental coach who had survived more than two decades of change at Winter Park High.

We never asked ourselves if this was a good fit. It was the only fit. We never allowed ourselves to reflect on the possibility that this wasn't a good situation for either of them. We knew what Ethan's goals were: to grow as a player, to make it all the way to a big Division 1 college program, but we never asked Coach King what his goals were beyond winning. We never understood, beyond his "brutal honesty," what his personal priorities were as a coach. Did he just want to win, or was he interested in his players growing into young men as well? Was it more important to him to follow the practice plans he'd developed in 24 years of coaching at Winter Park, or could he adjust to the different needs and personalities of players as unique as Ethan? If we had, if we had stepped back and thought about these complicated issues we might never have pushed Ethan to stay. We would have realized that Ethan and Bob King were not compatible. We would have wondered why, in 24 years, King had only sent 5 players to Division 1 schools to play baseball, when other schools in Central Florida sent two or three players a year. We would have understood, clear as day, that a coach who kept records of every practice he'd ever held would find himself in conflict with a boy who regularly forgot his homework, misplaced his keys, couldn't find his uniform, lost his gloves, missed appointments, and struggled with the concept that actions and consequences were intrinsically linked.

This fall the Scorpions announce that they are going to do things a little bit differently. They're going to have two 18-under teams like always, but players will have to earn their way to the end of season Perfect Game wood bat tournament in Jupiter, the largest and most highly scouted tournament in the country. The tournament takes place at the spring training complex shared by the Florida Marlins and St. Louis Cardinals. The complex is immense, with a dozen secondary fields and a bright, classic stadium for the big games. Because there are so many teams and so many scouts there, Perfect Game provides golf carts for all the college and professional scouts to scoot from game to game and field to field. During the final games of the tournament, the parked golf carts can be six rows deep and stretch all the way from first base to home and up the third base lines.

The players with the best statistics will make an all-star Scorpions squad, while the rest will attend an alternate tournament elsewhere. The glove has been tossed, the challenge accepted. In order to make it to Jupiter, you have to be one of the best.

Ethan proceeds to go on a wood bat hitting tear. He doesn't have a bad game, and midway through the season he leads the Scorpions in almost every hitting category. He is batting nearly .700 with doubles jumping off his bat like it's corked and on steroids. The ball looks like a watermelon to him. He can pluck it out of the air and squash it like it's ripe and succulent and just sitting there waiting for him. Almost every time up he hits a bomb, over the center fielder's head, down the first base line to the fence. He's in one of those rarefied hitting zones that occurs a few times in a ballplayer's career, and the timing couldn't be more fortuitous, because he's carving his name in the Jupiter lineup, taking the next great step after his coming out party from the summer before.

The fall is also training time for Winter Park's baseball team, and Ethan takes a weightlifting course with Coach King to build a connection with King. He does his homework during the class and talks to his coach, and gets his workout in after school with the rest of the baseball team. In King's enormous weight room Ethan goes from squatting 200 to 385 pounds, from benching 55 to 85 pound dumbbells, and the results are showing up in his power at the plate. King has the boys work with medicine balls as well, holding them far behind their heads and flinging them against a block wall building. During one of these drills, while Ethan is throwing the med ball without supervision, he feels something pop in his lower back. The next morning he wakes up stiff and sore and struggles to bend over, but during the course of the day it seems to loosen up, and I think sore muscles, not bad back.

That weekend, Pat calls me with an update on his performance at a weekend tournament in Clearwater. He was still hitting well with wood bats. One ball flew over 400 feet to a cavernous dead center. It would have been a home run on most fields, but he settled for another double. When he came around the bases, however, he complained that his sore back was hurting him more, and I schedule an appointment with an orthopedic surgeon and family friend.

Now I'm worried. More than worried, I'm scared. On occasion I have a sore lower back, attributed to degenerating discs. My wife is another story altogether. When she was 32 she herniated a disc in her lower back. Even with a pain threshold that's so high I can't imagine it (I suffer with splinters and hangnails), she experienced almost unbearable pain. During a trip to Los Angeles I watched her suffer as she shuffled alongside me, taking a few steps, gasping, holding onto me to take the pressure off her back. On the flight home she curled up on two seats, unable to move or talk as pain radiated down her leg and her foot began to go numb, and by the time we had driven from the airport home I had surgery scheduled for her the next day. While the surgery provided immediate relief, she has dealt with lower back pain (and another herniated disc) ever since. I feared the worst for Ethan.

Our orthopedist checks Ethan out and assures us that, based on the symptoms, and without any pain radiating down his leg, he's sure all Ethan has is a nerve tweaked by a pulled muscle. A week on anti-inflammatories and he'll be good as new. And while Ethan is on the muscle relaxants, he does improve, does feel better, but within days of the prescription running out he's in pain again, only now he's having a hard time getting up when he sits down, getting out of bed, and an MRI reveals what I feared most – a herniated L5 disc just like his mom.

Ohmygod, I think as I sink into a depression as deep and profound, maybe deeper than the one I felt when Ethan sat on the end of the bench with Team Easton. His dreams are over. His playing days may be at an end. How can a young pitcher reach his potential with a damaged back? How can he pitch if he can't bend over? And my dreams, I realize, may be at an end as well.

$$\bigcirc$$

On the walkway to the Winter Park High School baseball field are bricks inscribed with names and phrases and dedications to the great players of the school's past. "25 Years of Coaches Larry Wright Paul Suce Harry Lovegood George Royal Bob King," "Jack Billingham WPHS 1959-61 Orange Co. All Conference Major League Pitcher

Cinn. Reds," "John Hart WPHS 1965-66 Major League Coach General Manager Cleveland Indians," "Davey Johnson Winter Park Baltimore Orioles 1965-72 13 Years in Majors," "James Younger LHP 1989-90-91 9-10-73 – 2-23-95 Gave His All Now With The Lord," "Matt Incinelli Class of 98 Play Hard and Honor God."

I imagined Ethan's name inscribed alongside theirs, remembered as one of the great left handed pitchers to ever grace the playing field of his high school. "Ethan Bornstein Class of 2009 Do It Well and Do It Your Way." I had long imagined going through the recruiting process for college with him, listening to the shpiels of different coaches, prepping him on how to say no to many and yes to one. I imagined walking with him and his mother during Senior Night, the game to honor senior players, and listening to his speech thanking everyone, including us, for the great time he'd had playing ball in high school. God, it wasn't just his future that was vanishing. It was part of mine as well, memories I'd already lived that hadn't yet occurred. I wanted them badly. I wanted that walk down memory lane, and I was being denied it, not by anyone, but by a lack of supervision, perhaps, by a genetically predisposed back, perhaps, by a fate I had not considered possible. I'd imagined it all, and watched it evaporate in the amount of time it took for a medical opinion to be written.

If I was depressed, Ethan was worse. After visiting a back specialist he was put on rest and rehab for the rest of the fall, but there could be no pitching, no hitting, no running or working out. He could rest and rehab, rehab and rest, and hope that his young body stabilized his protruding disc. For the first time in his life, Ethan was injured and unable to perform for a season of baseball. He grew lethargic and lazy, sitting on the couch all day eating and watching TV. He put on at least 20 pounds in a short period of time. He got out of shape, and there wasn't much he could do about it besides starve, since he wasn't allowed to do any of the work that had been his regular routine at this time of year.

To make matters worse, the Scorpions go on a winning streak at the Jupiter tournament. As we followed them online, the team got performance after performance from its key players, grinding out close games, beating teams they should never have beaten, until in the semi-finals Anthony Figliolia, a University of Central Florida signee with a fierce competitive fire, a low 90s fastball and a filthy slider, pitched a complete game in a 2-1 win. And then, in the finals, the Scorpions played the Atlanta Braves Scout Team to a dead heat, with several pitchers throwing outstanding games until, arms and bats depleted, they lost 3-1 in front of hundreds of college and professional scouts. Ethan laid on the living room couch realizing moment by moment that he had earned his way on that team, that he would have been selected, would have been hitting, and probably would have been one of the pitchers in that final game to put the Scorpions over the top. It is a regret he carries with him to this day.

⚾

While Ethan lies on a couch recuperating and getting out of shape, Matty Tralka, the senior catcher for the Wildcats and one of the catchers for the Scorpions, finds himself shuttling back and forth between games for both teams. With catchers in short supply, during one weekend he makes the drive to and from Vero Beach, two and a half hours away, three times in order to make sure Winter Park isn't left without a catcher during a weekend series. Bob King gives a speech to the fall high school squad, talking about the lack of leadership on the team, and Matt quits, taking the comment as a personal insult, choosing instead to umpire little league games. He's not the only one. Keith Merkel, the bright, athletic first baseman who Ethan competed with the season before, quits to play lacrosse. He doesn't want to play baseball if he's not going to get a chance to hit. Steve Garvey goes to another school. The high school team we thought would be in place during Ethan's junior year has dwindled to a handful of juniors and seniors. More than 20 players projected to be on the team have left for a variety of reasons, including everything from injury to personal issues to resentment of the coaches. It happens at schools everywhere, just not to this extent. This is extreme. The core group of players who had been expected to carry the team are gone, to other sports, other interests. The stars projected to start rarely quit. In this case, it had become the norm.

Ethan goes through two months of physical rehabilitation, and we're told that while it is not necessarily a baseball ending injury (note all the professional players with bad backs) it could be unless he takes it seriously. I don't know if he's taking it seriously, but I know I am. I buy him an inflatable exercise ball for his back exercises. I buy him chondritin and glucosamine supplements to help his back heal. I buy a bed pad full of magnets for him to sleep on, and I read and read about back injuries and herniated discs. I study far more than I did when Pat was hurt. I learn about laser surgeries and disc replacement experiments, and while I feel guilty about this and acknowledge to myself how much more I'm doing for my son than I did for my wife, I can't stop myself. I'm becoming an expert on back injuries in youth sports, and am filled with hope and dread at the same time – hope that his back can actually heal, resorb the disc and he will recover, dread that he will never be the same. I read about inversion tables, cold lasers and electro-stim therapy, about clinics that specialize in back surgeries and promise miraculous results, and I'm ready to try it all.

Slowly, Ethan does recover, though his flexibility isn't near what it once was. Where he could bend at the waist from a standing position and put his palms flat on the ground, now he can barely reach his knees. His stride appears shortened, and his gait has stiffened, but it's only been two months, and he still has time before spring tryouts. I buy a cold laser device that is supposed to accelerate the healing process, reduce inflammation and promote blood flow to the injured area, and have Ethan lie down on his stomach twice a day to receive treatments, which I give him while we watch TV.

In November for Thanksgiving he and I take a road trip to visit Clemson and the University of South Carolina, driving from there to stay with family in Charleston. At Clemson we meet with an academic advisor and get taken on a tour of the campus via golf cart with their pitching coach. We see the 80,000 seat football stadium, the gorgeous baseball field that can accommodate more than 6,000 fans, the 4,000 square foot state of the art weight room. At South Carolina we walk the campus with the pitching coach, get shown the site of the new baseball complex, see the new student recreation center and meet with a young academic advisor who used to play baseball for the Gamecocks. Go Cocks! Best name ever for a college mascot. The coach at South Carolina tells Ethan he's interested, but wants to see him pitch at 86-88 consistently. "I can do that," he tells the coach. I can tell his confidence and forthrightness make a good impression.

He starts throwing again, jogging again finally, in December. He's carrying the extra twenty pounds, but at least he can move, run, and I begin to believe that he can be ready in time for his junior year. We haven't told Coach King or anyone, for that matter, the extent of Ethan's injury because, well, because we don't want anyone to know.

It's too early to tell how he'll recover, and besides, this is the year the recruitment process starts in earnest, and we don't want schools to be scared away because a pitcher they might have interest in has a bad back. So we tell Bob Ethan has a sore back, and Bob's reception is warm, concerned, and welcoming.

Ethan attends the Perfect Game Junior Class showcase Ft. Myers, and although he hasn't had much time to practice, he plays well. He pitches two solid innings, throws 87 mph, and picks a runner off first, a clip that Perfect Game shows on their website. In batting practice he's one of the only boys who hits the ball hard and deep with wood bats. It's an auspicious return, and even though his uniform fits him snugly, and he tires quickly, both his physical therapist and I declare him good to go.

Where Ethan was the first freshman to make the varsity team in a half-dozen years, this year three freshman make it: Dante Bichette, Jr. the anointed heir to Stephen King at shortstop, Alex Carter, David Carter's son, a goofy, scruffy blonde catcher with a reputation as a great hitter, and Nate Winters, a right handed pitcher.

Along with the young varsity players a new group of "power parents" arrive on the scene. Some I have heard of. Others I have been warned about. Particularly noteworthy are Dr. Tom Winters, whose older son Zach was summarily "dissed" by Coach King, relegated to the bench and rarely used, and who in the past had issues with King because of this. Winters is a prominent orthopedist who is also a part-owner of a minor league baseball team in Florida. But perhaps the most talked about, most watched and most distrusted new members of the Winter Park baseball parents club are Dante and Mariana Bichette, he of major league baseball fame, with a lifetime batting average of .299, and she with her own history, reputation, and agenda. Dante, Sr. seems like a nice guy with a hot temper and a hotter wife. Easy going and approachable, he was always available to give motivational talks to young ballplayers, to provide instruction and pontificate on his approach to power hitting. Ethan had met him on several occasions, watched him hit towering home runs and listened to him talk about making it in Major League baseball.

When a group of boys from Maitland Little League advanced to Williamsport to play in the Little League World Series, not only was Mariana widely credited with organizing and shepherding the team through the playoffs, but when Maitland was on the field, the TV cameras were focused on her more than they were the action on the field, with her Brazilian dark hair and skin, curvaceous figure and pretty face, she was a TV ratings winner. She is also bright, strong-willed, and manipulative, with all her energy focused on moving her sons through the maze of baseball teams, scouting, and recruiting.

What people who knew the Bichettes said was simple and straightforward: Mariana is all about her boys. As long as they are in the spotlight, and you don't steal any of the spotlight from them, she is charming, wonderful, helpful, and will do whatever she can to promote other players. She'll get them on good travel teams, hype them to coaches, become the best friend to them and their parents. But get in her way, cause a problem, outlive your usefulness or overshadow her children, and she'll discard you like yesterday's fashion trend without any awareness that you were ever important to her in the first place.

Besides being the guiding force that took a Maitland, Florida Little League team to Williamsport, she'd molded and crafted a number of travel teams around Dante Jr., who swung a bat just like his dad and carried all the aspirations, perhaps only the aspirations of his parents on his shoulders. If there was ever a child destined to be a star ballplayer, a pro athlete, it was Dante Jr. It was one of the unspoken truths of Central Florida baseball. The sun rose and set. The summer lasted a long time, and it was hot. And Dante Bichette Jr. would be known as one of the elite players in the state.

I'd heard the rumors too. They take over every program with which they're associated. Their influence on Winter Park will be pronounced. I dismissed it all. How could they possibly influence a program that had been chugging along without them for 25 years? How could they insinuate themselves into the good graces of Bob King, or pose any threat to the continuity of his coaching reign? It just didn't make sense. Besides, given the established hierarchy of high school ball (seniors first, then juniors, etc.), Dante Jr. would be a lowly freshman, while Ethan was the star upon whose shoulders the team's hopes and dreams were pinned.

But it became clear from the first day of practice that they were a force, unstoppable and relentless in their own way, frightening and irresistible as an earthquake that rumbles through diamonds of grass and clay. The Bichettes immediately work to develop a relationship with Coach King. They take him out to multiple dinners, and he frequents their New Smyrna beach condominium, spending days and weekends there with them. Mariana becomes team mom in the fall, and there she is, organizing drinks, sending out emails, helping with schedules and talking to boys about helping them get placed in college. And Dante becomes the assistant hitting coach. The Bichettes had the entire team in their back pockets.

At the first team meeting of the year, all eyes are on two people: Coach King at the front of the room, and Mariana seated at a high school student desk with everyone else. All the dads keep flicking their eyes, straining their necks to catch glimpses of Mariana without anyone noticing. While Bob goes on and on about expectations and nutrition and no outside coaching and the sins of showcase baseball, dads are squirming in their seats while Mariana sits, chest out, back straight and smiling.

King expresses his excitement about the upcoming year, the Bichette's involvement, the possibility of a great season, and introduces Dante to everyone in the audience. "I'm looking forward to this year more than I have in a long time," he tells everyone. "Bringing Dante in to help the boys will be great. He's going to add a whole new level to our program."

Dante Sr. stands and states that he will be helping the team with hitting, an exciting prospect since he was, in his prime, one of the outstanding power hitters in Major League baseball. He emphasizes that he has no interest in doing anything other than assisting Coach King, who already has a good thing going. There are smiles all around, handshakes, compliments. It is, in short, a baseball lovefest.

As the meeting breaks up I wait until the room clears. Lyndon Modomo, Chad's father, is talking to Coach King, and when he leaves I walk up to King just to reassure him that Ethan will be ready when the season starts.

"I usually don't make juniors captain of the team, but I'm looking at Ethan for that," Bob tells me privately. I'm excited. What a great opportunity. Captain of the team. Dante Bichette as the hitting coach. The Bichettes start drawing up plans for new, state of the art batting cages for the team. What a year this will be.

⚾

We start sending out letters to Division 1 schools about Ethan, listing the most basic of his credentials – 6'2" left handed mid to upper 80s pitcher – just to find out if they're interested in him. We contact the biggest schools in Florida: Miami, the University of Florida, Florida

State, the University of Central Florida. We reach out to Virginia, Clemson, South Carolina, North Carolina, Georgia, Georgia Tech, Ol' Miss, Texas, Michigan, LSU, Vanderbilt. Some, like Michigan and Texas, recommend Ethan attend their baseball camps. Some like North Carolina, Vanderbilt, and Georgia, never respond. Others respond immediately, and we begin to build our list of possible colleges.

I commence my spring ritual of attending the entire two weeks of tryouts in the afternoons, taking my seat in the bleachers, doing whatever work I have to do from my cell phone while I watch. I like to form my own opinions about the team, who's likely to make it, who looks good where (and who doesn't), trying to guess the coaches' decisions and understand the rationale for doing what they do. In this, Ethan's third season playing for Winter Park, nothing has changed with the exception that Dante Bichette roams the field and the batting cages, watching the boys take swings. They field fungoes hit by King, throw the ball to first, run double plays, and go through a set rotation of hitting drills. There are still no bullpens, no instruction given to pitchers other than King's occasional exhortation to be balanced and pitch with rhythm while they throw batting practice from forty feet. And while there's nothing wrong with all this, there's nothing right about it either, nothing that will lead to improved skills, increased knowledge and understanding of the game.

Two things become quickly apparent during the preseason tryouts and practices: Dante Jr. has replaced Bob King's son as the anointed favorite on the team, and Ethan is not going to get the positive reinforcement we'd hoped for this season. Over the ping of the hard fungoes and the slaps of the gloves as balls are caught, I hear, again and again, King call out, "Nice play, D!" "Way to move, D!" "Attaboy, D!" Dante Jr., or Little D, has been handed the shortstop position as a freshman, the same position Stephen played his entire varsity career. Whisperings and grumblings can be heard in the bleachers. Parents are already voicing their secret concerns. How can an untested (though pedigreed) boy be given such a high profile spot on the team...without any real competition. King has an answer, of course, one that makes sense. He'd rather have a shortstop who makes 90% of the standard plays and can't make the spectacular play than a shortstop who makes 90% of the spectacular plays and can't make the "gimmes." At the moment, Little D has limited range and an average arm. He's only 15 years old. But he has baseball smarts and a good glove, and does make the average play consistently. Interestingly,

King's son Stephen was just the opposite, often booting the routine play while making brilliant, almost impossible plays with his athletic ability.

The contrast is striking. Where Dante Jr. is the favored son, Ethan has already landed in the doghouse. There's no doubt that while we tried to mend fences in the off-season, Ethan still carries a grudge on the ball field. It's odd, because off the field he sits with King every day during weights class, the second year in a row Ethan has taken weights class with his coach, and they chat and talk baseball without any issues. On the field, however, Ethan does what he's told, but he's struggling to maintain a level of respect for his coach, and it's becoming obvious his attitude borders on disdain. He doesn't agree with the no bullpen policy. He doesn't agree with the no outside lessons policy. He doesn't believe in King's pitching philosophy, and while he abides by the coaches during practices, he does so skeptically.

He wants to be liked and respected by his teammates, and does everything he can to be a leader.

"Way to go, Q!" he yells loud enough for everyone to hear. "Great play! Good throw! Good throw! Way to back him up! Run! C'mon, you got this!"

He exhorts them to play hard, shouting encouragement, acting in many ways like a field general, a "mini-coach" on the field (the coaches get on him about this; they remind him that he's not the coach, they are). Unfortunately, since he has not been named captain (or anything else for that matter) most of the boys blow him off. Ethan has never learned the art of humility and leading by example. He's trying to earn leadership with his mouth and force of will, not his actions during games.

King prides himself an expert on physical conditioning and nutrition. If the example of his son's physical prowess and the outfitting of the Winter Park High weight room are evidence, he has grounds to make a claim. Every year he preaches the value of peanut butter sandwiches before hard workouts, eating healthy and staying slim. And every year he measures the body fat of the boys on his team as a barometer of fitness. It's the first quotient Bob uses as a determining factor in a boy's readiness to play. Not what a player does on the field, but what his body fat measures in the weight room. King is a caliper freak, and pulls out the pincers and squeezes the boys arms, bellies, thighs, to determine the percentage of body fat. 12% is good,

14% passable. Ethan is measured at 18%. He makes King's fat list. Ethan swears King measured him differently than other boys, and while there are other players who are overweight, Ethan comes in with the highest body fat number.

Pat and I begin to hear stories, told by parents who are at the practices I miss, by players who are Ethan's friends. King is using Ethan as an example of an overweight kid. Perhaps he's upset that Ethan came into spring out of shape. Maybe because he feels, deep down, that a lot is riding on Ethan this year, or believes that Ethan hasn't worked hard and come in ready to play. But Ethan's been hurt, laid up, and King knows this. We get constant reports of the public humiliation Ethan endures from the coach.

Ethan tries to bunt his way on base during a scrimmage, and King yells out, in front of the entire team, "What are you doing? You're the slowest kid in Orange County!"

The players are taking a break during a long practice. King encourages them to eat something to keep their energy up. He tells them, "Corey can eat pizza (Corey Conway is a sophomore outfielder), he's not fat. Bernie can eat pizza (Bernie Kissel, utility player). Ethan can't have pizza because he's fat. Chris (Quintero, Ethan's best friend) can have dessert. He's not fat. Ethan can't have dessert. He needs to lose weight. He's fat."

Ethan is invited to a baseball camp and tour at the University of Miami. It would involve traveling down on a weekend and missing a Saturday practice. Ethan asks King's permission, who tells him he can't go.

"Ethan, you're stooo-pid! You can't miss a practice right before the season starts. Besides, you don't want the Miami coaches to see you like this. You're too fat." Ethan lets Miami know he can't come down. For some reason, this has become a favorite topic of discussion for Coach King. While talking with Jared Incinelli one day one the field during a practice, King tells him that he wouldn't let Ethan go to Miami because he's so fat. Jared is taken aback by the frank talk about Ethan's weight, and Ethan starts complaining to us at home that he feels like the butt of all the coaches' jokes and negative remarks, even though there are other boys on the team who are packing more pounds, running slower, and in worse shape than he is.

During a scrimmage just before the season begins, Ethan is on the mound working on pick offs to second. He is supposed to throw the ball to the second baseman, or to the catcher so the catcher can throw the ball cleanly down to second. I watch from the stands. Ethan is struggling. He's not throwing the ball exactly where Coach King wants, but what's making matters worse, what obviously affects Ethan's composure, is that after every pitch he throws, whether it's high or low, inside or outside, King comments. Sonny Wolfe, an umpire who was helping out during the scrimmage (also the father of Ryan Wolfe, one of the lefties on the district championship team) reported it this way:

"Ethan was on the mound and _____ was the catcher. You (King) were talking to Ethan between pitches and asking that he follow your instructions about which pitch to throw and specifically you were asking that he attempt repeated pick-off attempts at second. He was having difficulty accepting these instructions from you and was very visibly showing his disdain. At one point he erupted, "What the fuck do you want me to do? You are yelling at me between every God-damned pitch!"

King remains seated and looks down at the ground. He doesn't say another word. I bow my head, and think, "There goes Ethan's captaincy." I didn't know how far gone he was.

What I saw and heard was somewhat different than what the umpire reported. As I sat in the stands I watched Ethan grow more and more flustered the more he pitched. It wasn't disdain. It was frustration that bloomed in his face and eyes. After every pitch he threw, after every pick-off that didn't work, every time the runner on first stole second base, King yelled out, "That's the pitcher's fault. That error's on the pitcher. That steal is on the pitcher. That's not where the pitch was supposed to be. Ethan, can you throw a strike? Can you throw the ball over the plate?"

Finally, Ethan exploded, and yelled loudly enough for everyone to hear, "Coach, I'm sorry, excuse me, but what the fuck do you want me to do?" At which point the game stopped, the catcher walked to the mound, and Ethan was taken out of the scrimmage. At the end of practice Ethan apologized for his outburst to the entire team and coaching staff, but the damage was done.

Bob later said he was testing Ethan, that he expected Ethan to be the butt of a great deal of ridicule, hostility, and heckling from other teams' fans this year, and he wanted Ethan to get used to the feeling. Perhaps that is the case, but the result was that a boy who already had issues with his coach, who lacked any level of safety and trust with the authority figures on the team, lost it. After weeks of feeling henpecked and belittled in front of his teammates, Ethan (inappropriately, mind you) suffered a mental meltdown and what he felt came unedited and unexpurgated out of his mouth.

$$\mathbb{D}$$

As a parent who believes that authority should be respected, I understand that Ethan could have been kicked off the team for what he said, for his rebuke of the central authority figure on the field – his coach - and the fact that Ethan was not kicked off the team, punished or suspended in any way shows the patience and flexibility and understanding the coaches exhibited in this difficult situation. And you know, Ethan wasn't suspended when he could have been. He wasn't kicked off the team for cussing at his head coach, when certainly that was within the coach's purview. But there's a bigger question here that begs asking, one that should be looked at more closely. And that's why, in this country, in high school sports in particular, in situations in which boys and girls in public schools have no choice who they play for, who they are coached by, is it acceptable for coaches to insult, denigrate, and humiliate these same students who, if they voice their opinions, run the risk of ending their high school athletic careers and beyond? Somehow it is all right for coaches to do to students what is completely unacceptable for students to even consider, and that is to show any true feelings, to get angry, to stand up for themselves, to not take it. The player who stands up to the coach risks excommunication. The coach who yells in the face of his star player, who berates or chastises his team, who criticizes, who castigates, who screams bloody murder, who jumps down someone's throat, rips out their tonsils and displays them like a trophy, gains acceptance, sometimes even solidifies their position of power. Why is this so?

The American mystique of the powerful coach, the rock of integrity while waves of indecency and teenage immorality and corruption swirl around him is widely accepted, part of our mythology. The coach has become the isolated hero, the only one who sees the true path, who can guide the misguided to the promised land, who wields a staff of high standards, who always strives for an ideal, and thus demands and deserves our respect and understanding. The coach works under tremendous stress striving to achieve something otherworldly, something beautiful and next to God – perfection. Thus, they get a free pass. They get leeway. They get to act in ways that would be completely out of bounds if done by a player.

One of the first rules of high school ball that I had to accept, however grudgingly, was that parents must fear the coach. They may pretend to be friends for the short term their son or daughter plays for them, they may be polite and respectful, but they live in fear of the coach's power and ability to cut, to bench, to diminish and minimalize their child. This absolute power (and it is real power, especially in sports like football where playing time can be the difference between a college scholarship and a job pumping gas) keeps parents at bay. There are no term limits for coaches. There is removal for abuse of their power, for hitting a player, for misconduct. But there is no universally accepted code of conduct, as there is for the student/athlete. While coaches may boast of their "brutal honesty," parents confess to couching their words, carefully selecting what they say, who they challenge, how they present themselves to a coach, because a wrong move, wrong word, wrong request may result in their child sitting on the bench. On the other hand, the coach who gives a player a hard time is tough, demanding, stern, strong, just what the kids need, a disciplinarian. Where's the sense in that?

Our society accepts the Vince Lombardi style of coaching, the yelling, the in your face aggressiveness. But maybe the standards we impose on our children should be the same standards used by coaches everywhere, in every sport. Maybe the best coaches understand the need to take the child into account. Maybe the days of public humiliation are coming to an end. Maybe. But they weren't for Ethan.

Ethan hand delivers a letter to Coach King before the first game of the season.

Dear Coach King – you've said you always want us to talk to you if we have things on our minds, and I thought this might be a good way to start a conversation and help me put my thoughts together.

I'd like to be able to pitch this spring as effectively as possible. That means doing things naturally and not having a lot of stuff in my head. One of the reasons I was so effective against Edgewater in the District Finals was because I knew you had confidence in me and the way I pitched. I'd like to get back to that space again with you. The way you get on me is not working for me. I can take your criticism when I know I also have your support. I'm sorry I talked back to you and blew up on the mound, but right now I feel like I've been humiliated in front of the team, and I don't feel like you're behind me. It's affecting my confidence and my composure.

I'd like you to please reconsider having me pitch differently than I naturally do and have been taught from the set position. There are a number of reasons for my request.

First, I'd like the opportunity to at least start the season pitching the way I know. You said that you don't believe in cookie-cutter players who all do the same thing the same way, and pitching from the set with a low knee is not the way I pitch.

Second, as a lefthanded pitcher I have a number of ways to control players on base. I can pause at the top of my kick. I can do a quick flip of the ball over to first. I can pause before I deliver the ball to throw off their timing. I can simply stare at them. The short leg kick throws me off more than the runners. Please let me keep the runners close the way a good lefty can. If there's a runner on third, I can understand throwing with a low knee kick. Otherwise, I'd like to be able to control them as a lefty looking right at them.

And finally, all the most important pitches a pitcher makes are from the set position. Making me change the way I throw from the set may not help. If it hurts my ability to throw strikes and my confidence runners will end up advancing because the batters get hits, and the best way to control runners is to not let anyone hit behind them.

If this doesn't work in the first third to half of the season I'll be glad to go back and do exactly what you want. But please, I'm asking you to give me the chance to pitch the way I know best. I want to be here for the team, and for you, but I need to know that you're here for me, too. Thank you.

Respectfully,
Ethan Bornstein

Coach King reads and acknowledges Ethan's letter and responds with mixed feelings. He indicates that he agrees with some of his points about pitching and others he disagrees with.

That wasn't the end of the preseason follies. Ethan is caught peeing in the bushes outside the fence on the side of the ball field. He swears he was peeing in the bushes because he had to go so badly. The coaches swear he peed on the side of the clubhouse. Ethan says lots of boys pee there. The coaches say they've never caught or seen anyone else. Ethan is told that he has to clean the clubhouse until further notice as punishment. He's not given any other direction or a time frame for the punishment. As far as he knows it could go on indefinitely. He feels picked on, and as he struggles with a lack of clear parameters with his punishment he haphazardly sweeps the clubhouse out a few times, then quits or forgets, and the coaches, though they're frustrated, don't say or do anything.

In preseason games Winter Park loses badly, embarrassingly, by 15 and 16 runs, to two of its main rivals, University and Olympia. For some reason Ethan has gone from hitting over .500 against the best pitchers in the nation with the Scorpions to pressing too hard and pulling the ball sharply foul every time up. Maybe it's his back. Maybe it's something else. Even though he's hitting the ball hard and far, his production has been minimal. The season of hope and promise begins to show signs of cracking and wear.

Dante Sr. has begun to have doubts about the way King runs his program. He and Mariana have always been associated with elite teams that reach high performance levels and compete for state, regional, national titles. He begins to hear frustrations voiced by parents, questions the treatment of Ethan, and even though Dante Jr. is the starting shortstop, Dante Sr. is not happy. Rumors start circulating among the parents. The Bichettes want to take over the program. Dante doesn't like the way practices are run. Dante wants to be the coach. Dante shouldn't even be on the field helping out. He hasn't filed all the correct paperwork. From what I can tell, there's truth and untruth to the innuendo. While it doesn't appear that Dante Sr. wants to coach the team, it has become apparent that he and King don't see eye to eye. Bichette doesn't like the practices. He stands with his hands folded over his chest, sitting close to the players in the dugout, away from the other coaches, watching. He doesn't comment. He doesn't try to change what is going on. He just watches. And he's not smiling.

In the first district game of the season Bob hands the ball to Ethan to start the game. Winter Park plays University, the same team that beat the Wildcats by 15 runs. University boasts three lefties who are all going to Division 1 schools, and one of them, Brian Adkins, who has signed to play with the University of Central Florida, gets the start. Even before the game begins, Ethan feels pressure. Coach King has told him that he'll never pitch successfully against University because of his high leg kick. "They'll run all over you and steal bases constantly," he tells Ethan in weights class.

"Why'd he even give me the start?" Ethan asks me after school.

This is how assistant Coach Rob Robison described the game:

"The Winter Park varsity baseball team opened up its district play on the road yesterday against cross town rival University. With the Wildcats off to an 0-3 start and one of those losses 15-0 to University, most experts didn't give the 'Cats much of a chance in this game. The

193

Wildcats proved the experts wrong and stunned the Cougars with a 3-2 victory.

"In the top of the first, Winter Park's lead off hitter, Chris Quintero was hit by a pitch and moved over to second on a Corey Conway sacrifice bunt. The Wildcats couldn't get anything else going and stranded Quintero. In the bottom half of the inning, the Cougars lead off man walked and a Wildcat mental error gave University men on first and second with no outs. Pitcher Ethan Bornstein then came up huge as he and shortstop Dante Bichette ran a perfectly timed pick play to nail the runner at second and end the Cougar threat. Energized by their great defense, Winter Park took the lead with three runs in the second. After Bernie Kissel moved Josh Bastian to second with another great sacrifice, sophomore Michael Boles' base hit gave the Wildcats their first run of the game. Ben Adams drilled a double off the left center field fence to give the 'Cats runners on second and third with only one out. Freshman A.C. Carter came to the plate in the biggest spot of his young career. Carter rose to the occasion, lining a base hit into left field and driving in both Boles and Adams.

"Now with a 3-0 lead, Winter Park looked to Bornstein on the mound. Ethan didn't disappoint as he kept the Cougar hitters off balance all day. Bornstein pitched a nearly flawless complete game. He struck out five and gave up only three hits on his way to the 'Cats first victory of the season. Bornstein also executed two perfect pick offs and was helped by a stellar defensive effort by the entire Wildcat team."

Ethan totaled three pick offs, including the one at second base in the first inning, the play that King had been on him about when Ethan lost his cool in spring training. With two picks at first he showed that he could control runners, regardless of his high leg kick. One of the hits off Ethan came in the first inning, when Bernie Kissel Jr. mishandled Ethan's throw off a bunt. That was the mental error that was so niftily referenced. Ethan completely outpitched Adkins, the UCF recruit, and up to that point Ethan had not heard a word from the UCF coaches, though he was a homegrown product and had attended many UCF baseball camps when he was younger. What the coach's report didn't say was that Ethan had been heckled by University fans all day, shouting obscenities, shouting that he was slow, fat, ugly, that he couldn't pitch. After his complete game, Ethan flipped the game ball into the University High stands, a "take that" gesture that was his way of responding to their nasty, virulent chatter. When the teams shook hands an assistant coach (the father of University's head coach), cursed Ethan out and told him he was classless. Dante Bichette Jr. jumped in, shouting to the coach that Ethan wasn't classless, the University fans were. Ethan pulled Dante back, putting himself between Little D and the coach. After the game Coach King took Ethan aside and chastised him for throwing the ball into the stands. "Don't ever do that again," King told him. Those were the only words King said to Ethan after the game, and during the next practice Ethan was punished by running poles, wondering all the while why he was singled out, why nothing was said to Dante Jr., though he appreciated his teammate's support.

It is now mid-February, and the season has taken on a strange, off-kilter sheen. In a home game against Bishop Moore High School, a local Catholic school powerhouse, Ethan is waiting in the on deck circle in the seventh inning. Bishop Moore has just put in their top reliever, a left-handed senior who pitches in the low 90s and has committed to the University of South Florida. We are down by a run with a runner on base, and the first batter to face the reliever strikes out. As Ethan walks to the plate, Coach King suddenly calls time and substitutes AC Carter, the freshman catcher, for him. It 's a cold night. Caught off-guard, AC grabs his bat and runs out to hit. Ethan remains frozen in place between home plate and the on-deck circle, a look of incomprehension on his face.

I am standing next to David Carter, AC's dad, and we exchange dumbfounded glances at one another.

"What's going on here?" David says to me. "Wasn't Ethan one of the top hitters on the team last year?"

"Yes," I say. "He had the second highest batting average on the team."

"This must be humiliating for him," David says. "I don't like this for AC either. He hasn't been in the game at all and now he's batting without any chance to warm up. He has a warm up routine. This isn't good at all."

While a good hitter, AC has never faced a pitcher like this. In fact, Ethan may be the only hitter on the team with a chance to connect, but instead, in front of everyone, he is suddenly yanked from the game. This wouldn't have been so bad if it had been done prior to

Ethan actually walking up to the batter's box, but the substitution at the last second combined with the look of abject humiliation on Ethan's face left many people in the stands wondering what was going on. Ethan didn't understand it either, especially after AC struck out on three pitches.

$\int$

Tension had begun to increase between parents in the bleachers. The parent who gossips the most about the players is Dr. Tom Winters. Winters, who once despised King over the coach's treatment of his oldest son Zach, now is firmly entrenched in the King camp with his younger son Nate pitching on varsity. Winters always has a cell phone to his ear, and inevitably can be overheard talking about baseball or medicine. As a well-respected orthopedic surgeon he is connected and influential in Winter Park circles. But as a baseball parent he has no trouble chumming up to a coach he once reviled to benefit his son. "King buried my son Zach," Winters told me once. "Here he doesn't allow a run his senior year and never got a real chance." When Ethan was pulled up to varsity his freshman year it was Zach Winters who never pitched again for the Wildcats. Winters now touts King's virtues, and Nate, a mid-level righty, gets more time on the mound.

"What a great coach," Winters says to me now about King. "He gets more out of these boys than any high school coach I've ever seen."

Dante Sr. hears rumors that Winters is bad mouthing his son. He's been told that Winters was whispering in King's ear, telling him that Dante was trying to get him fired. During one home game Dante Sr. storms into the concession stand and confronts him. "I've had it with you spreading rumors about me!" Dante screams, loud enough to be heard outside. "You quit right now or I'll make you stop!"

Winters cowers in the concession stands, accusing Bichette of threatening him, and yells out that he'll call the cops if Bichette doesn't leave. The police are, in fact, called, but no charges are filed.

At a game at Timber Creek, the exact same field at which, the previous season, Ethan was forced to throw from the slide step on every pitch, Chad Modomo throws a perfect game, the first one in Bob King's long coaching career. Chad keeps the ball low, and the team plays excellent defense behind him. Ethan is not on first base. He's been replaced by Bernie Kissel, Jr., a nice boy with modest talent who has never played the position before. As it happens, Bernie Sr. has been reporting conversations between parents to Coach King, including one in which Dante Sr. supposedly spoke about replacing King with a different coach.

Dante Sr. is allowed to run a Saturday practice, and every boy on the team says it's the best and most productive practice of the year. Ethan comes home ecstatic. He tells me that Dante threw batting practice and they hit more balls, fielded more grounders, and got more done in two hours than in any of Coach King's four hour practices. Coach King watches the practice and considers it a complete waste of time, and does not let Dante run another.

Ethan heeds what the coaches are saying about the team getting more involved and energetic during practices, and Ethan being Ethan, yells loudly and shouts encouragement and instructions to his teammates. The coaches complain that Ethan is making a mockery of practices by exaggerating his responses to them. Ethan tells me he's just trying to get himself and his teammates involved in the workouts. The coaches, obviously, feel otherwise.

On February 25, I send an email to Coach King.

"Bob – Ethan had to wait to see the physical therapist today, so it was too late for him to return to practice. The physical therapist expressed some serious concerns about Ethan. He told us that in comparison to where Ethan was in November after two months of rehab, he has regressed, not improved. He assumes this is due to the strain the baseball season is placing on Ethan's lower back. Ethan has lost flexibility and still complains about his back tightening up, which shouldn't be happening at this point. Unfortunately, the only thing that will help Ethan is rest. Robert (the therapist) compared it to having a cut that scabs over. When you pick at the scab it takes much longer to heal, as opposed to leaving it alone. We know Ethan can't shut down during the spring season, but there are certain things we can do together.

1) On our end, we are using a cold laser machine that is supposed to enhance the healing process and reduce inflammation. We will continue using this with Ethan on a regular basis. Ethan will also continue his pilates, which he does 2x week. This should provide him with core stability and strength, which will in turn help his lower back. We also make sure he gets regular treatments with heat and ice, and we limit any extraneous lifting around the house. This is all so he doesn't hurt his lower back again.

2) On your end, Ethan cannot throw a medicine ball again. I don't think he will do that form of exercise for a number of years. He may also not do the "inchworm" exercise the team performs, which puts a lot of strain on the lower back. We also need to discuss a way to get Ethan an extra day of rest during the week. If he is going to get through the season without reinjuring himself, we believe this is necessary."

At the end of the next practice, Ethan comes home and asks me what I sent Coach King, because he's been told he's going to be shut down for the rest of the season. I shoot off another email to the coach.

"Bob – this email is to clarify a misunderstanding. Ethan informed us today that you told him that we were requesting that he be "shut down" and not play again this season, and that you also believe that the best thing for his back is harder work, not rest. Please be advised that nowhere in our previous email did we recommend that Ethan stop playing."

Shortly thereafter, at their request, we have lunch with the Bichettes. Dante Sr. and Mariana tell us they have important information they believe we need to know. At the lunch their message is simple and clear. Dante is at every practice and he's never seen a coach pick on a kid the way Coach King picks on Ethan. Mariana emphasizes that if it were her son she wouldn't allow the behavior of the head coach to continue, and she encourages us to see the principal of the school, Bill Gordon. They tell us that other parents are considering filing a lawsuit against King for hurting their son's chances of getting a college scholarship (this never comes to pass). Both tell us that if enough parents complain about the way Coach King treats boys on the team the school will have no choice but to act and replace the coach, and that they have some ideas about who would make a good coach for the team. Dante makes it clear he has no interest in the position, but knows good people who would. Pat and I tell them that we don't care whether Bob stays or not. That's not our issue. All we care about is that our son is treated fairly. By the time we leave both Pat and I are stirred up, angry, ready to take this fight to the next level. Of course, as circumstances would have it, the timing is impeccable.

A few days after our lunch, Ethan pitches against Boone High School, one of Winter Park's arch-rivals. Ethan has not had a single outing as impressive as the one he started the season with against University. He complains after every game he pitches that Coach King is making it impossible for him to be effective by calling almost all changeups when he throws. Instead of mixing up pitches, King has turned his changeup into a slow fastball by calling it more than 75% of the time. I have noticed that Ethan's been throwing the change a lot, though I couldn't swear to the percentage, and he has been getting hit and knocked around in games. Against Boone Ethan takes matters into his own hands. In the first inning he calls off four pitches. King goes out to the mound and tells Ethan if he shrugs off another pitch he'll be yanked out of the game. Ethan looks shell-shocked. He goes comatose, emotionless, suffering internally with every pitch. His fastball is coming in hard, but now he's only throwing it 20% of the time and he's getting hit by a mature Boone team. King has him pitching inside and the Boone players are turning on the pitches and crushing them. One of their players, Casey McElroy, has signed to go to Auburn, and he is the first boy I've ever seen who hits three different pitches by Ethan to three fields. He manhandles E.

Dante Sr. starts yelling at the home plate umpire early in the game. He stands at the edge of the dugout closest to the plate, and says something after every called ball. "C'mon, blue, you're squeezing our pitcher!" "That's a strike in any league!" "How can you call that a ball? That's the worst call I've ever seen!" In the third inning Dante gets thrown out of the game.

Ethan lasts into the fifth inning. They're losing 7-3 when he's taken out, and the final score is worse. When Ethan comes out of the game he motions to me to come see him behind the stands. He looks down, frustrated, anxious. It's apparent he's worn down, defeated.

He says, "Dad, I can't take it anymore. I can't play for Coach King. He jumped all over me for calling off a couple pitches, but the way he's calling games I'm getting killed."

"Are you allowed to call off pitches?" I ask.

"No, I don't think so," he tells me.

"Well then, you shouldn't have, but we'll talk about the rest later. It's a long season. Let's figure out a way to get through this."

Ethan rejoins his teammates, and we wait for him at home after the game to console our upset boy. And wait. And wait. Boone and Winter Park are only 20 minutes apart, and the way I figure it, Ethan should have been home almost an hour ago. I call his cell phone and leave a message. "Where are you?" He calls me a few minutes later to tell me he's just leaving the Winter Park clubhouse, and it's apparent to me he's shaken up, near tears. Ethan tells me that Coach King accused him of mutiny.

King told Ethan, "There's one thorn in this team's side and I'm looking at it. If this keeps going on you're going to be off the team. Every run scored in the first inning was entirely your fault. You are spineless for not throwing inside to that left-handed batter. You're showing me you're scared. You'd better hope no colleges call me in the next week because I'll tell them this is a kid who basically does whatever the hell he wants."

Ethan also tells us that he was drilled with questions by Coach King. When he tried to answer Coach King cut him off. When he told King he had a "game plan" when he went out to pitch, King blasted him, saying the game plan was up to him, the coach, not Ethan. The questions were stated in such a way that Ethan felt as if he was being forced to incriminate himself. He is stunned at Coach King's furious reaction. Ethan comes home totally deflated and dispirited. I ask him if he wants us to intervene, because in the past he's told us to leave things alone. This time he says he can't take it anymore and please do something.

I wondered, at first, how much of this could be true. How could a coach lambast a kid to such an extent, regardless whether it was a misunderstanding or a direct rebuke of authority? Either way the obvious action was to tell Ethan not to do it again, and that if he did he'd be pulled from the game, and let it go at that. But as I went over and over what Ethan told us, I came to the inevitable conclusion that he was telling the truth. Ethan didn't have words like "mutiny" or phrases like "thorn in this team's side" in his vocabulary. He didn't have the capacity to make up a statement about a kid who does whatever the hell he wants. Those were someone else's words, not his.

After calming him down and getting him to sleep, Pat and I stayed up late into the night discussing what to do. We decide it's time to meet with both Coach King and the school administration. I e-mail King and request a meeting with him.

The day after the Boone game I call the athletic director, Mike Brown, and request a meeting with him as well. He wants to know why, and when I tell him he asks for any notes we might have that relate to incidents with Coach King. Pat and I put our heads together to come up with a plan and figure out what to do to salvage this season for our son. Finally satisfied that we have a cohesive, organized letter that laid out our thoughts as well as the many incidents between Ethan and Coach King, we make perhaps the most egregious error of our entire time in baseball: we send Mike Brown our notes. Worse, we preface them with an introduction, which my wife, in her intensely protective mode, crafts to include a single sentence – the last sentence of the first paragraph - that changes all our lives.

"Mike – Per your request, below are notes my wife and I have taken during this season and last year. We feel that each of these incidents in and of themselves reflects inappropriate treatment of a student athlete. Taken as a whole we see a recurring, repetitive pattern of negative reinforcement, mistreatment and verbal abuse of our son.

"On a positive note, Coach King has always been cordial and friendly with us and we just heard from one of the colleges that Ethan is interested in that Bob sent in a very positive recommendation. The issue is not what Bob thinks of Ethan as a baseball player, but how he treats Ethan as a human being.

"There have been numerous instances where we have seriously considered talking directly to both Coach King and the school administration. We have not done so in the past because we were afraid it would make Ethan's situation with Coach King worse, not better; jeopardize his position on the team, and negatively impact Coach King's recommendation to colleges on Ethan's behalf. When we've talked to Ethan in the past about us approaching Coach King he has discouraged us. In turn, we have encouraged him to deal with Coach King directly to improve their relationship.

"We did meet with Coach King last year, after the season. We did not discuss the specific incidents cited in our 2007 season notes. We made a conscious decision to discuss the themes of negative coaching vs. positive reinforcement, the pitching program or lack thereof and the detrimental impact on Ethan's confidence and attitude. We felt we had a positive meeting and that Coach King received us well.

"We are six weeks into this year's season and we have observed directly, heard repeatedly from other parents, and been told by Ethan that Coach King is once again treating Ethan inappropriately on a regular basis. Regrettably, we have reached the point where we believe the Coach's treatment of Ethan has crossed a line that is unacceptable. It is unfortunate that it has come to this point and it is time to bring this to the attention of the administration. We have requests in to Coach King for a face to face meeting to discuss these issues. Our hope is for change and resolution, in whatever form that takes, but the current status quo is unacceptable."

We sent a list of nine different issues to the athletic director, and then, thinking twice about it, we followed it with another.

"Mike – Please keep our notes in our previous e-mail to you in the strictest of confidence. This information is intended for your eyes and Principal Gordon only at this time. If you wish to share it with anyone else please consult with us first. We

do not want Coach King to have this information at this time because it is our intent to meet with him one on one to address our issues and concerns with him directly. We do not want anyone to speak to Coach King until we have had a chance to do so ourselves. That only seems fair and is the approach we'd like to take. We have sent Coach King two emails in the last day or two requesting a meeting and giving him our available times. We would still like to have a confidential meeting with you. Please contact us to schedule an appointment at your earliest convenience. Thank you for honoring our request. We look forward to meeting with you and Principal Gordon soon."

Mike Brown forwards our notes to Principal Gordon, and as soon as Gordon sees the words "verbal abuse" he does two things: he tells us not to meet with Coach King at the present time, and without informing us, he sends our e-mail and notes to the State of Florida Department of Children and Families.

The following day the team has a game against a highly touted private high school in Jacksonville. Ethan and I drive up to the game with the Kissels – Bernie Sr. and Jr. I've been warned at various times not to trust Bernie, but I consider him my friend. We sit together during games. He comes to me asking for advice for his son, who wants to play college ball but wasn't being recruited. At my recommendation Bernie Jr. attends a University of Florida Labor Day camp which, as it turns out, hurts his cause rather than helps it. He hits, fields and throws poorly, while Ethan has an outstanding camp, hitting two balls off the wall at the Gator's ballfield, and throwing a bullpen in front of coach Kevin O'Sullivan that's good enough to have the coach tell him they'll be watching him this spring.

Bernie Sr. is a strange guy. Standing over 6'4", he has a wisecrack for everything, laughs loud and lives large. He's put on weight since his swimming days at the University of Texas, and lives in a small, cluttered, kid-friendly house with an ant-filled front yard with his two daughters and son. He claims many things: that he would have gone to the Moscow Olympics if not for President Carter's boycott, that after his Olympic bid fell apart he made money as a part-time escort, and whenever I ask what he currently does to make money he's evasive and obtuse. I never get a straight answer from him. What is he – a spy, a hit-man, or just some guy who'd gotten a big legal settlement somewhere and was living off it? I have no idea.

On the way to Jacksonville I receive a call from the DCF. At first I don't know what to make of it. Then, as it becomes clear what has happened, I begin to get nervous, and talk to Bernie, rambling on and on as I imagine what lies ahead. "It's going to be a war now," I tell him after letting him know about the involvement of the state agency. "If King tries to do anything to Ethan because of this, I won't hold back. I'll come in with guns blazing. He hasn't dealt with anyone like me before. The law firm that represents me (because of my real estate business) is the best in the state. They won't let anything happen. If they need to, they can open doors. They have connections on the school board. They know all the local politicians. They'll protect us." And on and on, for the last hour and a half of the drive. I don't hold back. I fantasize. I get worked up. I prepare for battle. During the game I speak with my attorney, who tells me to do nothing until I have more information. As it turns out, I never ask the law firm to do anything. We decide it isn't appropriate to try to influence peddle over this issue. We want to trust the system, the school administration, the school board and the state for a fair and equitable resolution. In our naïveté we never consider the possibility that life will be unfair, that events will backfire on us, that the simple thing we hope for – positive change – will be the one thing that never happens.

Ethan doesn't get in the Jacksonville game in any capacity, and on the way back Bernie Sr. asks if I can wait a minute before we take off. I see him walk over to talk to the coaches, but I have no idea he's telling them what I'd said, that he was informing on me as a way to get his son more playing time. Self-motivated and Machiavellian, it was an act of dishonor that I could never have imagined possible – one father sacrificing another father's son to benefit his own. But that's what happened.

Ethan comes home the next day after practice complaining that none of the coaches are talking to him. Every one of them gives him the cold shoulder, not so much as looking at him. He is put in the outfield and doesn't practice at all at first base. He goes through his drills like a ghost, a vague presence taking up space but with no real existence, purpose, defined role on the team.

That Friday we meet with the school administration and Coach King. Present are the school principal, Bill Gordon, Assistant Principal Heather Hilton, a bright, positive, pretty young administrator who oversees the baseball program, and the school athletic director, Mike Brown. The meeting is both eye-opening and non-productive. King is told that he cannot, in any way, be vindictive towards Ethan, or take anything out on him. King is convinced we used the words "verbal abuse" intentionally to get him reported to the Department of Children and Families.

"We had no idea," my wife says firmly.

"Quite honestly," I add, "we've never been involved in anything like this before."

"Ethan is a tremendous problem on the team," King tells everyone at the table. "He takes more time and attention than any other athlete I've coached in 25 years."

"Coach, remember Ethan is ADHD," I say, "and needs to be handled differently."

"That's new to me," he says, though it's something we've gone over with him and the other coaches many times.

King tells us, again for the first time, about the various abuses Ethan has been responsible for during the short season – peeing on the clubhouse, not fulfilling his punishment of cleaning the clubhouse, doing, as King says, "whatever he wants."

"If Ethan has been non-responsive to you, you can always talk to us and we'll support you in disciplining Ethan for his misbehaviors," Pat says.

"We'd be the last people on earth to insist Ethan is a perfect angel," I add. "He's not. By the same token, we know he's not a bad kid."

"He just needs a firm and understanding hand, someone to direct him, someone he trusts," Pat says, looking around the table for understanding of her own. The meeting ends with forced handshakes, and an acknowledgement that the matter is now in the hands of the state.

And from that moment forward Ethan loses everything once and for all – his place in the batting order, his position in the starting pitching rotation, his sense of place on the team. We ask if he wants to stop playing for the rest of the season, but he insists on grinding it out.

Ethan has one at bat since the Boone game. He is on the bench against Olympia. When Ethan pitches, King calls changeups almost exclusively, and Ethan's outings continue to worsen. Coach King is not talking to him at all, which may or may not be a bad thing. He no longer visits Ethan on the mound. Coach Robison does. Ethan is the only pitcher to be spoken to by the assistant coach. Ethan transfers out of Coach King's weight class and into a regular phys. ed. class. He is not in the starting pitching rotation either. Ethan pitches 3.6 innings against Bartram Trails, but only because another reliever was hurt. He doesn't hit in the game.

Ethan is not in the lineup against Colonial High School. He finds out that every player on the team except him is told by one of the coaches whether or not they will be playing in a game and/or pitching the day before. He come home and tells us that he believes the coaches are trying to "break him" by their overall treatment of him.

We also hear that rumors are flying among the team parents about us and Ethan. We made up stories about Coach King. We reported King to DCF. We are part of an organized conspiracy to remove King from his position. We are told by a Lake Highland parent that Coach King called Ethan's old prep school to get information on Ethan's baseball history there. Dante Bichette tells me that in a meeting with Coach King he is told that King is just going to keep Ethan on the bench, after Bichette questions him about Ethan not being in the batting order.

It just doesn't get any better than this.

During games now it's not only Ethan who sits on the bench; so do I. As bad as it was towards the end of our stint with Team Easton, this is far worse. I sit by myself or occasionally with Bernie Kissel, who I still consider a friend - I don't know what he's done behind my back. My wife calls Bernie in tears, thanking him for remaining my friend as this terrible season has progressed. Those tears come back to haunt us as one of the most regrettably misdirected gestures we could have ever made. I catch the offhand glance, the whisper, watch as people turn a different way when I approach. I have become the leper of the parents, the deviant, the coach molester. I am a bad person. The mothers especially look askance at me, want to have nothing to do with me, avoid me like the plague with a few exceptions – the Bastians, devout Christians whose son Josh has always been a quiet, admirable player of above average ability. They home school their children, so the selection of Winter Park has been, for them, by choice and design. Both parents – Mike and Cheryl – are cordial and friendly, come up to me and make small talk, and I can tell their feelings of dismay and sadness for what has occurred to Ethan are genuine. Cheryl runs the concession stand, and she is one of the few people who, when I come up to place an order, looks me in the eye. Their gestures are small kindnesses for which I will always be grateful.

Mariana sends a 1,600 word email out to the entire team as an attempt to rebut rumors that are swirling about their attempts to manipulate the program. In it she writes:

Dear Wildcats parents and coaches,

    I begin with the end, that on Sunday Dante decided to remove himself from any position with this team and did let Bill Gordon know that intent. Bob let him know he was unable to be on the field due to paperwork that had not come through Orange County. Dante has no desire to take over this team. At a coaches meeting on Friday, where Dante spoke to Bob personally about any of his observations, Dante was asked to run Saturday's practice. He denied the request a few times before agreeing to it. He did not ask to run it. Dante has always been willing to help if asked, but has never wanted nor requested to take over any baseball program he has been involved with. He is a hitting coach and that is where his love lies.

    I spoke with a friend Tuesday night who asked me why I have any role other than that of just a mom on the team. I'll hopefully be clear here as well; I do not want any role other than mom. But, there was a wonderful welcome from kids and families this summer, and I organized and ran your Fall team, so I became more than just a mom. I think this is where much of this began. Since June I have listened to unsolicited pleas for help from parents and from kids. Someone told me a few years ago to worry only about the well being of my child and not to worry about the others. That's not in my nature; I love to bring people along if Dante or Bo experience success. But, I am acutely aware at this moment that I should have heeded that advice.

    All of you that spoke to me said you either have spoken to Bob to no avail or that you feared confronting him because of how doing so might affect your children. I shared some concerns with Rob and was counseled by one person who has known Bob well not to directly approach Bob. I desperately wish I had just followed my gut and laid out for him my frustration that there was so much negativity (at least shared with me) around. Because of one person's future intent that I thought could be devastating, I went to Bill Gordon and told him I would like for him to intervene to SALVAGE the situation. He asked directly what I would like to see happen and that is exactly what I told him. I did NOT say I thought Bob should go.

    Now for our intentions and to clear up some of the rumors I heard last night: Contrary to apparent opinion, we do not want an all freshman Varsity team. What Dante did want was to take what he has learned and ADD to Bob's program. Dante did not have some master plan, as I have been told some of you think, to come in and dethrone Bob! He actually turned down jobs with the Washington Nationals and the Tampa Bay Devil Rays, colleges and other high schools in order to come and work with Bob.

I heard some of you have heard some Edgewater kids were planning to come once the coaching situation changed. I have not spoken to ANY Edgewater kids or parents. I have commented and wondered why so many of their kids were WPHS kids first, and their assistant coach was the coach for our 14U team last summer who's come to watch "his kids" a couple of times. That's what I know about that.

Again, I am sure, absolutely positive that nowhere in our team was there ever intent to take Bob's livelihood, as I heard it put, away from him. In fact, Dante has not been quick to impose his ideas because of his understanding that Bob has had 25 years here. I can't imagine DCF was contacted by one of our parents. Even in negative discussions with concerned parents no one saw this coming. I haven't met anyone on this team with evil intent.

You know, our family is the last family who would feel intimidated or threatened that their son's position on the team is at risk; we have a freshman playing SS and batting third. We don't need another coach to improve Dante's situation, baseball wise. Any missteps I made came from a sincere desire to see everyone succeed, love baseball, and feel valued as a member of this team. We look very forward to everyone coming back healthy and to finishing the season well. Go Wildcats!

Mariana

$\oslash$

We have become friends with the Bichettes, and I must admit, there's something alluring, seductive about the relationship. We have them over for dinner with the Carters. David has become a good friend through baseball. His level-headed, pragmatic approach to what has become a highly charged situation has helped calm me down again and again. Mariana is intense, passionately focused on her boys and baseball. I can almost hear the gears in her brain grind away as she thinks about the options regarding Coach King and the high school. We've been warned she's all about her boys, but she seems so sincere in her concern for Ethan. It's hard not to get swept away by her praise of him. "I don't know how King can keep the best hitter on the team on the bench." "Ethan's the most important player on the team, and look what King is doing to him. It just isn't right." I feed off it, swallow it whole, nod my head in agreement and thank God there are others out there who understand how I feel. It isn't right. The world is unjust, and we are on the narrow path to righteous redemption. We will be vindicated, and all will be made good and whole once again. The process has taken on the feeling of a crusade. It's not that I'm out to get King's job. Truthfully, I could care less who coaches the high school. A dog could be the coach, a goldfish, a teacher. Bill Gordon could take the helm, just as long as he's fair and evenhanded. Or Bob King could stay where he is, if he only changed or modified his approach to our son, understanding in some capacity that Ethan needs both limits and understanding, and with that both parties can succeed.

It's equally exciting to sit next to Dante Sr. and listen to stories about major league baseball, how he broke in, who he played with, what his routine was at the plate. It's like having an inside seat to a top secret discussion, getting clues on how to capture the dream or a ticket to our son's ultimate goal. It's enticing, and I feel special, honored just to be there, able to ask questions and be the recipient of privileged information. They are on our side. They can't believe what's being done to our son. Dante tells me he thinks Ethan is one of the best, if not the best hitter in Central Florida. What am I going to say to that besides thank you, God bless, amen? With the Bichettes on one side and the counsel of the Carters on the other, with a great law firm backing us up and goodness and justice buttressing us, how can we lose? How can we fail to come out ok? We have done nothing wrong. All we are doing is trying to protect our son from a coach who doesn't get him.

The question of when to intervene haunts me to this day. We squelched ourselves during Ethan's sophomore year, and only when he finally came to us and said, "enough," did we move forward in an attempt to create change. What we didn't realize was that we were bucking more than a single man. We were bucking a system. There was a reason Bob King had been in charge of the baseball program at Winter Park High for 25 years, and it wasn't about baseball. He steered a ship without the need of administration oversight. While there had been some complaints and problems over the years, there had never been a tragedy on the field. There was never a controversy that made its way to the press or the school board. He had special privileges. His was the only sport that received all the income from its concession stand. His was the only sport that sold memberships and kept all the proceeds without distributing them to the other athletic programs. In exchange, he didn't cost the administration any additional time, money or headaches. No effort was wasted searching for new staff, worrying about legal repercussions, fretting over what would happen next. King ran a clean operation. Until now. Until me and E.

Now Heather Hilton is assigned the task of monitoring the program. She has a presence during practices and games. Oftentimes so does her husband, a police officer who was stationed at the Winter Park High School 9th Grade Center when Ethan was there, and he and Ethan are friendly with one another. Heather smiles at me during games, standing in the background by the Winter Park baseball walk of fame, and I nod at her, worried, fretting, wondering how Ethan's doing sitting on the bench watching the game, or, as he often does, shouting encouragement to his teammates in a boisterous voice that's loud enough for everyone to hear.

At the same time the recruiting process has begun. Thanks to the previous summer with the Scorpions, and even though Ethan disappeared from action in the fall, he is on radar screens nationally and has received letters of inquiry from virtually every major program in Florida and a number of others throughout the south: the University of Florida, the University of North Florida, the University of South Florida, the University of Central Florida, the University of Miami, Stetson University, Louisiana State University, Clemson University, the University of South Carolina, the University of Virginia, the University of Louisiana-Lafayette, Georgia Southern University, Ole Miss, Alabama, the University of Kentucky, the College of Charleston, Georgia Tech, all have sent, at the very least, form letters requesting more information, while some have been more persistent and seemingly have sent personalized letters.

Prior to the debacle with King we had given him all the requests for the coach's evaluation. Now, fearing some sort of backlash, we hand the forms over to Sal Lombardo, the owner and manager of the Scorpions.

Both Ethan's grades and his ranking at Perfect Game have taken a precipitous fall. For years we have hammered Ethan to work at school and keep his grades up, but his focus and energy have all been directed towards baseball. He's not a big reader and just doesn't care that much about getting As. While he's bright and capable, he never applies himself to the task at hand – to studying, to completeness, to putting in the extra time to get the few extra points. We have emphasized the value of education and even kept him at Winter Park High School because it is so highly rated academically and the alternative that would be his choice – Edgewater High – is not. And yet, when it comes right down to it, Ethan doesn't care. He's not in school for school. He's there for the social life and for the notoriety that comes with starring at baseball. We are on him all the time, struggling to keep him focused on his grades. We remind him he has to graduate in order to go to college, but he pooh-poohs our advice. He knows what he can get away with. If he has two hours of homework, he breezes through it in 20 minutes and then goes back to playing video games. No additional time spent studying. No development of study skills or good academic work habits. Ethan has become the master of the low B. He does just enough to get by, and that's good enough for him.

His ranking at Perfect Game, on the other hand, rankles him and me both. He began by being ranked 113 on the PG Class of 2009 list, and the goal of breaking into the Top 100 seemed attainable. We'd been told by both Matt Gerber and Sal Lombardo of the Scorpions that the most important thing for a player was to be on the list. Once on the list, you were guaranteed the attention of college coaches. If you were good enough, lucky enough, to break into the top 100, you put yourself in an elite category. The top 100 players ranked by Perfect Game got instant consideration for major scholarships and perhaps even big bonuses and early round selection in the major league draft.

But without playing in the fall, Ethan's ranking dropped to 133. By the time spring practice had begun, he'd fallen further, down into the 200s. This wasn't the direction he was supposed to be going, and there were no grounds for it. I dashed off emails to Perfect Game staff. What's going on here? Why is my son dropping in the rankings when he has done nothing to deserve it? Have you seen him? Have you watched him pitch? Did you see him throw 87, hit bombs at the National Junior Underclass Showcase? I am reassured by the Scorpion coaches that it doesn't really matter. Major programs know about him, are watching him. That's their job, to make sure he's recruited, and they have no doubt that he's on track. They advise me to chill out and let them handle the media. I try, but his ranking continues to plummet, and it feels like a splinter inching its way towards my heart.

Perfect Game responds. It's not Ethan so much as it is staff becoming more familiar with the entire class of 2009, with new, previously unknown players being added to the rankings. They know Ethan's a quality player. Send them his spring stats, and they'll watch him this summer and evaluate further.

OK, I say to myself, I'll bite my tongue and bide my time, neither of which come naturally to me.

○

What the people at Perfect Game, and other national ranking organizations fail to realize, is the impact rankings have, not so much on colleges and the pros, but on parents and players. The more astute college coaches have come to understand that all rankings do is send out a signal that a player is worth watching. For them, the true tale of the tape is seeing boys play ball. The coaches who rely almost solely on outside rating services often get burned. They may recruit the good looking athlete, but they overlook the winner. They may become enamored with the player's statistics – how hard he throws, his time in the 60 yard dash (both of which are important, of course; it's better to throw hard and run fast than the opposite) – but they fail to take into account efficiency, effectiveness, clutch play, intelligence on the field, desire, hustle, all the intangibles that turn a player with great skill into a great player.

Scouts still evaluate players based not on the complete package – the skills plus intangibles - but on appearance and quick impressions. A catcher can frame the ball poorly, drop pitches, watch ball after ball pass by, but if he can throw the ball to second at 90 mph, if the scouts happen to see him hit a towering home run once (even if he strikes out the other nine times), if he walks out onto the field with broad shoulders and a tight ass and when he takes off his catcher's mask his chiseled chin and ice blue eyes stare off into the sunset, he could go to a big division 1 school or get drafted in one of the top rounds, all because scouts think they can train him, teach him, coach him to greatness. Why? Because he looks the part. He looks like a player. While the kid who galumphs out to the plate with shaggy hair and a dumpy body and maybe a little bit too high of an IQ, the kid who speaks his mind intelligently and is a bit of a rebel or iconoclast, even if he bats .400 and blocks every ball and frames the ball well and calls a smart game, that kid will probably get overlooked by all the so-called top scouts. Why? He doesn't project. He'll clog the base paths (even if he just plain hits all the time), he doesn't look the part. On the basis of that formula major league baseball is made up of a higher ratio of beautiful physical specimens than the human genome should produce, and the soft-bodied winners, the efficient but ugly players, the team-makers, can all go play sandlot somewhere in the hinterlands of America.

And there's another layer of truth here, one that the Perfect Game scouts may acknowledge in back rooms and amongst themselves, but never publicly. Never as part of their ranking service. A lot just boils down to sheer laziness. As more players come out of the woodwork, as more and more high school athletes garner attention, they are simply slotted into the rankings, and the players behind them fall. There's no evaluation, no comparison. A new lefthanded pitcher appears who throws 88-90, and he has to fit in somewhere. And when he does, when someone new pops up, others fall. It's a simple process of making room.

It's this sense of painful, inexplicable falling, this unspoken critical evaluation of boys that the scouts at Perfect Game fail to take into account. Even as our friends and coaches told us not to worry, the gnawing erosion of self-confidence occurred. There's an arbitrariness to the rankings that Perfect Game reps never seem to take responsibility for. Boys move up and down their charts, and in some ways, whether large or small, so does self-esteem (or a lack of), confidence and doubt. While most athletes who play at a high level are trained to disregard or at least balance outside opinions with their own, the young athlete may spout worn out clichés, and Ethan was no different.

"Everyone's entitled to their own opinion," he told me. "It really doesn't matter what other people say; all that matters is what I do on the field."

But the truth is that I still saw the hurt, the downcast eyes, the fumbling with his hands as he spoke and the quick turning away so dealing with it could stop. And the rankings still cast a pall on a player's ability and performance when they drop, without reason or explanation, and the whole (baseball) world watches the downward spiral. It takes a toll on the families involved, and the organizations responsible for their rankings take no responsibility whatsoever. They don't post their reasoning. They're not in contact with anyone other than themselves and a select few baseball organizations, and this just doesn't seem right. At the very least, what ought to occur is for a player to receive an evaluation with explanations from scouts. You would have moved up if.... You fell in the rankings because.... This could serve as both motivation and education. Players could use it as a tool to improve, and if they wanted, the rankings organizations could sell their evaluations and use them as a means to increase revenue. Nothing says they couldn't charge a fee, and then everyone would reap some benefit. Instead, ball players watch their positions on the charts change without feedback or input, and Perfect Game moves on in a void, an institution with limited vision and an apparent inability to share its knowledge and resources with those individuals they impact most.

What the rankings do, and what a fall in the rankings does, is create questions in everyone's minds. The colleges want to know if something has happened – has he been injured, has his velocity topped out, is he getting hit, is he having trouble hitting good pitching, is he out of shape? In Ethan's case, it was a combination of new players being added to the list, players jumping ahead of him, and his coming back after injury out of shape. In this case Bob King was not altogether wrong. Ethan was getting a reputation for having a "soft body." How much it affected his rank can't be determined, but I heard from enough sources that he needed to shape up. Ethan didn't buy it. He was still one of the dominant players in Central Florida. He didn't think he was in that bad a shape. He didn't feel the need to work any harder than he already was. And if he dropped in the Perfect Game rankings, who cared as long as the right colleges were still interested in him?

Of course, I cared, and the questions that seeped into my mind were more insidious, and filled with more self-doubt and self-criticism. Had I done something wrong? Why couldn't I motivate Ethan to work harder? Had his pitching velocity reached its peak? It hadn't really increased in a year, the first time that had ever occurred. I saw the opportunity Ethan had before him, laid out like a red carpet pointing to the open door of a unique, paid for college experience. It had always been my hope and Pat's that Ethan's baseball would help him get into a college or university for which he otherwise wouldn't qualify. But now he was dropping in the rankings! It felt like freefall, and combined with the ongoing investigation and our ostracism and alienation from the team, we were plummeting without a safety net in sight.

The plot thickens.

On March 7, at the request of DCF, Bob King writes a statement that he sends to Heather Hilton, who forwards it on. He writes:

To whom it may concern,

My character, integrity, and the program that I have devoted the last 25 years of my life to, have come under attack. A few people were involved in a calculated plan to have me "fired", and destroy my reputation and a career of public service that has spanned over 30 years in Orange County. This was all going to happen so that these few people could make sure that the program was run with the style, priority, and values that they adhere to, and with the ultimate goal of their children attaining professional status. Both by word of mouth, and then in writing, they spell out their "vision" for Winter Park High School Baseball, which centers around a program that will become a "magnet" for all the great talent in the entire Central Florida area. They wanted things run in a professional manner, by a former professional "star", where the only focus of the Head Coach is to "put the best eight players on the field and WIN!" Of course, a professional would have to oversee such a program that is in total contradiction to the very purpose of sport in secondary education. They were willing to have this loyal and devoted public educator's reputation ruined, and his job taken from him. They were willing to exaggerate, embellish, influence, twist stories, and just outright lie, as this quote implicates, "We're going to get him fired, even if we have to lie". Thank God for those who are not so consumed in athletic "hero-worship" for helping me uncover this despicable plot. I have been waiting for a reply from DCF all week, as my initial step is to file a complaint that their report was filed with criminal intent and purpose.

I believe King refers to us in the last line, since the only report filed was our notes regarding this season and last, and so in his mind we became part of the grand conspiracy to have him removed, to destroy his livelihood and career. Little wonder, then, that he responded like a wounded, cornered animal, beleaguered on all sides, and went on the attack and defended himself as if his life depended on it. In his mind, it did.

☾

Gordon and Hilton encourage me to deal with the ongoing problems with Coach King face to face. If I have issues or concerns about Ethan's treatment or position on the team, I should talk to the coach like any other parent. So I do. I schedule another meeting with King, hoping to share information and clear up any lingering misconceptions. Personally, all I want to do is to make the rest of the season better for Ethan and the team. We meet after practice in the baseball locker room the middle of March. I sit on one of the low benches in the room, and stare straight ahead at King and Coach Robison, who sit on folding chairs in front of me. I wonder if I should have brought a second person along, a witness, someone to back me up, but I don't want to go there. This is a meeting between the coaches and me, and I want it to be as normal and productive as possible.

The room smells of boy – sweat and wet clay and sour shoes. I spy Ethan's locker, and somehow that relaxes me. For all that's happened, it's proof that he still exists as part of this team, as fixed and permanent as the lockers that line the wall.

"It's about the boys," I tell King, "not the coaches or parents. I want to reiterate that we had nothing to do with DCF being called."

Even though I emphasize this, it's apparent that he is still angry and believes that any informed individual would know that using the words "verbal abuse" would get authorities involved.

"We never even considered the possibility." I assure him. "We have no experience in matters like this. It was my wife's anger, not any attempt to get him reported, that got the phrase inserted. We are not part of a conspiracy to get him fired. In fact, I don't care who coaches the team as long as positive change occurs."

King repeats that he has never spent more time working with any kid in 25 years than he has with Ethan. He calls Ethan defiant, difficult.

"Ethan consistently ignores the instructions of the coaching staff," he says. King repeats the story about telling Ethan he was too fat to visit the University of Miami. He explains that they were still working to get Ethan's body fat down and get Ethan into shape.

"That incident was not part of our complaint," I tell him. I don't mention the number of times he called Ethan fat or the time he called Ethan the slowest kid in Orange County in front of the team.

I attempt to talk to King about three incidents he brought up in our meeting with Bill Gordon: Ethan walking out of a hitting station early, making a mockery of an outfield drill, and peeing on the side of the clubhouse. I tell him that Ethan's perspective on these matters is that the coaches told the boys when they were done with their hitting drill to move on (they deny that); that Ethan has a loud voice and was trying to follow the coaches' directions, though he may have gone too loud. They call Coach Lutz in to confirm that Ethan was way overboard and that this is something he does on a regular basis. I tell

215

them that Ethan peed in bushes not on the clubhouse and didn't think it was a big deal. Ethan later pointed out to me that many kids pee in that spot. I tell them that this doesn't justify the behavior and I don't condone it but it is obviously a blind spot for Ethan, not an intentional misbehavior.

"I never used the f-word on the pitchers mound with Ethan," King says. "I apologize for inadvertently swearing in front of the boys even in much more innocent circumstances."

"I have it corroborated by another student," I tell him.

When he asks by whom I tell him, to which he responds, "Oh, I discount that. That kid has bones to pick with me."

"Mr. Bornstein, I'm frustrated with Ethan not cleaning the locker room," Coach Robison says. "Ethan cleaned the room a couple times but not regularly like he was supposed to. He just sort of stopped."

"I'm willing to speak with Ethan about this and any other matters where Ethan was not following team rules," I say. "Just let me know."

"I've spoken with other past players from Winter Park who were shocked Ethan wasn't kicked off the team when he called off pitches in the Boone game. 10 years ago," Rob says, "Ethan would have been kicked off immediately, and this is how far Coach King has bent to accommodate him."

I try to explain to the coaches that in Ethan's mind having his own game plan did not mean an actual plan for each school he pitches against (an impossibility for a kid who doesn't know the teams or players), but rather that he had an order he liked to throw his pitches in. They don't buy it. They think Ethan pitches to his own piper, that he intentionally disregards Coach King's strategies, and there's no refuting their belief. I also tell them that I recommended that Ethan ask Coach King what the game plan is prior to any game. Up to that point Ethan has not done so.

Time and again both Coach King and Coach Rob make a point of how difficult Ethan is and how much time he takes up. There is no give and take, no introspection. There is no sign that they are willing to concede that their treatment of him may have in any way exacerbated the situation. There is never a point when they say they will look at themselves and try something different with Ethan. It is all about Ethan and the problems he causes.

Suddenly, Dante Bichette bursts into the locker room. The door flies open and he thrusts himself in, angry and frenzied, his arms waving, shouting at Coach King. I look up at him for a moment, then bow my head low and try to become as small and insignificant as possible. I don't want to be in the way of this tirade.

The following are Coach King's notes, as reported to the DCF, about the confrontation:

"We had a nice practice (third one this week), and I addressed the JV about their game tomorrow, and the varsity about practice tomorrow. Coach Robison congratulated both teams on a good effort, and we dismissed everyone in good spirits. I asked Dante Jr. if I could see him for just a minute, with Coach Robison present, standing just outside the office, I told him that he needed to "pick up the pace" on some of the drills that we do early in practice (cords, stride work), so that he can get more out of them...that over the last few days I thought maybe he was getting sick due to an obvious lack of intensity in certain drills that he appeared to not enjoy. I then go on to explain in a little more detail, something that I picked up on in the last few workouts...just a minor technique problem that can make it difficult to get some balls to his left. He listened, did not respond, but seemed fine with it, and left...the entire thing lasted about one minute, and we didn't even sit down. It was calm, in an instructional tone of voice, and it was just the three of us. Dante had struggled some with the glove last week, and so I have been watching closely to see if I could figure out why he was getting caught between hops. We know that his arm has been bothering him, so we had suggested he not throw for a couple of days in practice to give it a rest. Coach Robison had told him at one point in the practice that we were contemplating playing him at third base for Friday's game to help his arm out...we play the third baseman even with the bag the vast majority of the time, so the throw is considerably shorter...and he didn't seem to have a problem with that either.

"I was sitting with Mr. Bornstein and Coach Robison, in the locker room, after practice, discussing strategies to use with Ethan, when Mr. Bichette stormed into the locker room yelling something about what I had done to his son...and that I was going to have to deal with him now because his son was not going to become another Ethan. I told him that we were in the middle of a meeting, and asked him to leave the locker room, and I would talk to him when I was done with Mr. Bornstein. He seemed to grow madder, "bowed" his back and came toward me continuing to shout about how great his son is, and how dare I ever correct anything that he does...he shouted "what do you know, you never played at the level that I did...you don't know what you're doing"...and that now I was "messing" with him, and that would be trouble. I felt in danger from my seat across from Mr. Bornstein, sitting so low, and so I got up and he grew madder...now he is shouting that I am playing "head games" with the kids, and that is why my "best player", Ethan, is on the bench (Ethan was the starting pitcher Saturday) while we are LOSING! I told him he could speak to Mr. Bornstein about Ethan's playing time, and that there were much more important things than wins and losses...this seemed to enrage him as he shouted "What? Character? Your best player is on the bench, put him in! Everybody's down because we're losing, put him in!"

"Coach Robison coaxed him out of the locker room, and tried to resume with Mr. Bornstein, but was too upset to continue. I apologized to him, and we agreed to finish at a later time. I waited a bit and left to finish cutting grass. As soon as I left Mr. Bichette started again saying that since I had not corrected that problem earlier I had no business working with it now, and that it proved that I was just "picking on his son". Even as I type this letter I have NEVER had a single cross word with Dante...and he is a 9th grader starting at SS, and batting third in the order! Mr Bichette then started back on how negative I am towards the kids...and they don't get enough ground balls...and I hit one too hard to his son...and we need to throw more bullpens. When I went to cut grass Coach Robison said that he complained that we did not prepare the team properly, and that that is why we were losing. I asked Mr. Bichette why he kept his son on the team if I was not allowed to talk to his son, and was such a bad coach, and then I asked what credentials he had for high school baseball instruction...which is NONE!...and then I wondered (out loud) why a win at all costs professional mentality was so desirable at the High School level...and then I reminded him that just last week he told me what a great coach I was, and how much respect he had for me and the program I have looked after for a quarter of a century...and that he "only wanted to contribute to the program"...and he keeps bringing up my son, who graduated two years ago, with all kinds of resentment and jealousy in his voice, and I have no idea what that's about either."

Beneath the typed letter King hand wrote:

"I keep coming back to his comment on Friday night, February 29, which was made to all the coaches..."your job is *put the best 8 guys on the field and win championships. I have a lot invested in this team, and if THINGS DON'T CHANGE FAST, kids are going to move out of here, and the kids that are going to move in will NOT move in...and you'll not win for a long time!"

Coach King's notes are accurate as they relate to our meeting. I have no knowledge about the practice he refers to, whether or not he hit fungoes too hard to Little D, what their post-practice conversation did or didn't include. All I know is that the coach did hit hard fungoes on a regular basis. He had for years. And he failed to mention that as Dante Sr. yelled at him, so he hollered back, shouting at Bichette to leave or he'd call the cops. By the time the frothing face to face had moved outside, I bolted, my heart pounding, hoping to never be caught between the two of them again. King and I agreed to try to pick up our conversation again, but that never happened.

After the meeting I sent Coach King an email regarding Ethan that included the following:

"I'm not asking that he hit in a certain spot or get a certain number of at bats. I am asking that if he is not hitting for a reason, please let me and Ethan know. If he is being disciplined, please let me and Ethan know. If he is not, please explain to me why he is not somewhere in the lineup."

At the same time King and Bichette were having their toe-to-toe, Mariana was pounding out another lengthy email to Coach King, who forwarded it on to Principal Gordon who forwarded it to DCF.

Dear Bob,

I mentioned to Rob that I wanted to get with you guys to assure you that there was no sinister plan against you and that the rumor mill has gone crazy but all I can really be responsible for is what I know to be true. However, I now see that maybe all this unfolded like it did for a reason and will no longer defend any of your actions as maybe coming from misunderstanding. I believe today that you wholly understand your actions and choose to continue them because you feel you are above any consequence. For your information, whatever you are saying is not being kept confidential; maybe that's what you want. The email I wrote that was meant to put a lid on things was immediately – I mean within minutes – sent around town and people were warned of the lies I was telling, etc. Some called to apologize for their initial response because once they read the email they realized they fell for some wretched spewing of mal intent and that they had no business or need to have been forwarded the email in the first place. So, if your goal is truly to keep this under wraps you should know that the people you are trusting with your "side" of the story are all too happy to spread this juicy gossip around.

I wanted to tell you for a month now that a family told me that they were going to sit tight but were working on a lawsuit against you because of how you have treated their son. That would have been out of a sincere desire to let you know that there was still time to salvage this team and maybe avoid such an ugly event. I will not rehash things that have happened, but I will say that your actions since this whole thing has been in the open have proven me wrong. You do not seem like a man who can accept responsibility and who does have good intentions toward the kids....

Today Dante Jr. became the "Ethan." Actually, I knew when I saw how you responded to things that he would be. But you will not find anyone in the world who can say Dante doesn't work; he has always been made to work harder. You will not find a child who has been held to a higher level of respect for authority. He has never quit anything in his life and will not be allowed to do so now. What you have done is to take a FIFTEEN year old child's LOVE for a game and made him want to stop playing it for his coach. That's quite an accomplishment and I will absolutely say you should be ashamed of your attempt to get that done. What a horrible thing to do to a child because his parents disagree with you. You continue to prove all the people who said to stay far away from your program to be right. Some of them by the way are now your greatest advocates and guess why that is? Not too hard to see.

Today you singled Dante out to yell at, you hit ground balls to him "with loud grunts" and when one hit off his ear you yelled at him some more. You are bordering on crazy to think you can get away with such TRANSPARENT and blatant actions. Dante may be 6 feet tall, but he is a freshman. Imagine if someone treated your girls that way. And you aren't even fooling ANYONE who has seen this before....

One of the lovely rumors I heard this weekend is that things here have come down to either you or us leaving Winter Park. I never had that hope and do not see things that way. But how you treated Dante today shows me that maybe you are hoping for that to be the outcome, with us leaving of course. I hope you can be man enough to apologize to Dante for taking your frustrations with his parents out on him. You have another uncomfortable, discouraged, disillusioned child on your hands as a result of your actions. Dante will not be the last victim, I can be sure, unless you are made to stop acting like a child.

I look forward to speaking with you.
Mariana Bichette

And Bernie Kissel provided this letter (reproduced as it was written) to Coach King and the DCF, helping to solidify his son's spot at first base that year and the next.

Sunday, March 16, 2008

To whom it may concern,

This correspondence is in regards to events that I have witnessed in regards to the current Winter Park baseball season. I was first approached at the Winter park baseball fields after our second game by Mrs. Bichette. She was very careful to whisper to me that she had made arrangements for my son to be on a summer league with the UCF Nights traveling team. She also informed me that she had spoken with the recruiting coach at UCF on my sons behalf. Then her discussion moved towards Coach King. Mrs. Bichette informed me that she had spoken with four parents in regards to complaining to Principle Gorden about Coach King's attitude towards players. She also informed me that she had met with Principle Gordon already. I point blank asked her what she wanted me to do and she replied that I should make an appointment to see the principle and inform him as several other parents would be doing to say how unfair coach king was and how he insulted the players. She gave me examples which included

As the talks stated to circulate around the field I received an email from Mrs. Bichette warning me to keep quite because Mr. Bichette had not sat down with coach King yet. At first I did not know what she meant but I latter learned from Dave Bornstein what she meant. Dave told me that he had lunch with both Mr. and Mrs. Bichette and they informed him of a list of items that Mr. Bichette witnessed while coaching regarding his son. Mr. Bornstein informed me that he was taking these items to the A.D. and to the principle. At this lunch he also informed me that Mr. Bichette was going to talk to coach King about taking over the baseball program and if certain changes where not made that he would remove his son and several other players. I was not sure of this hearing it second hand but then a couple of days latter as practice was ending Mr. Buichette walked up to the fence where Mr. Madommo and I where sitting. He started his discussion at first as to all of the things run wrong in the practice then he went into the changes he was planning. After about ten minutes of conversation Coach King came out of the concession stand next to where we where talking and got into his truck parked at the track. As I turned back to Mr. Bichette he had turned white with fear. He asked several times if we thought that Coach King had heard his discussion. It was clear to me now that what Mr. Bornstein had told me was true.

What brought everything to a stop for me was during a car ride to a game in Jacksonville with Mr. Bornstein. The school called Mr. Bornstein and informed him of a meeting set with Principle Gorden the next day and that DCF was getting involved. This opened up the floodgates for Mr. Bornstein. He informed me of an email to AD with complaints, he informed me that he had already met with his friend on the school board about King and he was hiring an attorney to sue. Dave went on and on how he was at war and Coach King would be removed as the baseball coach.

It is my opinion from these first hand events and discussions by other parents that it is the intent of several people involved in our team to have Coach King Removed.

Bernie Kissel

I didn't see the Kissel letter until well after the season's conclusion, at which time I requested a copy of the complete DCF report. I don't recall Dante Sr. ever telling me that he would remove LittleD and others from the program, though there is no doubt that the Bichettes were unhappy and more than willing to fuel the flames of parents like me and Pat, using us to help get King removed. And sadly, Kissel misunderstood me in many ways when he reported on our conversation in the ride to Jacksonville. I had no friends on the school board. Nor had I, or did I, ever meet with anyone even vaguely connected to the school system other than Winter Park administrators. I never hired an attorney, though I did seek advice from one of my closest friends who is a lawyer. And I never said Coach King would be removed, though I may very well have said, in the heat of the moment, that if it came to a war we would not be the losers. That only goes to show how little I knew.

In a game against Oak Ridge High, a poor school in a heavily Black and Hispanic school district, King pitches two sophomores. Ethan sits on the bench. Normally a "gimme," an easy win, the game is high scoring and tense. Oak Ridge has one quality pitcher, and he's hanging tough through the late innings. Winter Park's pitchers have given up eight runs, and are losing 8-7. With a runner on second and one out, King scans the bench, thinking hard over his decision, until he finally tells Ethan to grab a bat and hit. It is the first time Ethan has hit in awhile, the first time he has moved off the end of the bench. He runs to the on-deck circle, takes a few hasty warm-up swings, and enters the batter's box.

After a few pitches Ethan tags a ball, skying it a mile high. The fence in right field at Oak Ridge is ridiculously deep – over 350 feet – and Ethan's ball clears the fence, goes over the light pole behind the fence, and lands somewhere in the parking lot behind the field – foul. Ethan gets under the next pitch and pops up to the infield. Out two. King tells Ethan, when he walks back in, that it was a selfish at bat, that all Ethan was trying to do was hit a home run instead of advance the runner. Ethan doesn't respond. The next two batters hit singles, and Winter Park goes on to win the game 9-8.

After the game, King publicly berates himself for putting Ethan in the game. He tells everyone who's interested that he was wrong to put Ethan in because Ethan didn't deserve it and he had a good boy – Josh Bastian – sitting on the bench who could have hit, but he put Ethan in because he was greedy and thought at that moment that Ethan gave them the best chance to win. He swears to all within earshot that he'll never do that again, never put his own self interests ahead of what he knows is right. Of course, the judgments implicit in his pronouncement are clear: putting Ethan in made it wrong. Josh is good. Ethan is…something else.

Ethan pitches the first 3.1 innings of a doubleheader against Gainesville Buchholz in Gainesville. He doesn't hit. Gainesville Buchholz boasts an outstanding athletic program, and Ethan gets hit hard, giving up four runs in those few innings. Nate Winters comes on after Ethan and pitches well. He gives up three runs, but looks better doing it. Several parents come up to me between games and ask if Ethan's arm is ok. He was pitching so slow. The reason, I realize, that he had no velocity was that he threw nearly no fastballs. Virtually every ball he threw was a change-up. Change-up change-up change-up. No wonder he got hit. No wonder he was throwing 78. I also wondered how intentional this was on the part of the head coach to make him look bad, or if it was simply a matter of the coach loving Ethan's change-up.

A week later, Coach King and Ethan have another issue over the order of groups batting. Coach King accuses Ethan of disrupting and disrespecting practice, when Ethan says he merely understood the coaches to say that it didn't matter which order groups batted in. Could this have been cleared up with a simple question by the coach asking Ethan what he heard or understood? Perhaps. Instead it becomes another accusation of insubordination.

The next week the team prepares for its spring tournament, something that hadn't happened in several years due to problems during previous trips. This year, the baseball team goes to Sarasota for a five-day tournament with other schools, including Sarasota High, a perennial powerhouse that has won several state championships. We hear that there will be a number of college coaches scouting the tournament, including Gino DiMare, the assistant head coach and recruiter from Miami, one of Ethan's top choices. At the meeting for players and parents, Coach King reviews the do's and don'ts, clearly laying out the rules, expectations and consequences for misbehavior.

There will be a curfew. No drinking. No drugs. No reckless behavior in the hotel rooms. No crossing the busy streets that surround the hotel. Players would bunk together. Parents can stay at the same hotel or elsewhere. Heather Hilton and her police officer husband will accompany the team as chaperones.

"I expect it to be a good time," he says.

I have eyes focused solely on Ethan during King's talk and, as I fear, Ethan drops his head, scratching the back of his neck and ignoring the coach. I pull him aside after the meeting and have a serious heart to heart. I'm concerned that this is the worst possible situation for him – away from our protective shell, under the scrutiny of a coach he detests who now despises him, surrounded by his baseball playing friends he wants to impress but to whom he feels disconnected. It's a recipe for disaster.

"E, did you hear what the coach said?"

"About what?"

"About the rules for the trip. You realize you've got a target on your back? You can't do anything, and I mean anything wrong. No stepping out of line. No back talk to the coaches. The only way you can go on this trip is if you promise me you'll do everything exactly as you're told. The whole world is breathing down our necks. We can't afford to have you slip up."

"Don't worry, sir, I won't."

I trust he understands, and let it go at that.

We make it our family spring vacation – five days at the beach. Rather than stay at the mediocre hotel with the team, I book us into one of the nicest hotels in town. I research restaurants, and plan some good meals with the Bichettes and Carters and any other parents who want to join us. We pack our bags, load Ethan and all his baseball equipment in the car along with our suitcases, and head down to sun-kissed, white sand Sarasota.

Within hours after arriving we find out that Ethan and another boy - Matt Toelke - have gotten in trouble for taking off and crossing the major highway in front of their hotel. All the boys were told not to go anywhere without proper permission and supervision, and no one is allowed to cross this dangerous road. Ethan and his friend disregard this. They say they just wanted to go to a convenience store to get sodas, and receive wrist slaps for punishment. Something doesn't sound right to me here. Ethan really doesn't drink soda, but I figure he just went along with his friend, and though I don't think anything's up,

I tell him no more. No more issues. No more attention drawn to him. Nothing else wrong happens, or we just pack it up and go home.

Ethan and I have agreed to meet with Coaches Robison and DiFrancesco the first night we are there. Coach Robison requested the meeting to discuss Ethan's status and recurring problems on the team. We sit in their hotel room, and Coach Rob proceeds to play bad cop, laying out one scenario after the other regarding Ethan's misbehaviors. Ethan ignores outfield fly ball drills. Instead he comes in and tries to feed balls to the pitching machine they use to lob balls to the outfield. He is told repeatedly to go back out and catch balls, and he dogs it out and then sneaks his way back to the machine. He ignores the coaches' instructions at the hitting stations. He goes where he wants, leaves each station when he chooses, spends too much time talking to other players. His attitude is that he does whatever he wants, a party line we have heard repeatedly from Coach King as well.

But this party line has some truth to it. Ethan doesn't refute what Coach Rob says. He just has a reason for everything he does. He sees no point in catching fly balls in the outfield since he's not an outfielder and has been told by the coaches that he's a pitcher and first baseman. Coach Rob replies that with Bernie Kissel Jr. entrenched at first they need to look for other places for Ethan to play. I visibly choke on this, and let them know that Ethan has been a first baseman all his life, and as a lefty has a natural advantage there. Bernie Jr. has been playing there for one season, his arm hurts, and (though I don't say this) he's not very good. Ethan tells the coaches that he only leaves the hitting stations when he's done what they've told him to do, and moves on so he can get extra batting practice in. They don't care. It's not following the rules. He needs to follow the rules. And Ethan does need to follow the rules. He does need to learn, to understand that he can't set his own standards of practice and play on the team. He struggles with this, especially in light of his near-complete dismissal of Coach King's authority. I watch him nod his head in agreement, but I'm under the impression it's not real buy-in. It's the "just say yes and move on" syndrome, what Ethan does to end a conversation he doesn't like.

Rob ends by letting us know that Coach King will not talk to Ethan or deal with him for the rest of the semester. All communication should go through him, not the head coach. We get it. There's the rest of the team, and then there's Ethan. It's all we can expect for the rest of the term.

Chad Modomo gets the start the first game, and throws well through five innings. The team holds a tenuous lead, but as Chad tires in the late going his fastball starts to rise, and he gets hit hard. Chad's pitching depends on keeping the ball low. King leaves him in one inning too long. By the time he gets through the sixth, Winter Park is behind and Ethan has come in to close.

Well rested and pumped up, Ethan mows down the side, pitching harder, perhaps, than I've ever seen him. The batters on the other team can't hit his offspeed pitches, can't catch up to his fastball. It's three up three down in a matter of minutes, but Winter Park can't score either, and loses the game. As we leave we run into Coach DiMare from Miami, and I ask if he saw Ethan throw. I let him know how well he did, and he promises to watch the next time Ethan pitches if I'll just give him the heads up.

Ethan doesn't play at all in the next two games. My frustration grows with each inning he sits on the bench. I had been told that Coach King was not allowed to take his feelings out on my son, but he's doing it anyway, using his power as a coach to ground Ethan completely. When the fourth game comes around, the third day of the tournament, it's become a joke among the parents that, no matter the situation, Ethan won't see daylight. He's the official team mascot. But while others joke, I grow furious inside. Ethan is being punished because we decided to stand up in defense of him, and then, when the school administration sent information to DCF Ethan gets punished for our actions – without anyone from the school stepping forward to stop this injustice and protect our boy.

I keep turning around while the fourth game is being played, staring up at the tower that rises between the four ball fields at the Sarasota complex, and pleading with my eyes at Heather Hilton who sits in the shade in the tower, shrugging my shoulders as if to ask, "What's going on? Can't you see how defeated we are, how this defeats everything you've said would happen? Everything that you promised would be fair has turned to dust, to straw in our mouths? Can you see how bitter this experience is for us?" She and her husband smile back at me from above, a smile without a word cutting across her face.

After the game, just as we return to our hotel, my cell phone rings. I need to come back to the team hotel right away. There's a matter of great urgency that has to do with Ethan. "Is he hurt?" I ask. "Has there been an accident?" Just come, I'm told, and I dash off, leaving Pat, my daughter Jerica and Gabriel behind.

When I get to the hotel I see Coach King leaning against the handrail of the hotel's second floor, staring seriously at me as I drive up. Ethan sees me, too, and runs up to me. "I'm sorry, Dad," he says. "I'm so sorry, and I'm really, really scared."

"What happened?" I ask.

"I blew it," he tells me. "The coaches searched the rooms, and they found some blunts and a water pipe in my bag."

"They what?" I don't understand. Blunts? Water pipe? The one thing I felt certain of was how important Ethan's baseball was to him, that he wouldn't risk it all by smoking pot. The idea goes right over my head. Water pipe? For what?

"I'm busted," he says. "I've ruined everything."

Now it begins to sink in. Ohmygod. It's over. The one thing Ethan couldn't do, he did. He got himself in more trouble than Coach King. He's shifted all the attention away from King and onto himself. He's become the bad boy, the troublemaker, the druggie. Every college will know. Everyone will hear about this. Everything we've worked for since he was five years old has just come crashing down.

"They want to talk to you, Dad," he says, his voice quavering, tears in his eyes.

I have no sympathy for him, no feelings of compassion or any willingness to comfort him at all. I'm mad. "Well, let's go then," I say, and walk up the outdoor steps to the second floor where the inquisition awaits.

King is in the room, along with Hilton and her husband. He has a frown on his face, but it feels like it's forced, a cover for a grin. He's won. He knows it's over. Hilton shows me the water pipe, explains that blunts are cigars that have the tobacco taken out and pot put back in. They found no marijuana in Ethan's bags or in the room. Just the paraphernalia, but that's enough. The Sarasota police will be arriving shortly. Ethan needs to come clean right now, to name names and tell them exactly what's been going on. If he does, she can virtually promise that all that will happen is a suspension and reinstatement to school. He'll have to go for drug counseling. If he passes the drug class there will be nothing permanent on his record. If he fails to cooperate, the high school could kick him out permanently. He might have to attend a school that specializes in delinquent behavior problems. The Sarasota police could charge him with possession. He could go to jail.

Much of this, I find out later, is a gross exaggeration. Ethan's a minor and no drugs were found, but the threat works. It frightens him and me, and that, combined with my volcanic anger, sets me off. I take him outside to talk.

"How could you?!" I say to him, deeply, darkly, barely containing my rage. "Everything your mom and I have gone through, everything you've worked for all your life. It's all undone. What didn't you understand? Why couldn't you keep it together, just for a few days?"

"I'm sorry, Dad. I'm really really sorry." It's all he can say.

I hammer him mercilessly, demand that he come clean, do anything they ask to minimize the damage to his future. "You're going to tell them whatever they want. You're going to name names. I know other boys must have been smoking with you. You're going to tell them the whole truth. Do you understand? You could go to jail if you don't. You're going to tell them everything."

Ethan doesn't want to squeal on his friends. He begs me not to make him. He says it's the worst thing he could possibly do, that he'll never be able to walk the halls in school again. But under my constant pressure and intimidation, and the real peril he faces, he finally caves. He names three other boys who were smoking with him. One, the senior who crossed the busy highway with him, gets kicked off the team along with Ethan. Nothing happens to the other two boys, who deny ever smoking anything. We pack Ethan up, get our stuff from the hotel and quietly depart for home.

Ethan gets suspended for ten days, goes to a drug education class, and bears the stigma and the scars of a squealer for the rest of the year. If he had been demoralized, diminished, devalued by his playing time being taken away from him, now he is a true pariah, friendless, an enemy of the student body, a virus to be avoided and scorned. When he returns to school, it's hell every day as he walks the halls. Kids bump into him in the hallways, call him asshole, squealer, in whispers that follow him wherever he goes. They throw food at him in the cafeteria. Even worse, he's shunned, ignored like a leper as he makes his way from class to class. The senior who gets kicked off the team with him, one of Ethan's best friends, never speaks to him again, though word is out that he wants to find Ethan sometime after school and beat the crap out of him.

We all stay away from the ball field the remainder of the season, lock ourselves away, avoid the light of day. Pat feels the blight and shame of public humiliation almost as badly as Ethan. She is a deeply private person and for her, the idea that our dirty laundry is in plain view of the world is one of the most difficult consequences of this all-wrong semester. The Central Florida baseball community is small and insular, and Ethan had been a high profile player. Though it's supposed to be a confidential matter, word gets out. Everyone in the baseball world knows what happened to him, though they may not know the particulars, the extent and details of his misbehavior. Like Ethan, we are abandoned by all but a few baseball friends. The Bichettes are still nice, but they're playing baseball and we're not. Our dinners with them end. The Carters remain friends, and the Bastians are kind and compassionate.

"What really happened?" Vic Incinelli wants to know. "I love Ethan. I can't believe what I'm being told. How could a star athlete like Ethan not only jeopardize his career but do something as stupid to his body as smoking pot?"

But he knows Ethan's not a bad kid, and believes in forgiveness and second chances. Chip Gierke stays by Ethan's side. He gives Ethan a stern lecture about future behavior and has Ethan swear he'll show the world he's a good person, but Gierke remains steadfast in his belief that Ethan is a good kid. The coaches of the Orlando Scorpions stand by our side as well, though they insist, if Ethan is to be part of the team in the future, that he prove he deserves it. Good grades. NO MORE PROBLEMS. Hard work at the Scorpions facility so they (and the rest of the baseball world) know he's not getting a free pass. We don't know what the end result will be now with colleges, how many will drop any thought of recruiting him, whether King will report what occurred back to anyone he's written. Our son is damaged goods, and we spend the remainder of the year quietly trying to repair the breaks and leaks.

The Department of Children and Families concludes its halfhearted investigation. Without ever interviewing us, any players or parents who witnessed anything that had occurred during the past two seasons, Coach Bob King is fully exonerated. The only witnesses DCF calls on are Coach King and anyone he may have asked to make statements on his behalf. The school administration stands firmly behind him. The game, the sad season, the mistakes and abuses and manipulations and machinations are all over.

①

Now for the whole story. When Ethan and Matt Toelke crossed the highway, they went looking for cigars, not sodas, to make blunts. The reason Ethan wasn't caught with any pot was because he didn't have any. Other boys brought the weed on the trip. The coaches were tipped off in two different ways. First, housekeepers at the hotel reported a room (not Ethan's) smelled of smoke. Second, the Bastians were staying in the adjacent room, and they also reported the strong smell of pot smoke coming from next door. In fact, it was reported that when boys walked into the room smoke wafted out the open door in clouds. It was like walking into fog. The sophomores who were staying next to the Bastians were oblivious. They just smoked in their room to their stoned hearts' content. The coaches supposedly searched every boy's bags, but at least one of the boys in the smoke-filled room had a pack of cigars on the top of his clothes, and though he was named by Ethan, he was neither caught nor disciplined. Other boys had blunts, marijuana, and papers in their bags, but the only one who was discovered was Ethan, whose bag was thoroughly taken apart to find the waterpipe buried on the bottom. Was Ethan targeted? Does it really matter? No, he did wrong and deserved to be caught and face the consequences of his actions. Should other boys have been caught as well? Absolutely. And finally, was Ethan, in some way, asking to be found out, his subconscious begging to be let out of this hellish season? He swears no. When asked why he did it, Ethan's response was merely, "I didn't think I'd ever be caught." Simple, straightforward, utterly shallow. But perhaps this was his way out of the constant pain and humiliation of a demeaning, embarrassing season. Perhaps this was his way of telling the school, the world, to leave him alone, that he was going to do whatever he wanted, and what he wanted was to have the hurting cease.

①

What I really believe as a person and what I did as a parent were so diametrically opposed at the time that I have lived with my own hypocrisy and shame ever since. I have had to face the fact that I was not honest with myself, that I was hoodwinked by the administration, that I gave Ethan bad advice and, in my bollixed up fear and anger and exhaustion over his baseball season, I forced him to do the wrong thing. I forced him, not to lie, not to keep his mouth shut, but to tell the truth. And the truth, in this case, was a commandment I turned into a sin.

I think of myself as a moral person. My wife tells me, in fact, that one of my biggest "issues" is honesty, that I put it on such a high pedestal it's become almost a neurotic ideal. I have always emphasized the value and importance to my children of telling the truth, of not bearing false witness, of being honorable and upright, and how shameful it is to be otherwise. In doing so, I have taught Ethan that it's easier to lie than it is to deal with the shame of doing wrong. It's a convoluted logic, but Ethan struggles with the truth, that very value I uphold so strongly, because he is often ashamed to admit that he hasn't done something he's promised. He hasn't done something right or on time or to the exacting standards that were set for him, and rather than face the momentary shame of admission, he lies and hopes to make his mistakes right before anyone finds out. He does this when we ask him to take out the garbage. He does it when we ask him how his grades are. He does it when we want to know when he'll be home, or what he's done that night and where he's been – all to avoid, temporarily, the shame of admitting the truth.

In the situation where I strong-armed him to squeal on his teammates and friends, over time I have realized many things. First, I understand now that those who wield authority often do so simply for authority's sake. The threats that were leveled at Ethan were both unfair and, in all likelihood, unenforceable. A minor first time offense, without any drugs present, with a minor to boot, could never have resulted in jail time or permanent suspension from school. We were scared into submission, frightened into doing what they wanted – for nothing other than to get Ethan into trouble and diminish his credibility. Looking back on it, I should have stood up for Ethan right then and pushed back. I should have told them that I would not stand for him to be threatened. I should have called an attorney. Instead, I joined in the threats. My own anger so overwhelmed my better judgment that I allowed us both to be bullied and run over by an administration that couldn't have cared less about my son or my family. They were motivated to protect a coach who had built a stable program, no more and no less. We were incidental casualties who would disappear and be gone forever within a few short semesters. The coach had been there 26 years. They could live with our loss.

231

And I realize, now, that sometimes there are higher callings than the truth. Sometimes silence is better. Sometimes quiet is king. Neither lying nor telling the truth, in this case it would have been the honorable path to take. By squealing on his friends Ethan cemented his shame. He lost the one card he could have held onto – the support of his friends, and it was wrong, horribly wrong for me to take this away from him. Yes, it's important for parents to teach their children that telling the truth is right, that lying is wrong. But let's face it. Let's look in the mirror and answer the basic question, "Who among you has never lied?" Who has told the white lie in the name of kindness (You don't look fat. You just have a little belly. There's nothing wrong with that haircut. You didn't embarrass yourself. No one even noticed. Of course it will be all right.) Who has remained silent when the truth will hurt? Who then, has taught this valuable humane lesson to their children? Sometimes the little white lie is an act of kindness. Sometimes it's preferable. And sometimes there are more important actions to take than telling the truth. If it ever comes up again, I know what I'll say to my children. I'll tell them not to squeal. I'll tell them that silence can be honorable, that friendship can last forever or be broken by a failure to trust. I'll tell them that there are values in life that are equal to integrity and honesty, and that often, the highest form of integrity comes when you're honest with your heart, with the feelings you hold most dear, not with the cold, sometimes heartless truth. Thou shalt not lie may be a commandment, but thou shalt not squeal ought to be a strong addendum. I'll remember what I did to Ethan, and in the future I'll do it differently.

And when it comes to drugs, I have to admit something right here, right now. If I ever decide to run for public office, have at it. Use this paragraph against me. I've smoked, I've inhaled, and I've held it in for as long as I can. Though I don't smoke now, I did through my thirties. I smoked all through high school and college. Mexican dirt weed. Gold and black Columbian. Thai sticks. American homegrown buds. I've smoked them all. And I hate to break it to you, Mom and Dad America, but chances are your kid has, too. More than ¾ of all high schoolers have at least tried pot. They may not use it regularly, but they've been around it, they've probably toked a little, maybe taken some good hits, maybe gotten really stoned and decided whether they like it or not.

So who am I to say that smoking pot is a bad thing? Who am I to tell my children to never smoke marijuana? It's a virtually inconsequential drug. It makes you happy and gives you the munchies. It can increase your self-consciousness and make you giddy. It's not the best thing to do when you're driving, but it's not nearly as bad as drinking and driving. I believe it should be legalized. I'd like to see the drug trade end, to see the United States reap the benefits of new taxes on cartons of well-rolled joints. It's ridiculous that athletes in America can be punished for smoking weed when smoking cigarettes is so much worse for you, when the real issues of the abuse of human growth hormone, steroids, amphetamines, are far graver. Let the poor professional athlete relieve some of their stress by taking a few good hits from the bong. Heck, drinking more than 3 cups of coffee a day is worse for you than smoking a joint. Honore de Balzac, the great French writer, died from caffeine overdose. To the best of my knowledge no one has ever died from smoking too much pot.

Then who am I to tell Ethan that it's bad to smoke when I did and honestly don't believe it? The real message I should have been giving him all those years was that while I have nothing against marijuana and don't consider it a big deal, the rest of our behind the times society still does, and because of that the consequences of him being caught and punished for smoking pot far outweighed the benefits. It was the risk Ethan faced due to society's rules that made pot smoking so bad for him, not the effects of the drug itself. I needed to use this as an opportunity to teach a kid who struggled with connecting his actions and their subsequent consequences. I needed to draw straight lines between being caught with a bag of weed in his car (or driving with a friend who had weed) and the following: no high school baseball, no college baseball, no professional baseball, probably junior college and a couple years at a state university and then, if it's what he wanted, if he didn't mind not playing ball, he could smoke all the weed he wanted and make a living as a charter fisherman or even a high school baseball coach.

This is a kid who, from the time he was five years old, had been playing baseball and popping pills. Ritalin. Adderall. Vyvanse. Homeopathic remedies. Amino acids. Anti-inflammatories. All in the name of better health, proper brain function, pain reduction. And then we try to give him the message that drugs – in particular smoking pot – are bad? When almost everyone around him is doing it? The real lesson had to be one of appropriate use and behavior coupled with potential risks and consequences, and how a parent teaches that while making sure one's child isn't simply mouthing a false understanding (yessir, I get it, sir) may be one of the great challenges of raising a child. Of course, I had a child who had yet to connect action (smoking pot) with consequence (getting caught and having your whole life come crashing down). Amazingly, the possibility of paying for what he did was obliterated by the simple belief that he would never be caught. And did he, perhaps, in the furthest recesses of his mind, want to be caught? I don't know. With that in mind, teaching him and having him believe that using an easily obtained, popular, illegal drug could have disastrous impact on his future was a lesson we failed to impart, if it was ever possible to do so.

CHAPTER 10
Showcase Summer

With Ethan done for the spring, with mediocre statistics through half the high school season, and word spreading that he was kicked off his high school team for disciplinary reasons (most people knew it was for pot but because he was a minor that was not the official report), the only way he was going to get any visibility for college recruitment was through his showcase team.

The summer after junior year is perhaps the most important time for any ball player with dreams of playing college ball. After receiving months of bulk mailings and inquiries from colleges and universities, along with the occasional handwritten, personalized note, players can be spoken to by coaches directly on July 1, with commitment letters signed in early November. These are the calls that reveal a school's real interest in a player, not the mass mailings received by thousands. Boys are already talking about the calls they expect to receive on the first day of July.

During the recruitment process both players and schools cast wide nets. College baseball programs weigh their needs against which players are likely to sign professional contracts straight out of high school, which players they'll lose to other teams, and which ones will actually sign. On top of that, in the convoluted system created by the NCAA, baseball, for some reason, is the chosen sport to discriminate against, with less scholarships to dole out to its players than any other major sport.

In an article published on June 7, 2007 by Mark Schlabach at espn.com, Schlabach says, "Already hampered by having only 11.7 scholarships to award to more than 30 players each season, the NCAA has approved legislation that will dictate how those scholarships are awarded. College baseball has always had the short end of the stick in terms of scholarships. Division I-A football teams receive 85 scholarships, and men's and women's basketball teams have 13 scholarships. Women's equestrian can dole out 15 scholarships, and women's crew teams can award 20 scholarships."

Under new rules approved by the NCAA's Division 1 Board of Directors, starting in 2009 all baseball scholarships must be at least 25% of the equivalent of a full ride – that is, no less than ¼ of a fully paid scholarship. The number of players on baseball scholarships is limited to 27, with a maximum squad size of 35. With such severe limitations on scholarships, baseball coaches must be conservative in their offers, enticing the star high school players with offers in excess of 50%, tempting the good players with less, and hoping to capture others who have either fallen through the cracks or are destined to be backups with offers as preferred walk-ons – officially on the team but with no scholarship dollars at all.

In 2010 the University of Miami made offers to 13 high school players. For the first time in many years, the school decided to go after five big name players who would probably sign pro contracts rather than players they knew wanted to go to college. They lost all five to the pros. In the 1st round Christian Yelich, a 6'4" first baseman, signed with the Florida Marlins for $1.7 million. In the supplemental 1st round, 6'4" third baseman Nick Castellanos signed for $3.45 million with the Detroit Tigers, and immediately after, Luke Jackson, a 6'2" right-handed pitcher signed for $1.557 million with the Texas Rangers. In the third round Yordy Cabrera, a 6'4' 20 year old high school senior shortstop, signed a $1.25 million with the Oakland Athletics. And perhaps the story of the draft for Miami was AJ Cole, a 6'5" right-handed pitcher who had played with Ethan on the Scorpions for several years. Projected as a first round draft pick with a fastball that had been clocked as high as 98 mph, Cole fell in the draft to the first pick in the fourth round. Speculation on his fall centered on signability, that intangible question mark regarding how much it would cost to tempt him away from a school like Miami. The truth was probably more complicated than that. Never a stellar student, Cole's desire all along was to play pro ball. He had a below-par senior year, during which his velocity dropped and, in a few key games, he got hit hard by high school teams. Blessed with spectacular natural ability, Cole never had to work hard to throw hard. His arm, Ethan said, was kissed by God at birth. Even so, he fell. Out of the first round, past the supplemental round, the second, the third, and Miami had hope, albeit short-lived, that as a fourth round pick he would not get the money he wanted to turn pro and would come to school. After prolonged negotiations with the Washington Nationals, who had signed Stephen Strasburg the year before as the number one pick in the draft to a record signing bonus, and in the same draft as Cole signed Bryce Harper to a $6.25 million contract, Cole signed for a 4th round record $2 million, and Miami was down to an eight player signing class.

This is less a problem for a national power like Miami than a program that doesn't carry a similar cachet or reputation, but it happens all the time. And because of that, colleges begin the recruiting process by sending out hundreds of mailers to prospects, winnowing down the list after months (and sometimes years) of scouting to dozens they desire, hoping to land 10-15 players at the end of the day.

By the same token, the desirable high school baseball player, unless he is truly elite and commits to a college early in his junior, and occasionally even sophomore year, will keep his options wide open. We were advised by the Scorpion coaches to respond to every letter Ethan received, and to do so in a polite and timely manner. Unless we had absolutely no desire for him to attend a certain school, we were told to be respectful and fill out all forms and mailings that were sent to him. And we did, with the only complication being that now Ethan didn't ask his high school coach for an evaluation. He gave the questionnaires to the Scorpions. In every instance, every school asked which schools were recruiting Ethan, or to please list his top 3-5 choices for college. In every case Ethan listed, as his top two choices, the University of North Carolina-Chapel Hill and the University of Miami. But that number three spot changed with the wind. If he was filling out a form from Clemson, Clemson made the list. If he was filling out a request from Georgia Tech, Georgia Tech made the list, though Ethan was far away from being an engineering student. What was he to do? Leave the school asking about him off the list, letting them know that his response was perfunctory and he had no real interest in their program? No. He made them a solid number three, and so did almost every other player with whom we spoke. "Yes, of course, you're one of my top choices. It's UNC, Miami, and Whatever U." While schools were soliciting dozens of potential players, players did their best to play the schools and keep their options open. Everyone knew. Everyone did it. All that really mattered was what you said and did when a school made you a bona fide offer.

The other part of the recruiting process that is so convoluted and completely backwards from a normal college application is how little choice you have in going to a school you want. In her application process my daughter Jerica laid out the qualities she wanted in a college: class size, size of the school, location, programs and degrees offered, and so on. She then winnowed down the list to eight: three in-state, five out of state. She applied to each, and waited for their responses.

As an athlete (and not a top athlete that everyone wanted) Ethan first had to woo the schools. We sent out DVDs. We sent letters. We sent copies of the few newspaper clips we had, just to get a school's attention. Then we hoped he would make their list. When we heard from them we could respond again, and only if they were interested in him did he have an opportunity to attend. It didn't matter what his dream school was. He couldn't apply if they weren't interested. UNC never responded to us, and so Ethan never even got to peek in that door.

Then, there's a third side to being a baseball parent trying to guide a son to a wise decision for college. There are times when the school that wants you is a great academic institution but not a known baseball power, and the corollary – a great baseball school that lacks great academics. Do you shoot for mediocrity and balance both? Do you acknowledge that your son has a 2% or 3% chance of playing pro ball, while getting a good degree helps insure a stable future? If you were to choose between Harvard and Michigan, where would you go? Michigan is an excellent academic institution that plays Big Ten baseball, but Harvard is….Harvard. At one you might get scouted more, but the other can probably place you in a good summer league. Do you turn down Harvard because it plays Ivy League baseball, because the narrow path to the pros is that much more difficult? Where do you go?

After not playing the second half of the spring, Ethan is chomping at the bit to get back in action, and the Scorpions summer schedule starts early and gives him little time to breathe. It kicks off before school is even out, with a Perfect Game national qualifying tournament May 24-26. The winner of the tournament gets a guaranteed spot in the wood bat national championship tournament in July, the most highly scouted tournament of the summer. There are two prominent events Ethan hoped to play in – the Perfect Game National Individual Showcase in Minneapolis, in which 200 of the top players in the country are invited to attend, and the Tournament of Stars in Cary, North Carolina, the tournament that selects the Junior Olympic Team for that year.

In the qualifying tournament in Ft. Myers the team makes it all the way to the semi-finals before Ethan is called on to pitch. Ethan has never played on a team that is this good defensively. The middle infielders are graceful, polished and virtually error-proof. The outfield is unbelievably fast. There isn't a single boy out there who runs slower than 6.7 in the 60-yard dash.

Matt Gerber has saved Ethan for the semis because, he tells me, he wants a competitor to get us into the finals, and the game before we faced a team that was so bad we run ruled them in five innings. Ethan gets the first batter out, and then throws a mistake pitch over the plate to the second batter who crushes the ball. It shoots over the left field fence on a line in a millisecond. Ethan barely turns to look. He knows it's gone as soon as it's hit. And then he settles down. With the score 1-0 and Perfect Game scouts watching, Ethan proceeds to enter "the zone." He throws a complete game, allowing one other hit, striking out seven, and walking none. Over seven innings he throws 75 pitches, of which over 70% are strikes. In the seventh inning the Scorpions finally score twice, and Ethan walks away with the victory. It boggles the mind, in a way, to watch Ethan mow down a team loaded with some of the best hitters in the state, when he struggled to go four innings pitching for his high school team. His catcher calls the game. Ethan shakes off a few pitches, but they're in sync, in rhythm, and thoroughly confuse and demoralize the batters. In high school the hitters sat back and waited for Ethan's change-up, and hit it like they were sticking a fork into a meatball. Here it's less than 11 pitches an inning. There it was 75 pitches, sometimes in three. Here it's all praise and excitement. There he fought multiple battles on the field, in the dugout, against the competition and his own coach. What a difference it makes. Rob Haben, whose son Robbie plays third on the team, tells me he's glad Ethan was on the mound.

"That was really something," Rob tells me. "He was wheeling and dealing out there today."

The representatives from Perfect Game tell me if Ethan keeps this up he's sure to move higher in their rankings. When the rankings are revised later in June, he's dropped another 50 spots.

After a small tournament held at the University of Central Florida campus, the team travels to Minneapolis for a special four team round robin tournament played in the Metrodome. We've never seen the cavernous dome before. It's like walking into a concrete bunker when you look down to the bottom, a hot air balloon when you see the light, buoyed ceiling above.

We play host to a black kid from Philadelphia for the summer. Coach Gerber found Ricky Moses at the National Underclass Showcase in December. Ricky was blazing fast, and Gerb had visions of the fastest outfield in the nation. Pat and I agreed to house him, and when we pick him up from the airport I can only describe my first thoughts as, "What did we get into? This kid is so…ghetto." Big swagger, full of himself. All attitude. He wears his pants halfway down his ass with his boxers ballooning out. My first impression is completely wrong. Ricky turns out to be one of the nicest, easiest boys to play second parent to that I could ever imagine. I am Pops to him, and Pat is Mom. Helpful, easy, considerate, I ended the summer hoping Ethan had learned some lessons in kindness and generosity from him. And while he was fast, he had never played baseball at a level like the Scorpions. In Philadelphia, the fields had no fences, so when he approaches the wall in the Metrodome he stops, confused, not knowing what to do. He stares at the wall while the ball bounces beyond him. Then he wakes up, fields it, and proceeds to throw it in from right field, but not to the cutoff man. He thinks he'll throw out the runner going from second to third. Instead he watches the ball carry, carry, over the third baseman's head into the seats beyond third base. He tries to be the hero he was at home and gun the base runner down, which only leads to disastrous errors and more confusion. He runs fast, but he had a lot of ground to make up in his baseball education.

The Scorpions expect to be anchored by two all-star middle infielders, Nick Franklin (who is later drafted in the first round by the Seattle Mariners) and Nolan Fontana (who attends the University of Florida and, in his freshman year, starts at shortstop and makes a total of four errors during the entire season, which includes a trip to the College World Series in Omaha). Nolan travels with the team, but Nick drops off to focus on his own goals, and this causes a shuffle in the lineup. After Minneapolis, Nolan also falls by the wayside to concentrate on his recruitment. With the infield changing, Ricky in the outfield and erratic pitching, the four games become a comedy of mediocrity. The only game the team wins is the one Ethan pitches, another complete game in which he controls the opposition. His velocity starts at 87 and drops to barely 80, but he holds them at bay and gets the win. The Perfect Game reps there, preparing for the Individual Showcase the following week, give Ethan a late invite based on his performance. Ethan is tired and coming down with a cold, but he's got his first big wish of the summer, and we extend our stay another four days. Ricky goes back to our house, where he's hosted by my wife and daughter, and Ethan and I get a bigger dose of Minneapolis.

I am bored out of my mind. I'd expected to be in Minneapolis for four days, not eight. We've been living in a hotel near the Metrodome. Ethan barely ventures out with a massive head cold. I'm sick of the hotel's breakfasts. Enough with the made to order omelettes and tiny cereal boxes. For entertainment I walk the streets near the hotel and discover coffee shops and clothing sales. I am mesmerized by the heated walkways that connect the downtown buildings in response to the long, frigid winters, and wander them, figuring out how to get from one location to the other without ever setting foot on the ground. I pull him out of bed to go to the zoo one day, where we see wolves, elk, a northern lynx. I take the metro to the Mall of the Americas, the world's biggest mall, a sprawl of indoor mayhem, so many shops and restaurants I feel like I'm on a roller-coaster just walking around there, without ever getting on one of the mall's 25 rides. The mall is so big it has its own tourists. But I'm only a wanderer, a time killer, waiting for a reason to visit the Metrodome and watch someone from the Scorpions play.

The Perfect Game Individual Showcase is fascinating in and of itself. Nearly all the top 200 players are represented. The Scorpions have a half dozen boys there – Franklin, Fontana, Joe Lovecchio, now a 90 mph righty, Nate Gonzalez, a brick wall of a catcher, Zeke DeVoss, one of the fastest, smoothest outfielders in Florida.

One boy, Levon Washington, runs a 6.21 sixty-yard dash, the fastest time ever recorded at the event. There are so many right-handed pitchers who throw 90-92 mph that they seem cheap, commonplace – virtually all the 100 or so righties throw that fast, and most of the lefties as well. I learn a new term – JARP – just another righthanded pitcher. A handful throw in the mid to upper nineties, but Ethan quickly assesses himself against the throng and comes to the harsh realization that in this crowd he's at the bottom, not the top. At first base he is dwarfed by the other first basemen in attendance. At 6'2" he looks small and feeble. We hope he can pitch well, but even if he throws his hardest he probably won't seem like much to the hordes of scouts and college coaches in attendance. By both our accounts he's in the bottom 10% of the talent.

We run into the coaches from Virginia and South Carolina hobnobbing at an outdoor café. We see LSU, Clemson....heck, we see every school Ethan has an interest in represented. Ethan doesn't get to play first, but he is given an opportunity to hit, and when he does, as luck would have it, he's almost immediately plunked in the ass by a 92 mph fastball. He turns away from the pitch and it hits him smack in his right cheek. That's embarrassing enough, but Perfect Game decides to show the video again, over and over. Wherever I look as I walk the corridors of the Metrodome, I see Ethan getting hit in the ass, bending over in pain, rubbing the spot where he was hit. It's how he makes the tournament highlight reel.

When he pitches his allotted two innings, finally, he's running a fever. He can barely breathe. He's tired, congested, worn down, and it's only been three days since his complete game for the Scorps, but when he's told to throw, he throws. Pitchers face a maximum of five batters or three outs, whichever comes first. The first inning goes great. Ethan hits 86 and goes three up, three down including a strikeout of Max Stassi, one of the most feared hitters in the class, a catcher and later a first round pick. I suddenly have high hopes that, though he may not throw with the velocity of other pitchers, the scouts will see his competitiveness and pitchability, his ball movement and command.

The second inning doesn't go so well. He gets hit. They figure out his changeup, and it's five batters up with no outs this time. Whatever equity he built up the first inning disappears the second. But two good things come out of Minneapolis. First, he realizes, perhaps for the first time, that if he wants to be recognized and compete on a national stage with the best players, he's going to have to work harder. He sees what's out there, and knows he's the bottom of the best, not the middle, not near the top. At breakfast conversations with other ball players who are staying at our hotel, we hear about their long toss programs, their running and conditioning. "How far do you throw?" one boy will ask another. "350-375 feet," he answers. There's a belief among trainers and ball players that a 300-foot throw in the air equates to a 90 mph fastball. If you do a long toss program and get the ball that far, you should be able to throw 90. Ethan has never made a concerted, extended effort at long toss. These boys do it in their sleep. They eat it up like chocolate cake. They're so quick and strong Ethan feels like a peasant standing at the feet of Olympians. It's the most humbling experience he's ever had.

If he wants to go to a big-time college program, he has to ramp it up. He's not in as good a shape as he needs to be. He needs to get leaner, work on his footwork, and increase his pitching velocity. So far everything he's done has come with a good, but not a great work ethic. He knows know that it's time to take it up a notch. He makes an internal commitment to working harder than he ever has before, beginning with the end of the summer season.

And his second wish comes true. He's invited to attend the Tournament of Stars in Cary, NC. One of the teams needs a lefty, and he goes as a pure pitcher, not a hitter or first baseman. I change travel arrangements again. I fly home, but send Ethan off to the Raleigh-Durham airport where he'll be picked up and hosted by a local family for the tournament. Pat and I make plans to attend the latter half of the games during the weekend, and Ricky – poor Ricky – is left at our house to fend for himself, play pickup basketball games at our gym and some minor tournaments with the team in Central Florida.

In Cary, local families host the 250 or so boys who come in to try out for the Junior Olympic Tournament, which will be held in Edmonton, Canada at the end of the summer. Ethan gets to stay with a sweet family of five, with three children below the ages of nine. There are supposed to be two other players staying with him, but one has an injury and doesn't show up, and the other changes to another house to be with his friends. Ethan is in a house with three children who glom onto him like he is the next baseball god. At first it's pleasant, gratifying, even fulfilling, and he does his best to tell them baseball stories and talk sports and let them know what it's like to play in big tournaments. But they don't leave him alone, and when he's by himself, he has nothing to do, no one his own age to share anything with. He is all alone in a house of caring people whose children are, after the first day, driving him nuts.

The tournament is a big deal for the people of Cary. It's one of the major summer events, and the baseball field and facilities are out of the Field of Dreams. Picturesque. Manicured. Brilliant green against a pine country backdrop. The people who volunteer to host players and help put on the event put themselves into it wholeheartedly, to the point that the boys who stay with them become extended, adopted members of their family. That's the best part about the family watching over Ethan. He is their player, their only player. They go to his team's games to cheer him on. They're his biggest supporters, his only supporters at the tournament. We don't arrive until Thursday afternoon, and I had hoped that the schedule would work so we would see him pitch, but alas, he's scheduled to throw on Wednesday.

Against the top hitters in the nation, Ethan holds his own, tossing six hit ball over 4.2 scoreless innings and gets the win. He tops out at 86, which probably isn't going to get anyone's attention, but he hopes his effectiveness will catch some coaches' eyes. When he calls us up to tell us about it, he can't wait for us to arrive, not to see him play, particularly, but to take him with us into town to our hotel. We oblige him that, and during the next few days, while he recovers from child shock in his own hotel room on Franklin Street in downtown Chapel Hill, Pat and I explore the town, the university, visit Carrboro and the best food co-op we've shopped at since our college days, eat country cooking and imagine our son playing ball in Carolina sky blue uniforms. In our minds he's going to Carolina. In reality he never gets their attention.

He pitches once more as a closer, and throws another scoreless inning. He gives up a walk to the first batter he faces, speedster Levon Washington, always a threat to steal. Ethan lobs a ball over to first to keep Washington close, and hears him trash talk. "That pitcher's got nothing," Washington says. That is Ethan's fake pick-off, meant to lull the runner asleep, and it works. The next time he fakes Washington out of his cleats with a hard, perfect throw and picks him clean.

Even so, even with 5.2 innings of scoreless work, even with a pick of one of the fastest players in the nation, Ethan isn't one of the 34 players selected for consideration for the Junior Olympics team. Of the final 18 players selected, 10 had previous USA Baseball international experience – Harold Martinez, Ryan Weber, Matthew Purke and Jeff Malm were all bronze medal winners on the 18U team year at the Pan American Games, while Andrew Aplin, Colton Cain, Nolan Fontana, Nick Franklin, Austin Maddox and Max Stassi all competed for the 16U national team in Venezeula, winning the gold medal at the World Youth Championships. Both Nick Franklin and Nolan Fontana from the Scorpions make it without having stellar tournaments, but their lengthy resumes and reputations guide them in.

And the fact is, even though Nolan in particular had a terrible tournament batting, anyone who watched him knew what kind of player he was, and he goes on to have a spectacular showing at the

Junior Olympics. It points out the obvious: most of the team is pre-selected, and it's not about how well you play. More often it's about how well you're known, and, if you suddenly bust through with a 95 mph fastball, how hard you throw.

$$\bigcirc$$

Ethan has thrown four times in 12 days, hasn't been home in two weeks, and now we travel together from Raleigh to spend one night in our own beds before driving down to Miami, where Ethan is slotted to pitch at the University of Miami's baseball field as the starting pitcher in a tournament sponsored by the Florida Bombers, the Scorpion's counterpart showcase team in south Florida. He says he feels all right, but I have a gnawing feeling in my gut that tells me this is all wrong. Pitching five times in two weeks, one night at home and then driving four hours, stepping out of the car and walking onto the ball field to pitch. It doesn't add up to a good performance.

I can't blame the Scorpions coaches. If anything, I'm grateful to them. They know Miami is one of Ethan's top choices, and they're giving him the opportunity to show his stuff in front of the Miami coaches on their home field. It's exactly why we decided, several seasons ago, to throw our lot in with the Scorps, and they're coming through for us.

The Miami stadium is hot – furnace hot. The plastic seats absorb the summer heat, and I feel like my ass is getting fried through my pants. Even though Pat insists we all wear gobs of sunscreen, I'm baking, shriveling under the cloudless sky. She takes Jerica and Gabriel down to a shaded area on the third base side of the ballpark where there's a large camphor tree, picnic tables and benches. Gabriel's happy. He finds a stick to play a game of "Hit whatever's nearby" with, and Jerica just sits and suffers.

The stadium itself is in the beginning stages of a $14 million renovation. As we've entered the recruiting world, we've discovered that a whole new element has entered college baseball. With the advent of ESPN and more broadcast dollars, college baseball, for the first time ever, is becoming profitable, watched, even popular to a mass audience.

All the big programs in the country are renovating or expanding their facilities. South Carolina is building a $32 million stadium. LSU boasts the largest home audiences in the nation. UNC is renovating their historic Bokamper Field. And Miami convinced Alex Rodriguez, the great and infamous New York Yankee third baseman, to donate millions towards the new, expanded facilities – a new locker room, media room, more seating, a complete upgrade to a worn ballpark. I look out over the ball field and I have to say I'm not impressed. It feels like the sun has peeled back a layer of skin and exposed thin, raw dirt, washed out signs, weather beaten seats, dusty base paths. I know it's the middle of summer, but even so, this doesn't feel like one of the premiere programs in the country.

Then again, I know it is. Miami went in to the 2008 College World Series ranked #1 in the nation with a power hitting, pitching loaded team that had won more than 50 games. Even though it got knocked out of the tournament early, the "U" had as impressive a season as was possible, and it still managed to knock its great rival, Florida State, out of the tournament. And it had Jim Morris, the legendary coach who had won three national championships, one at Georgia Tech and two at Miami. Ethan's on the field warming up when I look up and see none other than Coach Morris take a seat across the aisle from me. I don't know whether I'm boldly stupid or stupidly bold, but I strike up a conversation with the famous coach.

"Great season, Coach Morris," I tell him. "It's a shame you lost early."

"Yessir," he says in his slow, low-key southern drawl. "Our bats just stopped working."

"My son's pitching today," I tell him.

"Hope he does well," Coach Morris says. "Our pitching coach is watching."

There, in the second row from the field, is the pitching coach and assistant head coach, J.D. Arteaga, another big lefty who, though not a hard thrower, holds the record for most wins in a career at Miami. His number 33 has been retired. As a coach he would be a perfect fit for Ethan – clever, not overpowering, a competitor who commanded the strike zone. Now it's up to E.

And he does terribly. Facing an 18-under team from North Carolina, he looks stiff and slow, uncomfortable on the mound. He never gets in rhythm. Each pitch looks like it's being delivered differently, with an ill-defined arm slot, a pushing motion instead of any loose, snapping fluidity. He has nothing going on. No velocity. No movement. Not much control. He's tired, wiped out. Think of every cliché you can, and that's Ethan on the mound that day. No gas in the tank. No reserves. He gets knocked around at the caprices of the other team. By the third inning the Scorpions are down by six and Coach Gerber pulls Ethan. Arteaga has left the field. Coach Morris turns to me and says, "Too bad for your boy that J.D. was watching." That's all he has to say. It's over for Ethan and Miami.

$$\mathcal{D}$$

The summer fills with small miracles and contradictions. On July 1st, the first day that colleges can directly contact boys in the class of 2009, Ethan gets a half dozen calls, including one from Miami. Coach Arteaga tells Ethan he's still being watched, that the Scorpions coaches assured him what he saw in Miami was an anomaly. He's made the list with South Carolina, Stetson, Ol' Miss, and Jacksonville. Scorpion players are on the phone, comparing notes, comparing who got how many calls from where. It's a defining day, a winnowing day, a day that clears a path for all these boys, letting them know exactly how the outside world views them, where they stand, where they'll likely end up playing in college.

This year we turn the Perfect Game Wood Bat National Championship Tournament into a family vacation. We caravan to Atlanta with Matt Gerber's wife Bethany and their two year old son. The team takes a circuitous route to the tournament, stopping first in Columbia, SC at the University of South Carolina for a pair of games. Ethan pitches again, in front of coaches from schools in North and South Carolina as well as the University of Virginia. He tells me he was throwing hard, and afterwards in his zeal he chased after the Virginia coach to ask if he saw and what he thought. Ethan is summarily chastised by Coach Gerber for being too anxious. "That's my job," he tells Ethan. "I talk to the coaches. You play baseball." It appears that the Virginia coach is put off by Ethan's approach. We never have any contact with them again.

Since we have to be there for a week anyway, we may as well make the best of it, and as it turns out, we end up as the official family chaperones for three other boys – Ricky Moses, Ethan's best friend Chris Quintero, and Kyle Andre, a quarterback and pitcher who has just come on the scene this summer. He's been a great addition to the

Scorpions, with a high 80s fastball and a good changeup and curveball. Instead of staying with the team, we opt for a more normal hotel – a Residence Inn where we have room to spread out, a pool to enjoy, and we're only ten minutes away from everyone else.

Nearly 200 teams are in attendance from across North America. The ball for the first game gets put in the hands of Joey Lovecchio. Ethan has known Joey for five years. They've played against each other, played with each other on the Florida Tars, and now are teammates once again. Joey is a pretty pitcher, a graceful pitcher who points his front foot elegantly when he throws, with long legs and a flat fastball. When he's on, he's very good. But when he leaves the fastball up he gets in trouble because it doesn't move. In the past he's shown glimmers of a plus changeup and curveball, but he's always gone back to trying to throw as hard as he can, with his father chattering away in his and everyone else's ears. Joey did well at the Individual Showcase, touching 92. I sat next to his father, Rick Lovecchio, when Joe pitched at the showcase, and Rick's comment to me, after I'd told him how well I thought Joe had done, was "If he'd only touched 93 that would have been icing on the cake." Rick has done something that I've wished I could do for years and never brought myself to do: schmooze with anyone who wants to talk about my son. Rick is the consummate marketer. He comments on every pitch Joey throws, talks to anyone who's interested, and has managed to make friends and inroads across the country. Rick may be a gadfly, but he's an effective gadfly, always getting Joey placed on excellent teams, always making sure Joey has a high profile with the right people in the right places. And Joey does his part by looking the part: a 6'1" athletic pitcher who throws in the 90s.

He and his dad are both enamored with velocity, and they're not off the mark. It's what seduces every major league scout, every big time college program out there. Forget the real mainstays of pitching: movement and location. For a right handed pitcher, all anyone wants to see is that he can throw hard, regardless of whether he's effective, whether he wins or loses, gets hit or commands the game. It's the old school philosophy of baseball that has yet to really change, and Rick has pushed Joey to throw hard and then harder still for years. Forget the fact that Joey has lost movement, lost the command he had when he threw in the mid to upper 80s. Everyone notices velocity.

At East Cobb he faces a high school team from Louisiana that won their state championship. Through five innings he has no hit them, but he's also walked five, and his fastball is up up up. They're just swinging at everything. He's also touched 93 a number of times. I think it's a mixed performance, but the scouts are impressed. Zeke DeVoss has a great game, making two fine plays in center field and going 2 for 2, hitting the ball hard both times. The Scorpions lead 2-0, but then, in the fifth inning, with runners on first and second for Louisiana, the skies break open and the rains come down. We try to wait it out, 20, 30 minutes, but the rain falls in relentless sheets. The fields flood, the game is called until the next morning, and we go back to our hotel to dry off.

The following morning the Scorpions proceed to lose the game. The first batter up is walked by James Mannara, a crafty, competitive lefty who has consistently given the Scorpions three or four quality innings with every outing. This time he gets taken long by a hitter who's committed to LSU. Suddenly the score is 4-2, and two innings later Louisiana wins 5-3, with Joey taking the loss.

Not that it really matters. The night before the Lovecchio's meet with Sal Lombardo, the head of the Scorpions organization, when J. D. Arteaga from the University of Miami calls. He offers Joey a scholarship rumored to be around 75%, a huge number for such an esteemed program. Rick hesitates. "Should we just take it, or should we shop around?" he asks Sal. "This is only the first offer Joe's gotten. Maybe he can do better."

Sal and Mat Gerber are quietly, politely stunned. Gerber chimes in. "Rick," he says, "Are you kidding me? Miami is Joe's dream school. It's his number one choice, and he's gotten a monster offer. How are you going to do any better? Take the offer." And Joey does, becoming the first Scorpion of the summer to sign with a Division 1 school.

Ethan gets to pitch the second game, in what should be a walkover against a 16-under local team. In front of more than 20 scouts from schools like Florida State, Miami, Vanderbilt, LSU, Tulane, he pitches one of his worst games ever. The catcher, Mike Russo, doesn't help. Russo tries to control the tempo of the game by slowing it down to a crawl, but everything begins to crawl. The time between pitches takes too long. Each at bat becomes interminable. Ethan talks to him to speed things up. He works better when the pace is fast, but Russo keeps it plodding along like a tortoise. The Scorpion coaches have been struggling with him. They've reminded him that it's about working with the pitcher to make the pitcher comfortable. The game is not about the catcher, but he hasn't caught on. It doesn't help that, for some reason, Ethan has no velocity. He's living around 80-82 mph. The scouts at the game turn their radar guns off by the second inning. They watch Ethan and Russo mishandle a bunt that stops between them. They see this young team score three runs in the first two innings against Ethan. In the third inning, Ethan finally forces the pace, pitches quicker, gets his arm going and touches 84, but that's as good as it gets. He's yanked before the fourth for Matt Zettler, a big strong righty who's been coming on all summer. Zettler doesn't allow another run, and the Scorpions come back to win the game. Zettler gets the win, Ethan the no-decision.

After the game Ethan is visibly upset. He knows he stunk. "Every school out there just wrote me off," he tells me, slamming his fist into a pine tree as we leave.

"That was your right fist, wasn't it?" I ask.

Ethan scowls at me. "Yes, dad, of course that was my right fist. Not that it matters anymore." He sighs, then says, "When I woke up this morning I raised my left arm above my head 'cause it felt stiff and my whole shoulder cracked and crackled and popped a bunch of times. It sounded like my spine was being cracked by a chiropractor, and afterwards my arm felt dead."

"Why didn't you tell anyone?" I ask.

"It was my time to pitch," is all he says before hopping in the car and slamming the door.

There's one more tournament in Ft. Myers, and then it's time to shut down for a month. Ethan gets no more calls from colleges. No one who's seen him shows any further interest. The topsy-turvy summer of high recruitment hopes and redemption after the loss of his junior year comes to a quiet, crashing close.

CHAPTER 11
Senior Year

Just a few weeks before school starts Ethan gets a call from one of his buddies on the Winter Park High baseball team. There's been a terrible accident. Nate Winters has been hit by a boat propeller. He's lost one of his legs and is being operated on. No one knows yet whether he'll live or die. Ethan doesn't stop to think about what he should do. He doesn't ask what other players are doing, if the family has asked people to wait, to stay away, or to come by. He doesn't consider the fact that he is not a current member of the baseball team. All he knows is that Nate is a friend and he ought to be there. He hops in his car and drives to the hospital. He is the first player to arrive. When Nate's dad, Dr. Tom Winters, walks into the waiting room, Ethan is the only boy there. They talk, and Winters leaves, and other players start to trickle in. The waiting area fills with people from all walks of life in Winter Park, including Bob King, who makes it a point to say hello to all his players, to shake hands, and to act like Ethan doesn't exist at all.

The Bichettes and Carters have transferred to Orangewood Christian Academy, a private school in Maitland, Florida with a young baseball coach who played at the University of North Carolina.

E makes good on his promise to himself. He puts together a regimen with the help of Coach Sal to retool his body and arm. He has ten weeks to change himself before the biggest, most highly scouted tournament of the year in Jupiter. That's what he's aiming for. That's what he works so hard for – to make new impressions during the fall, and secure a scholarship to a good school by signing day in November.

We await word from Orange County Public Schools about our request for a psychological transfer. We apply for it mid-summer, just in time to get an answer by the beginning of the new school year. It is supported by the Winter Park High School administration (so we're told), with supporting documents from a reputable local psychologist. While we are warned that the school board will not allow transfers based on problems with coaches, we believe that, given the far more serious problems Ethan had with his classmates the latter half of his junior year, he has a chance at getting his transfer approved, a chance to start over at a new school, and have a positive, uneventful senior year. We had tried, over the summer, to move him to any number of private schools, but because he is a senior none of the better preparatory schools will take him. They have rules against seniors transferring in and getting diplomas from their schools for one year of work. We can't send him to a Christian school because...well...we're Jewish. And it's too late to get him transferred to a magnet school, a school with a special course of study because he doesn't have time to take all the required courses. He's stuck.

His workout regimen includes treadmill work and four days a week with a trainer who works out of Lombardo's Next Level facility. He watches what he eats and drops down to 210 pounds. He also starts a long toss program for the first time in many years. At one point, when he was 12 and we had the pitching mound in front of our house, we had spray painted marks in the street every 60 feet, and he had gotten up to throwing 240 feet. I couldn't throw it back to him that far; I'd get the ball in the air about 150 feet and it would skitter and roll and bounce the rest of the way back to him. We couldn't move back any further because his throws started hitting the canopy of oaks hanging over the street.

This was a far more serious program, designed to strengthen his arm and get him back to 300 feet. He did it religiously, three times a week, and within a month was tossing the ball over his goal, beyond the 300 foot mark with relative ease. When Chip Gierke saw him do his long toss one day he shook his head with astonishment.

"That boy's gonna be throwing 90 this spring," he said to me.

When school starts E tells me he thinks he's in the best shape of his life. Even Coach Robison, passing him in the halls, notes how good he looks. We're still awaiting word from the school board, expecting it any day even as the first week of school comes and goes. It comes the next week. His transfer request is turned down. Ethan has no choice but to finish high school at Winter Park.

In a story posted in the June 9, 2010 sports section of the Orlando Sentinel, it was reported that "Austin Keel, a rising senior regarded as one of the top high school basketball shooters in Central Florida, said Wednesday he has transferred from Winter Springs to Class 6A state champion Winter Park.

Rumors of Keel's impending move have circulated since shortly after Winter Springs season ended with a regional quarterfinal loss to Winter Park.

"I want to win a state championship. I feel like this is the best opportunity for me," Keel said, adding that the resignation of Winter Springs coach Travis Jones factored into the decision. Keel, a 6-foot-3 guard, said he enrolled at Winter Park last week and planned to take part in the Wildcats' first summer practice on Wednesday."

On June 22 the fallout from the story began when the Sentinel followed its first post with a report on Orange County Public Schools investigation of the transfer.

"Predictably, it took about the time elapsed for a 30-second timeout for Orange County Public Schools to launch an investigation when stellar shooter Austin Keel said he wanted to win a state championship in a June 10 Sentinel story on his transfer from Winter Springs to Winter Park.

"Even before that story broke, there were questions in basketball circles about Keel's rumored relocation to the reigning Class 6A state champs as a senior. And since any mention of athletics by a transfer student raises red flags, the OCPS' office of pupil assignment is on the case.

"Until an eligibility determination is made, Keel has been barred from participating in team camps and practices with the Wildcats since taking part in an initial summer workout on June 9.

"Keel's father, Rick, said the family is answering all questions OCPS is asking. Mr. Keel said there are legitimate family reasons for his son to move into the Winter Park zone and switching schools. But he said he wants to give OCPS administrators time to sort through the case before he elaborates.

"Once Austin came out and told the world he wanted to win a state championship, this whole thing blew up and became a nightmare," Mr. Keel said. "That was an enthusiastic 18-year-old kid with a sports-related response because you are a sports writer. We understand the questions, and we understand Orange County Schools has to do its due diligence. That's OK."

Finally, on July 16, the Sentinel concluded their mini-series with a small paragraph inserted into a larger column about a variety of sports, in which they said that "Orange County Public Schools has cleared Winter Springs transfer Austin Keel to participate in interscholastic athletics for Winter Park, where he enrolled last month...

Keel's father said Austin is 18 and has his name on a lease agreement for a Winter Park home he is sharing with family friends."

Because he was of legal age entering his senior year and could sign legal documents for himself, the Keels managed to find a loophole, albeit an honest one, that allowed their son to move to the school of his choice simply by claiming that he was renting a room from family friends in the Winter Park school district. It doesn't matter if he lives there or not. It doesn't matter who he has dinner with every night. It doesn't matter if anyone tries to check bank records to see if Austin has, in fact, paid rent to his family friends for the room he rented. All that matters is that he got to transfer, and he may very well get his state championship.

Eligibility rules on the matter are clear if fudgeable. A family must reside in a public school district for their children to attend schools in that district. There are exceptions, however. If a child wishes to take and qualifies to take courses that are not offered at his or her high school, a specialization in law, for example, or engineering or the arts, or the highly touted international baccalaureate program in certain Orange County high schools, then a transfer no later than the junior year may be approved. If there are bona fide psychological grounds for a transfer – a death in the family that necessitates a change in environment, or a documented socially negative situation at the school that could seriously impact the student – then a transfer may also be allowed.

But to move to win a championship? To move to a better team or for a different coach? That, supposedly, is never allowed.

I am reminded of all the hoopla that surrounded LeBron James when he became a free agent and eventually joined the Miami Heat. In one of his many, many televised statements, he said that at this level of basketball, it's all about winning championships, and that's one of the big reasons he left Cleveland. But is that a good reason? Is that what we want to teach our children, that it's all about winning? Somehow the perspective has gotten skewed. As one of my own high school buddies once said in the most obvious and brilliant statements, winning's better than losing. There will always be great joy in winning, suffering in losing. But it's not everything. Winning ought to be a goal, not the goal in sports.

Imagine for a moment, a baseball game in which two exceptional teams play a tight, competitive game. The pitching is excellent, the defense exceptional, the hitting timely. All the plays that should be made are made. No errors are posted. In the last inning of the game, one team squeezes out the winning run. The pitch hit is an excellent pitch, the right pitch thrown to the right spot. It's just that the batter got his bat on the ball and manages to drive in a run. One team wins, the other loses. But if all the players on both teams played to the best of their abilities, perhaps even better, is one team a winner while the other becomes a loser? In my mind, the score, not the game, is the only indicator of a loss. I believe that a coach in that moment should congratulate his team for playing well, whichever side of the score they came out on. He or she should speak about the quality of play, the well executed game, and then move on. The coaches in that situation (and the players as well) who focus on the final score instead of the complete game miss the beauty and joy of competition, which takes place in a continuum of movement and thought and precision, not in the moment the last out occurs.

Wouldn't it be incredible if the goals in sports were reaching one's potential, helping a team become as good as it can possibly be, learning that the sum can be greater than the parts, discovering the euphoria of collaboration, teamwork, as well as posting a winning record? If all that matters is championships, then the vast majority of athletes are failures. And yet they're not. Participants in sports often look back at the time they spent competing for their club, their high school, their college as some of the finest, most quintessential moments of their lives. LeBron James was wrong. It's not all about winning championships. It's about the search for greatness within and creating the greater good amongst all. That's the lesson we need to impart to our children. That's how success can be judged, not by the final score but by the constant growth of the players and the team.

For years we heard about families who used the rental ploy to move their child to a different school with a winning sports program. They would rent an apartment or a house in the school district and claim it as their primary residence – for all of a year or two prior to moving back to their permanent home. Or they would file a notice of separation, claiming that there were marital problems, and one parent would rent an apartment in a school district while the other stayed at home. Miraculously, after the year or two of high school were up, they would reconcile and be back together in their original home.

This goes on all the time. It rarely gets contested, unless an Austin Keel says something that garners attention, or a student is so good or so reviled that a challenge to his eligibility is raised.

255

After everything that happened during Ethan's junior year, and because we didn't want to be deceitful or dishonest or manipulative, we decided to take the high road. We requested a transfer for Ethan his senior year, abiding by the process outlined by Orange County Public Schools. We had him psychologically evaluated, and we turned in all the documents the school system wanted, openly, on time, and without any strings pulled or influence pedaling. We didn't ask that he be transferred to Chip Gierke's school, his first choice, of course. Any other school would have been acceptable. And we were summarily turned down.

Something's wrong here. The school system allows people to shallowly bend the rules to get what they want, but people who try to do it "by the books," without the benefit of back door deals or transparent shams regarding their living situation, get slammed.

Now he's stuck and his desperation grows. While Scorpion players are signing with schools left and right, he's getting nowhere. No responses from anyone. No offers. It's as if he's being excluded from a select club. The big schools that were interested have all gone cold. South Carolina, Clemson, Virginia, LSU have signed other lefties, have told us no thanks, he's not what they're looking for, best of luck. One by one the boys he's played with are getting scholarships to good, sometimes great schools: Nate Gonzalez, the catcher, to Vanderbilt, Zeke DeVoss to Miami, Matt Zettler with offers to North Florida and the Air Force Academy, Nolan Fontana to Florida, Nick Franklin to Auburn, Robbie Haben to George Washington University. One by one they commit, a dozen or more, and Ethan's panic grows. Now I'm managing his time, helping him with his long toss and his workouts, and trying to keep a lid on his ever expanding anxiety. He can barely talk about college. Every conversation begins and ends with "What are we going to do?" He paces. He frets. I try to convince him that everything will work out. Everything will be all right. But that's not our history. Everything has not worked out all right. It's as if forces (and sometimes my and Ethan's actions) have conspired against us. Occasionally he blows up, ranting against Coach King, yelling about how life sucks, how he should have never gone to Winter Park, how we should have known, we should have let him go to Edgewater High School when he had the chance, how it's our fault, not his, that so much bad has happened. I do my best to take it, to remain stoic, quiet, to absorb the verbal punches, but there are times when I've had enough and I throw it back in his face, and that's what he wants, a reason to explode, a wall to hit, not a sponge, an excuse for his anger to escalate. We all live as if we're on the edge, a family teetering all because so much of our energy for so long has gone towards this moment, this time in Ethan's life, and it's crumbling. It's falling down and we have nowhere to go. E could be one of those players who falls through the cracks, who doesn't get picked up by anyone, who gets overlooked or ignored or cast out.

We're all worried. I talk with the Scorpions coaches regularly, and they're aware and working on possibilities, but so far nothing. All I can do is try to remain calm in contradistinction to Ethan's internal frenzy, his fear and rage. I train myself to stay quiet when he boils over. I speak slowly, in low tones to help him relax. I tell him over and over that it will be all right. There's all fall left. There's Jupiter coming up. The Scorpion coaches won't abandon him. But we get no phone calls, no more letters. It's as if the baseball world has moved on, and he's been left behind.

A scout from the St. Louis Cardinals asks if Sal can set up a special workout for some of the top players in Central Florida. Sal obliges, of course, and asks 25 players to show up for an afternoon of hitting and pitching. I find myself in the same category as Ethan. While parents mill around the bleachers, talking to one another, commenting on who's been invited, who's not there, I am summarily ignored as if I don't exist. It's a funny feeling, awkward and empty, to be watching my son compete as we both stand in vacuums, detached, not part of anything. Many boys wear their high school t-shirts. Ethan wears his Scorpions colors.

Nolan Fontana looks good hitting. So does Nick Franklin, and so does Ethan, who sprays line drives around the field. During the bullpen Ethan throws harder than anyone else there. Steve Ewing, a lefthanded pitcher from University High who has signed with Miami throws 87. Ethan throws 88. The Cardinals scout comes up to me afterwards and says, "I had your son down as a soft bodied kid, but it looks like he's changed. He's a hard body now." He gives me his business card and tells me he's going to keep an eye on E. It's the first good news I've had in a long time.

And then Vic Incinelli asks me one day over lunch if Ethan would consider the University of North Florida, the school where Vic's two oldest sons went and thrived. He tells me that the coach, Dusty Rhodes, is very "old school," but he's honest and straightforward and as good a baseball mind as there is in the country. Vic's son Matthew tells me that, even though he was a two time All-American and the winningest pitcher in UNF history, Coach Rhodes only complimented him once, in his senior year. That concerns me, but Matthew also says that Rhodes was the best coach he ever had, and I give Vic the green light to put in a good word for Ethan with the North Florida staff. Matt Gerber from the Scorpions follows up, and within a week the recruiting coach from the school is in contact with us. He watches Ethan during Scorpion tryouts that fall, and afterwards, we have lunch together.

"We're prepared to make you an offer," the UNF coach says almost as soon as we sit down.

Neither Ethan nor I are prepared for this.

"Really?" Ethan says. "OK. What is it?" He sits on the edge of his seat. I can see that's he's ready to jump at anything. I put my hand on his leg to slow him down, steady him, anything but have him jump and say yes.

"Thank you very much," I say. "That's a great compliment. We'd definitely be interested in talking."

"Talking?!" Ethan interjects. I squeeze his leg.

"I've spoken to Dusty, and so have a number of other people on your behalf." I know he's referring to both the Scorpion coaches and the Incinellis. "We'd be looking at you as a weekday starter right away. And I'd want your bat in the lineup too. You'd definitely get a chance to hit with us."

That's a plus. Most big schools want pitchers to be pitchers. The chances of Ethan doing both in college, I'd always told him, were slim and none. The offer, when presented, is more than fair. With other monies available through the State of Florida, Ethan's college education would be virtually paid for completely. The cost to North Florida: less than $6,000 per year, but they would be invested in him, and we're told Ethan would have the largest scholarship of any pitcher on their staff. I ask if it's all right for Ethan to visit the school first. We're assured it is, and the following weekend we drive up to Jacksonville to see the school and meet the coaches.

The University of North Florida touts itself as Florida's best education value. It is a new school, an expanding school, and its two big sports are baseball and basketball. There is no football team. The red brick buildings are built around your typical college green, and there's a pretty, northern-feeling wetlands with walkways running through it, a new, large, contemporary library, and construction everywhere. New buildings, new student recreation facilities, everywhere we look something new is going up. It's exciting. It also has a sense of becoming, rather than being established. We're told they're getting approval for a new baseball complex, but find out later that the funding has been delayed, if not turned down altogether. When asked about academic counseling and support, we're told that the best tutors the baseball players have are other, older ballplayers. Red flag number one. No organized academic support for athletes. When Ethan sits down for a private chat with Coach Rhodes, me and Pat by his side, the first words out of the coach's mouth are, "Normally I'd never consider a kid like you, but enough good people have vouched for you to convince me to take a chance." Red flag number two. I watch the color drain from Ethan's face. A kid like you. Coach Rhodes may be a great baseball mind, but he definitely comes from the old school of brutal honesty. He's Coach King with integrity and baseball smarts. He's of the grudging compliment, make 'em tough by riding them school of thought. I'm worried immediately. Ethan would have to give this man his respect, but I don't think they'd see eye to eye. I see another storm coming, only this is one I'd rather skirt around.

"Don't keep us waiting," the coach tells us. "The offer's on the table now, but it won't be for long."

When we leave that evening, smiling, shaking hands all around, none of us are excited. We decide to lay low for a little while longer and hope something else happens before Ethan has to commit. I'm not happy about the choice at all, and go back to discuss it with the Scorpion coaches.

"It's a good fit," Gerb tells me. "He'll be one of their top pitchers. And it's all we've got right now."

"I'm just not comfortable with it," I answer. "Isn't there anything else you can do? Can't you talk to any other schools again? How about Miami?"

"Miami? One of the best programs in the country? If he goes there he'll be at the bottom of the barrel. A little fish. Do you get what kind of pressure that is? He'll be competing with studs up and down the lineup. Stick with UNF."

"Call," I tell him. "Please. Make some more calls."

(D)

We catch Ethan one Friday night lying about where he's been. He gets home late, and I have my ways of finding out. A few text messages, a little cross referencing. Ethan's not where he said he'd be. It's not all that bad or unusual for a teen to tell his parents one thing and do another. I know that. I did it all the time when I was in high school, but we're trying to teach Ethan a simple rule. Tell the truth. It may hurt at first but the pain doesn't last nearly as long as lying. Plus, it's easier. It's hard to keep track of all the untruths, all the cover-ups, to piece them together and create a cohesive picture. And if there's one thing at which Ethan truly fails, it's cohesiveness. He leaves clues behind him wherever he goes. He tells a story and I could walk an elephant through the holes. I catch him when it matters, and when it doesn't, I'm still suspicious. Pat and I can tell the minor fibs from the majors. Sometimes we just bookmark them. Our antenna go up, but it's not worth the fuss or the fight. And sometimes, like that Friday night, it is. The consequence? The only thing that matters to him. No Scorpion baseball that weekend.

Ethan erupts. He tries to bowl us over with his anger. He screams at us about how life is unfair, how the Scorpions are counting on him, how we're hurting the team as much as him. He paces in circles. He slams his bedroom door. I catch him before he punches a hole in the drywall and send him outside.

"I'll call Gerb and tell him you won't be there." But when I get on the phone with Coach Gerber he tells me that, in fact, they really do need him that weekend. They're short pitchers and have him scheduled to throw on Sunday.

"Can I make a deal with you?" he asks. "You let Ethan play this weekend and I'll discipline him. He won't play on Saturday. Then he can pitch on Sunday. Or he can stay home. His choice."

Ethan chooses to have Gerb be the disciplinarian. The games are in Daytona Beach. Hot. No shade. Ethan's been told to wear his running shoes. "Ok," Gerb tells him. "There's a Burger King about a mile down the road. Bring me a packet of ketchup. You have 15 minutes." Ethan takes off and brings him a packet of ketchup. When he gets back the game is in progress. "Who wants a candy bar?" he asks the boys on the bench.

"I do!" James Mannara calls out.

"Ethan, run to 7-11 and get James a candy bar and bring me the receipt. Make it quick." Ethan runs the opposite direction, two miles down and two miles back to the nearest 7-11. He hands over a crumpled, sweaty receipt along with the melted Milky Way bar.

"Coach," Ethan says, panting. "If I run to the water tower...." He points to a water tower, shimmering in the heat in the distance.... "can we call it even?"

"Sure," Gerb replies. "Take a picture of the legs of the water tower with your cell phone camera. Close up. And you're done." Neither of them realize quite how far the water tower really is, but it's far – over three miles away. When Ethan gets back he collapses, falls on the ground, puts ice on his neck, and then pitches the next day with no legs beneath him, holding the junior college team he faces to three runs off an error, a walk, and a home run he gives up on a mistake pitch. Not bad, given the fact that he can barely move.

Ethan gets invited to the Florida Diamond Club Tournament, an individual showcase similar to Perfect Game's, but for Florida's top 200 players. He's invited as a pitcher only, but still gets to hit in batting practice. He's there with some of the other top lefties in the state: Brian Johnson, a 6'4" mammoth (who Ethan says is easy going and nice) who has committed to Florida, Patrick Schuster, another Florida commit, who throws four no-hitters in a row his senior season, Miami commit Ewing. In batting practice Ethan hits a half dozen home runs with a wood bat, including one that flies over the fence, over the batting cages behind the fence. Where other pitchers get two innings to showcase their stuff, Ethan only gets one, but he makes the most of it.

He pitches after Ewing, and while Steve does well, in his one inning of work Ethan does a smidge better. He works fast, looks aggressive, almost angry on the mound and throws 88. Of the five batters he faces, he strikes out three, gets one to ground out to third, and walks the other, though the umpire admits to him afterwards that he blew a pitch and the kid should have struck out. The recruiting coach for North Florida comes up to me, excited.

"Ethan did great today," he says. "We're all excited about him." I smile wanly. The hitting coach for Miami is watching too.

"Gerb's asked me to keep an eye on your boy," he says. "I'll tell J.D. how good he looked."

When we get home at the end of the weekend an email awaits us from UNF. Ethan's scholarship offer has been revoked, divided between two left handed pitchers. They'd waited as long as they could, and then moved on. Ethan flips out.

"What now, Dad?" he screams at me. "Where am I now? I've got nothing! I'm going nowhere! Call them and say yes. Get my scholarship back! I need a place to land!"

"E, be patient," I advise. "You're doing so well right now. You look good to everyone. Can you just hang in there a little while longer? You'll end up at a good school. I promise."

"Promise? You've promised a lot, Dad, but nothing's happened. You have no idea what I've been through! You have no idea what school's like. It's hell, Dad! Worse than hell!"

He's almost uncontrollable, pacing back and forth, his arms flailing, his temper escalating the more he talks. It's times like these when he punches holes in walls, throws whatever's in his hands, trying to find a way to release his unrestrained anger. I try to calm him down, put my hand on his shoulder, but he shrugs me off, the wild, irrational look in his eyes a combination of fear and rage.

"Call them!" he shouts at me. "Call the UNF coaches and tell them I commit! Ask them for my scholarship back! Please!"

I get on the phone and speak to their recruiting coordinator. Of course they still want him, but because they hadn't heard from us, they figured we weren't interested, and so gave Ethan's scholarship away. I chastise them for not getting in touch first, not giving us a chance to say yes or no, and the coach hears that, acknowledges that he could have made a call, and he'll see what he can do.

And as it turns out, within a week something breaks. After his official visit to the Air Force Academy, Matt Zettler gives them his commitment, opening his scholarship to UNF up for Ethan. It's a little smaller, but it's what E wants and needs right now: security, something solid and grounding under his feet. Ethan gives them his verbal commitment.

But I'm not done. There's a month before signing day in November, and I'm not convinced that North Florida and Coach Rhodes, as great a coach as he may be, are the best fit for E. Word is out that Ethan has committed, but I ask the Scorpions not to post anything on their website yet. Give it a little more time. Be patient. Wait until after the Jupiter tournament. Play this out until the very end.

◎

Jupiter. The tournament Ethan missed last year with a bad back. Pro scouts and college coaches cruise the dozen fields behind Roger Dean Stadium. Unlike the Perfect Game tournament in East Cobb during the summer, in which just about any team that signs up early enough can play, this tournament is by invitation only and is considered by many to be the top amateur baseball tournament in the world, consisting of 80 of the top elite travel teams from across the US, Canada, and Latin America.

In the first game the Scorpions play Gerber throws both Cole and Lovecchio, the two hardest throwing righties on the team. The area behind the home plate fence is ten feet deep with scouts, all with radar guns pointed at AJ. It looks like a gun range, or an invasion from outer space. Every time he throws a pitch, the guns jump into the air, point at him. Click click click. The triggers pull, the scouts look at the number, cock the guns to the side, whisper to one another. Every pitch it's the same thing, and AJ is doing his job with velocity. The problem is he's also getting hit. A single. A home run. Then he gets pissed, throws even harder and shuts them down. After facing his 95 mph stuff, Lovecchio comes in and his 92 mph fastball looks like a fat meatball. The other team tears him up. With the loss the Scorpions are almost assured of being out of the tournament after the first game.

Ethan pitches the second game the next day. The pitching coach from North Florida is there, and I make small talk with him. It's the first time he's seen Ethan pitch. He watches for two innings then moves on.

"Tell Ethan nice job today," he says.

J.D. Arteaga watches as well. Ethan's not throwing his hardest, living 84-86 mph, but he's got his off speed pitches working and the other team is off balance. He throws a changeup, a slurve, a two seam that tails away like a cut fastball.

"He had a rough summer, didn't he?" Arteaga says as I sidle up beside him.

"Yes he did. He realized he had a lot of work to do. But he's worked hard."

"I've heard about how he's done. I'll tell you right now, Mr. Bornstein, if he throws like that he could be successful with us."

My heart skips a beat. I know I have to tell him the whole story. "He's verballed with North Florida, Coach, but…"

Arteaga cuts me off. "That's too bad. We can stop talking right now. We're friends with Dusty. We won't do anything to interfere if Ethan's made a commitment."

Am I hearing this right? If Ethan's made a commitment? What if he hasn't? Would the door be open then? Would Miami, Ethan's number one choice, the school that comes up in the Princeton Review as the best fit for Ethan nationally, be interested in him? Or would I be walking through a field of land mines once again, blowing it with the one school that's offered him a scholarship to go off chasing a dream? Is it worth it to take the risk, try to finagle something and possibly screw everything up once again, with Ethan in a state of sheer panic, and it all be my fault? I have to think about this. I have to powwow with my son. I have to talk to the Scorpion coaches. I have to keep my shit together.

Just then I overhear one of the Scorpion's assistant coaches talking on the phone to Sal, who's coaching another Scorpion team on a different field. I listen to him as I watch the play on the field unfold.

"Yeah….we're up 4-0….Ethan's cruising….they can't touch him….he's got it all under control…..he just struck the batter out. Russo (the catcher) dropped the pitch. The runner's going to first. No problem. He's slow as hell. Wait a second…..Russo overthrew first….the ball's in right field. Wait a second….the ball went through Dore's (the right fielder) legs. He's throwing it in to second…he's overthrown second… Russo's got the ball….he overthrows third…the runner's rounding third….the throw to home's overthrown."

Ethan stands on the mound, dumbfounded, his arms by his sides, spinning around like a carousel horse, his head following the ball as it careens around the field. I can hear Sal on the other end of the phone. "What? ARE YOU KIDDING ME?"

Thankfully, Arteaga leaves as the play begins. It wouldn't matter anyway. It's not Ethan's fault. It's just his luck. Ethan gets taken out after that inning. Everyone's seen enough, and the Scorps go on to win 4-2. Ethan becomes the talk of the tournament for a reason no one would ever expect, the only in the park home run off a strikeout anyone has ever seen.

On the way home we talk. And talk. And go back and forth, weighing and balancing the pros and cons of going to North Florida or decommitting and taking the chance that Miami will come through. As Pat and I chime in, it's clear that our choice is Miami. Not only has it always been one of his dream schools, it's probably the best academic school he could hope to get into. It's not that Ethan's a bad student, but the years of sliding, of settling for Bs and Cs have caught up to him. We had always hoped baseball would get him into a better school than his grades would allow, and now the opportunity sits before him, if he'll take the chance. We nudge. We cajole. Ethan is scared.

"I won't have anything again," he says.

"Not for a little while," I tell him.

"What if they don't come through?"

"That's the chance you'd have to take. Where do you think you'd fit in better?"

"Miami."

"You know you'd have to work your way up. You'd be in the middle or bottom of the pack there, not the top like you would at UNF."

"I know. I've done that all my life."

"Are you ready for the challenge? Is this what you really want?"

"I don't know, Dad. What do you think, Mom?"

Pat sits quietly for a moment, then speaks her truth, as she always does. "I think you should listen to your heart and do what it tells you to."

"All right then. Miami. It's my dream. But dad," he says to me, "will you make the call to the UNF coaches to tell them?"

When we get home I spend the next hour getting thoroughly reamed out by the recruiting coach at UNF. It's worse than a colonoscopy. It feels like I'm confessing to adultery. I've sinned. I'm unfaithful. I got on their case for giving Ethan's scholarship away without calling us, and now I'm stabbing them in the back. They were warned about me. I'm a bad guy. I'm not a man of my word. They should have known better. Now they believe everything they heard and me and E. Every rumor, every innuendo. They're all true. Don't ever talk to them again. They're better off not having us as part of the UNF family. This is something we should never live down.

I take it on the chin. I listen and apologize, and in the back of my mind I'm thinking, "This is bullshit. It's not the best situation, and it's certainly not the way I wanted it to go, but kids decommit on a regular basis. And we're doing it praying that another school - the dream school - comes through."

The previous year Ben McMahon, a Scorpion catcher, decommitted from Arkansas when the University of Florida coaches saw him hit a grand slam and catch consecutive games at the Jupiter tournament. Florida was his dream school. And it goes the other way, too. After AC Carter commits to Boston College, the coaches there leave for Notre Dame. The new coaches at Boston College make it clear that they are not invested in him, and don't believe he will ever be the kind of catcher they want. They encourage him to decommit, and AC gets a scholarship from the coaches who originally recruited him and heads to Notre Dame.

Then I get on the phone to Miami, and Arteaga gives me the good news and the bad. Assuming that Ethan's decommitted, and he has to confirm this and make sure the North Florida coaches know he had nothing to do with it and had promised nothing to Ethan prior to, then yes there's a place for Ethan on the Miami baseball team. He's the kind of pitcher Arteaga likes – a crafty lefty with lots of movement.

Now for the bad news. It's late in the recruiting season and they have no money left. No scholarships to give. If Ethan wants to come there he can – as a preferred walk-on. He'll be on the team like any other player. The only difference is that he won't be on scholarship.

The one thing we never expected has begun to unfold. Ethan can go to Miami, an excellent private school with a great baseball program, but to do so will cost us double every penny we've saved for his college education. And there are other concerns as well. The school won't have the same investment in him that they have in other players. While we are assured this won't matter in the coaches' eyes, that they'll play the players who perform the best, I can't help but think that Joey Lovecchio, with a huge scholarship propping him up, and even Steven Ewing, with a normal one, will get more serious consideration than Ethan. It'll be much easier to let E go if he makes a mistake, and history has taught me that Ethan makes mistakes, leaves a trail, gets caught, and pays the consequences more than anyone else. Ethan says yes, please, let him go, and after absorbing the shock of the cost, and looking at all the options, and explaining my fears and concerns, we say yes as well.

Now there's only one other decision Ethan has to make, one last call before he concludes high school and moves on to college: does he want to try out for the Winter Park baseball team one last time? It means playing for Coach King. It means working under his system, accepting his rules, doing whatever he says, biting your tongue and fitting in, and Ethan says yes, it's what he wants, not because he wants to play for King, but because he wants to play with his friends, with Q and Modomo and the other boys on the team one last time. He wants to make amends. He wants to show everyone that he's a good guy and not a problem, not a troublemaker. He wants a second chance.

I can't say no to that. I was taught by my father that everyone deserves a second chance. Not a third, necessarily, nor a blank check. What is done can't be undone, and what is said can't be taken back. As Jews, as human beings, we bear the burden of our actions, we live by what we do, but we all make mistakes, and thus deserve a shot at redemption. I want Ethan to have that shot. I hope Coach King will take advantage of it as well, and redeem himself in the eyes of all those who thought he treated Ethan too harshly.

What lessons can we teach our children that are any less important? Judaism teaches that who we are is defined, not by what we say, but by what we do here on this earth in this life, that we are held accountable for our deeds and must act accordingly. We are caring because we care for others as well as ourselves. We are loving not because we say, "I love you," but because we act in loving ways towards our spouses, our children, our world. We are moral because we live moral lives. We are good because we do good. It all comes down to what can't be undone – our actions that define us and give us shape and substance.

An act of redemption heals the soul. There may be no better way to repair the internal wounds of doubt, grief, shame, and personal contempt than by doing right with a second chance. It creates a bridge between the one who was wronged and the one who did wrong. It opens the door for discussion. It rebuilds friendships. While it can't revise history, it does add positive building blocks to what is often a stand alone negative incident that then infects opinions and distorts all perception regarding who a person really is.

I've often told Ethan that, besides the difficulty in tracking lies, in maintaining a story built on falsehoods, that each lie tears down trust. The truth, like redemptive acts, rebuilds trust. With each truth a foundation of trust and respect gets rebuilt, while one little lie tears it all down in an instant. A second chance made good does the same as building a tower of truth: it engenders respect and belief in the integrity of the individual. It blesses both parties: the redeemer and the redeemed. It teaches contrition and forgiveness. It builds internal resolve and a generous sort of kindness. It binds people together permanently, and it allows them to part peacefully. It changes individuals on the most basic levels, both in their attitudes towards themselves and the world's view of them. That's why it's so valuable, and why I so hoped that both Bob King and Ethan would find their way to try again.

When an employee is late for a meeting the first time, I watch to see what happens next. I tell them not to be late again, and if they are, I know I have a problem. If they show up ten minutes early the next time, I know I have someone special working for me, someone who listens, adapts, does the right thing. I put the first incident in the forgiven pile and the second good showing gets asterisked with "Redeemed." This is someone who has shown me they want to do well and are willing to work to prove it.

There is no question in my mind, as I look back on all that happened in that brief six week period of time during Ethan's junior year, that the acts of many people were wrong, ill-advised, self-serving, fearful, vengeful, manipulative, that many people were pushed into doing and saying regrettable things, and even now, years later, I look back on that time with shame, embarrassment, and pain. I can't forget what happened, and forgiveness comes with great difficulty. But I can give all those involved a second chance. I can believe in the ability of the human spirit to learn and grow, to right itself after doing wrong, to come to terms with the lack of generosity, compassion, and understanding through remorse, acceptance and a commitment to doing better the next time. That is how we teach our children about right and wrong. If they never had a second chance I doubt we'd ever let them out of the house to experience the complexities of a fractured, incomplete world with a moral compass that often spins more than settles.

I realized that it was important to me to see Ethan back in that troubled, dangerous situation on a number of different levels: to see if he could make a difficult scenario work, to see if he could humble himself enough to fit into someone else's world if it was important enough to him, even if it was uncomfortable for him, to see if he could control himself and let the world see who he really was under the "bravado" jock exterior – a kid who'd been hurt, a kid who'd worked hard and wanted nothing more than a chance to prove himself again.

In November I write Heather Hilton, the assistant principal in charge of Ethan's case, and tell her that Ethan has officially signed to play baseball at the University of Miami, and that it's his intention to try out for the Winter Park baseball team in the spring. I ask her to help make this move easier by talking to Coach King to see if he is willing to take Ethan back. I let her know that my hope is that he will be fair in his assessments of players, not hold unfair grudges, and give Ethan a second chance. She assures me that every year kids start with a clean slate. That's how it must be. That's how Coach King must be. Ethan's slate, she promises, is perfectly clean on a going forward basis.

She sends me the following email:

November 10

Mr. and Mrs. Bornstein,

I want you to know that we are making good progress here towards Ethan's participation in spring baseball. Mr. Gordon and I will be speaking with Coach King this week again, and I will be able to better update you at that time. Congrats to Ethan on signing! What an exciting year.

I appreciate your patience through this and providing me the time to aid in this situation.

Sincerely,
Heather Hilton, Assistant Principal

Before Thanksgiving King holds a meeting for players who plan to try out in the spring. Since Ethan has been working out on his own and avoided all team workouts in the fall, I encourage him to attend. Afterwards, he says most of what was discussed was how the team would be picked this year.

"Coach King said he's not going to have distractions this year or necessarily pick the best 15-18 players but is going to pick the players who will make the best team," he tells me. "He was looking right at me when he said it."

"Ok, maybe he was and maybe he wasn't. But you have to promise me one thing, E." He looks at me, eyes wide open, and nods his head. "You can't screw up at all if you're going to go out. They'll look for any reason to cut you. If you really want this, it's got to be all yes sirs and no sirs and you do everything they tell you. Understand?"

"Yessir," he says. I hope he means it.

I'm also hoping that just a little of what Ethan heard is tainted by his own fears and feelings towards King. I'm hoping King wasn't already sending a message. Ethan and I plan to go to Miami for Senior Scout Day just before Thanksgiving, but before we go I send Ms. Hilton this email, and her response follows.

November 21

Just emailing to see if you've got an update for us. We're heading to Miami today to meet the coaches, and will discuss with them the situation for next year. Any light you can shed will be most appreciated.

Best wishes and happy Thanksgiving,
David Bornstein

Mr. Bornstein,

I am glad to hear that you attended the meeting last night. We have been trying to meet with Mr. Gordon and each time it has been cancelled due to a variety of reasons. We will be meeting in December, but we are expecting Ethan to try out for the baseball team. I continue to work with Coach King to pave the way for a successful season. Best of Luck with Miami! You will love the campus!

Heather Hilton
Assistant Principal

It is the first day of spring tryouts. I go to the ballfield early, hoping to run into Coach King to talk to him personally before boys arrive. I see him beside his white pickup truck, unloading supplies for the concession stand. I walk over and offer to help.

"Whasssss-up?" he asks me in his extended drawl, looking askance in my direction. I can see the suspicion deeply etched in his face, but I ignore it.

"Can I give you a hand?" I ask.

"No, I've got it. What can I do for you, Mr. Bornstein?"

But before I can say anything, he launches into a disparaging monologue. "Just want you to know that Ethan's already started off badly. He picked up his fund raising cards late and got his physical in a day late. That's not showing senior leadership."

Both had been talked about at the pre-Thanksgiving meeting Ethan attended, and both had been instantly forgotten by Ethan. I managed to help him get his physical taken care of and turned in just a day late, and he had already sold half the discount cards the team used for fund raising by the time I ran into King. Other boys picked up the cards late and turned their physicals in late as well, but that didn't seem to matter. It was all about Ethan.

"I'm sorry," I said. "I don't think it's such a big thing...."

"Maybe not to you," he replies.

After this run in, I meet with Heather Hilton the next day, and she promises me that she and Principal Gordon have reached an understanding with Coach King that he must use purely objective standards to select the team this year, and that they must be applied across the board. Ok, I tell myself, if that's the case and the administration supports that I'll go along. Minor infractions like turning in his physical a day late won't count against him.

During the next week of tryouts Ethan shines. He throws seven no-hit innings against his teammates, bats .570 and hits a home run off Chad Modomo, the other top pitcher on the team. Ethan plays well at first base. I make sure I'm present during all the practices and scrimmages, just to keep my eye on Ethan. I want to make sure if anything happens I'm there to witness it, and as far as I can tell, there are no incidents, no behavior issues. If anything, Ethan is helpful, friendly, chatty with his teammates. He runs on and off the field. He helps batters with their form in the different batting stations. He slides hard into home when he has the chance during one of the practice games. He appears to be giving a good, hard, honest effort at everything he does. No reprimands come from the coaches. No harsh words are spoken. I have my Stealth radar gun out during the scrimmages, and Ethan is living at 86 while Chad tops out at 84. Neither are overwhelming, but both are pitching well. After the week goes by Coach Rob approaches Ethan, somewhat wistfully, it seems, and tells him he did really well, that he had a great week on the field. Even so, Ethan warns me that he did screw up.

"I wanted to take some extra swings in the cages and Coach King got on me for not moving on to the next station."

My frustration boils to the surface. It's tough to get on a kid for wanting to work harder and get better, but in this case Ethan knew he had to be the good soldier, the sheep following the leader, and he wasn't. Even though his intentions as a ball player were good, he went his own way and King called him on it right away.

"Ethan," I whine, "Can't you keep a low profile for once? Just for a little while?"

"I'm sorry, Dad." Mumble mumble. He hangs his head like a whipped dog.

"I told you you couldn't do anything like that. I guarantee you King is going to use that against you. This could come back to haunt you."

"I know, dad." Mumble mumble. "I'm sorry."

But it's a small infraction with no harm done and good intent behind it. I cross my fingers that King, in a redemptive mode, will look at it the same way.

That Saturday night the list of Varsity players is posted on a door at the back of the school. Pat and I are out to dinner when Ethan calls.

"I didn't make it, dad."

"What? You're joking, right?" I don't understand. I hear the words, but they could be Mandarin Chinese. They make no sense. He must be kidding.

"No dad, I got cut. I didn't make the team."

Another player, Michael Pietkiewicz, stands with Ethan reading the list. Michael has been hurt all spring with a shoulder injury. He hasn't been on the field to play. He makes the team.

"Gee, Bornstein," he says. "It sucks being you."

The next day Pat and I make an appointment to see Principal Gordon and Ms. Hilton.

It would be easy enough to say that Ethan wanted to go to a different school just because the situation with Coach King had deteriorated, that it was all about a coaching problem and thus should be denied. But in this case the situation had deteriorated to such a degree that it was bad for both of them. And in this case, after being dismissed from the team, after being publicly humiliated by becoming known as a pothead, after becoming a pariah because he "snitched" on friends, and after being forced to deal with an impossible situation on a daily basis without the support and fun of the sport he loved, Orange County Public Schools said suck it up and go back there. Go ahead and take whatever your senior year serves you on your chin. Go ahead and suffer the consequences of another season in the same situation with a coach who viscerally hates you, and who you hate as well. Why? Because you were honest enough to tell us it all started with baseball. Because you were told by your county's school system and your school's administration that you would be treated fairly and that you would be all right. And what happened? You got cut from your high school baseball team your senior year without any support from your school's administration, though they promised otherwise, losing something you will never get back. Friendships. Memories. Redemption. A second chance.

Something needs to change. Something needs to be done. What's lacking here is the school system's awareness that, for some students, sports is a college track, and perhaps, a career track as well. If that's the case, and there are grounds for a change, allow the change. For the student athlete who wants to make a move to win a championship, tell them sorry, go to a private school of your choice, but we're not a self-serving institution that bases its decisions on personal gain, but rather on the personal welfare of our wards.

Instead, the way it stands today, anyone with parents willing to lie, anyone who is over 18, anyone who doesn't mind working the system can beat the system. The ones who get shunted aside, the ones who are abandoned, the ones who get hurt by the rules are the ones who try to abide by them. What's wrong with that picture?

School systems should insist on a single primary residence, validated by the state's homestead laws. If a rental situation is approved, the school in question needs to be aware that if the family moves back to its previous residence within a year from the student's graduation, all games the student played in will be forfeited. Parents who are legally separated will not be allowed to use that as a vehicle to move a child to another school. Only finalized divorces will justify a child's change of address, unless a judge or certified therapist swears that the move is necessary for the child's well-being. In the event a student has suffered actual hardship in a sports related scenario at his or her high school, the case will be reviewed on an individual basis in an open setting by a group of teachers and administrators with testimony from all sides. That's my recommendation, but to date only deaf ears have heard it.

♪

I am told by the school administration that we need to meet with Coach King first. He came up with an approved list of "objective criteria." These criteria included coachability, work ethic, and attitude towards the team, all of which, sadly, are subjective criteria based on the coaches' opinions. But when I hear them, I think to myself, "All right, Ethan should have been ok. He's coachable, has always had a strong work ethic, and the boys on the team like him with a few exceptions. Even after the incident last year he seems to have mended fences and reestablished relationships with all but a few of the players."

But when Pat and I sit down with King and Robison in the baseball locker room it's a different story. Pat and I face the two coaches, whose backs are against the lockers. I take a quick backwards glance to the door, remembering the last time I was here when the meeting ended in a shouting match between Dante Bichette and Coach King.

"We evaluated all the players based on a set of objective standards," King begins, "because the school told me that's what I had to do this year so there'd be no questions about any of my decisions. Ethan graded out high on all aspects of baseball – hitting, throwing, fielding. Low on athleticism. But he started off badly by turning in his physical forms late and missing the deadline for getting the coupon books for our fund raising."

"He wasn't the only one…"I say, but King talks over me.

"He was the only one who missed both. And then in the batting cages I'd see him standing around talking….a lot….to other players. And I had to tell him to get out of the cages and move to the next station."

"He was just getting in some extra swings…" I interject.

King cuts me off again. "He was supposed to move on and he was disregarding his instructions. He was already being a distraction to the team, and he was proving that he was not coachable. I discussed this with the other coaches."

"And you all decided to cut him because he handed in forms a day late, picked up fund raising coupons late, and took extra swings in the batting cages."

Coach Rob nods his head, though I can see him hesitate as he does so.

"Ethan does whatever he wants," King said, his voice rising. "He showed no senior leadership. He set a bad example for the younger players. I said this year there would be no distractions. I said I'd pick the players who make the best team, not necessarily the best 15 or 20 players."

"So you're cutting him for three small infractions, two of which had nothing to do with his performance during tryouts."

Pat puts her hand on my leg to calm me down. She can see that I'm irritated, short-tempered.

"They had everything to do with his attitude!" King's voice begins to rise.

"Can we back up a minute to how he did on the field. If you're using objective standards I saw him getting along with all the boys…"

"That's your opinion."

"And when he pitched he was throwing 86 and Chad was topping out at 84…."

At this King erupts. "That's the problem right there!" he screams. "It's people like you with your daddy guns who are the problem! I have our radar gun calibrated every year and if Ethan was throwing 86 Chad was throwing 95! There's no way he threw harder than Modomo! You and your fancy equipment, thinking you know better than anyone! You're the cause of all the problems we've had the past couple years!"

"My gun's a daddy gun?" I shout back. "Yours is held together with rubber bands and baling wire! I'm not the problem. It's guys like you, coaches like you who can't deal with kids who are a little different! All Ethan wants is a chance to play and you're getting your revenge this way!"

Pat takes me by the arm and starts to pull me outside. "David, there's no point getting mad. It won't change anything," she whispers to me.

"I can see this is going nowhere," I shout back to the coaches. "We're done here!"

King's back is already turned to me. Pat pulls me into the parking lot and tells me to be quiet. She doesn't want me to embarrass myself any further. I'm still ranting, as enraged as if someone tripped me or poked me in the eye. And I'm equally mad at myself, for falling into the ugly pit of senseless anger that King made surface so easily.

Later, I regret everything about that meeting – that I lost my cool, that it ended in a shouting match much like King and Bichette, that no one listened, that there was no attempt to come to any sort of mutual understanding. But what I regret most to this day is that I never asked Bob King a simple question: why couldn't you give Ethan a second chance? You were the adult. Ethan was the child. Why couldn't you take this opportunity and perform an act of redemption for both of you? Why couldn't you give yourself the chance to show the world you weren't unfair, unreasonable, unforgiving, that you in fact were a generous man willing to give a difficult kid a take two? And at the same time, you would have given Ethan a chance to redeem himself. But maybe that's what you couldn't live with, Bob. Maybe you couldn't live with Ethan doing well, with Ethan having the experience of a successful senior year. Maybe you couldn't accept the possibility that, along with you, Ethan might also find atonement, might discover some bit of salvation from the unfair opinions of a judgmental world.

The radar gun Coach King referred to, the one he used, was an old Jugs gun that had been malfunctioning all during the tryouts. It didn't register any throw over 81 mph. In fact, almost every boy on the team was throwing 81 mph. The radar gun I used, the Stealth Sport gun, is the same radar gun used by policemen all across the country, and is accurate to within 3/10 of a mph. I wasn't trying to upstage King. I wanted to make the point that Ethan had a good tryout, like Coach Robison said. Instead I got a new name for my radar gun, which I inscribed with a Sharpie. My radar gun became The Daddy Gun. It was the last useful tidbit of information Bob King ever gave me.

A few days later we have an equally counter-productive meeting with Principal Gordon and Assistant Principal Hilton. Pat and I bring our notes, all the points we want to make, but they get shuffled under the hubris of Gordon's abiding principle of school administration: don't interfere with a coach's decisions regarding players. They asked King to set up standards. He did so. He made cuts on that basis.

That was all there was to it. As far as they were concerned, the issues King cited were enough to cut Ethan, regardless of the fact that other boys did the same things, that there were other discipline issues during tryouts that resulted in nothing. I talk for a half-hour. It goes nowhere. They've already made up their minds to stand behind their coach. Ethan's time is over. It is time for all of us to move on.

I emailed them a letter after our meeting, in which I said:

"Ethan is one of the lucky few. Because of his athletic ability and the support of the coaches on his showcase team and many other people who have vouched for his good behavior and integrity, he is going to a great university with an outstanding baseball program – despite being cut from his high school baseball team his senior year.

The student athletes who are at risk are those who need a coach to be their advocate, to help place them in a college program. Mr. King fails to do the two crucial tasks I believe are mandated for every public servant who works in the school system: to help students reach their potential, and to assist in giving them an opportunity to receive a degree from an institution of higher learning.

I realize now that it would not have been possible for Mr. King to watch Ethan have a successful season. While we were prepared to move on and put last year behind us, it is obvious that he could not. On that basis, the appropriate course of action would have been for Mr. King to tell you, or Ethan, that Ethan shouldn't even bother trying out, because he would not be allowed to play on the team. You could then have helped us place Ethan in some other program or some other school. That would have at least been understandable. Instead, Ethan was encouraged to try out, and he and he alone suffered the consequences – the loss of his senior baseball season and a measure of his dignity and self-esteem.

Ethan lost a chance to prove that he had learned from his mistakes. He lost the opportunity to play with his best friends. And he lost experiences that could have provided a lifetime of irreplaceable moments and memories. What your baseball program has lost is a level of integrity that may take years to repair, if it ever occurs under the current coaching regime.

I am personally sorry for all that happened. It was never our intent to have Mr. King reported to the Department of Children and Families. We should have never sent our concerns in an email as your Athletic Director requested and should have insisted on face-to-face meetings. At least then there could have been open communication rather than the breakdown we all painstakingly endured.

At some point it is my hope that you will hold your coaches to the same high standards you apply to your students. In fact, I would encourage you to establish a code of ethical standards for your coaches, standards that could be applied across the board, objectively and fairly. Ethan is moving on to a better situation, and for that our family is truly grateful. However you choose to do so, make the situation better for future student athletes at Winter Park High School."

Every year there are baseball players who stay away from Winter Park High School because of King, parents who have told me their children are going to different schools because of the coaching, but the school will never know. Their absence will never register or make a single dent in the structure of the school or athletic program, because those players will be ghosts. They will have never appeared on the scene.

At the end of school, during the graduation ceremony for Ethan's class held at the University of Central Florida's basketball arena, Principal Bill Gordon at one point asked every student who had participated in high school athletics to rise. Hundreds of students, wearing their tassled hats and robes, rose in acknowledgement of their involvement in athletics. I had spotted Ethan in the huge crowd at the beginning of the ceremony, and he remained seated. He looked up at me and shrugged his shoulders. I could see the scars of pain and regret etched deeply into his stiff half-smile.

As far as I know Ethan is the only player in the history of the University of Miami's baseball program to get cut during tryouts his senior year and still land a spot on their team. When we met with Coach Morris during Ethan's official visit in the spring, while baseball was going on everywhere around the country, his only words to us were, "I just don't understand what happened to you in high school. But we're glad to have you. We feel like we got a steal with you."

Ethan still resents the loss of his senior year. He resents being forced by me and others to name names, to squeal on friends he subsequently lost forever. Ethan could have paid for his actions in Sarasota, learned his lesson and been done, but his punishment was multiplied immeasurably. No one experienced any further consequences anyone except him.

Both Ethan and his coaches had lessons to learn and changes to make in their behaviors. And so did I. Perhaps the great lesson here is that no matter what your station in life, learning is never over, and sometimes we have a lot farther to go than we ever would have imagined. Sometimes life isn't fair. It doesn't matter how talented you are, how in the right you are, you still may not get what you want or what you deserve. As an adult and a parent I have had to come to terms with the fact that what I am left with in the end (and this is a hard concept to teach and have fully accepted) is my opinion of myself, my ability to look in a mirror without shame, to stand up straight and say, "I did the right thing and lived a good life." That's not much of a reward for a 17 or 18 year old. We may all want the money, the notoriety, the pretty wife and perfect children and ideal lifestyle. But a good name may be all we can count on.

Sometimes as parents it's the looking back and asking what we would want a "do over" for that we learn from the most, where we'd want a take two….to not get angry so quickly, to be quiet and listen instead of talk, to ask instead of advise, to give them the chance to think for themselves instead of doing the thinking for them, to not make the quick recommendation, to remember that our children always need us by their side to protect them no matter what, that protection doesn't mean saving but supporting. And then in lieu of a take two, which we almost never get in life, we have to be big enough, willing enough to ask for forgiveness for our weakness, our forgetfulness, our flaws, both from them and from ourselves.

How many take twos would I ask for? To not shout out at all the baseball games, to ask Ethan what he thought of himself, his performance, to sit quietly and enjoy the moment, to laugh more, fret less, to recognize danger and conflict when it arose, to acknowledge who my son was and who he wasn't, to protect him from an overpowering adult world that didn't see him clearly or have his interests at heart, to understand what their interests and priorities were, as opposed to his. These are some, not all the things I would do over, but it starts with E. With me and E. And this book, in a way, is my acknowledgement of my failings and my love and support, my way of asking forgiveness for a lifetime of indulgence and over-investment. It's taken me a long time to give him this freedom, though I must admit he took it, grabbed it, possessed it as much as I gave it away.

We're still close, but we have underlying resentments to work through, unresolved losses that can't be regained and pain that will never completely go away and heal. That's life, or part of it, but it's also the job of parents to minimize the haunting losses as much as possible.

If parenting is about limiting the amount we mess up our kids rather than the search for the perfect response or behavioral technique, then this has been an exploration of the mess on all sides. And that really is the story of growing up, from childhood to adulthood, and from adulthood to some glimmering of maturity.

And now my take two actually approaches. My youngest son Gabriel, age 10, has decided he wants to be a pitcher like his big brother. I don't think I'm ready to go through half, a tenth of what we went through with Ethan. I'm gritting my teeth just thinking about it. Gabriel's a lefty with no baseball experience, so I've spent the summer playing catch and catch-up with him, teaching him how to field ground balls and hit line drives. He's way behind other boys. He stabs at the ball when he catches it, flings his shoulders open when he swings the bat, lets the ball go way too early half the time he throws. Heck, in Florida most kids his age have already been playing for four or five years. But he's brave and tenacious and hasn't shown a sign of giving up, so I'm moving forward alongside him. I don't care if he's great. God knows, I sort of hope he's not. But I don't want him to be embarrassed either. I want him to have fun. And if he goes out for little league this spring, when the air is crisp and dreams of Williamsport and championship banners hang on every team and every boy starts off, in some strange way, as equal, with a zero batting average and no innings tossed, no wins or losses, if he goes out and has a good time, and I sit back and smile and applaud every boy who steps up to the plate and do nothing else, say nothing else beyond "How was the game? Did you have fun?" then maybe there was a point to the madness. Maybe there was value in the insanity I put my family through for fifteen years. Maybe, in truth, though I choke as I admit it, if baseball was nothing more than playing catch with my son, if it was just sitting in the bleachers one day and watching him run to first, if it was just a smile after a base hit or the sound of laughter from a dugout full of ten year olds, if it was any one of those singular, memorable moments, I could say it was enough.

In August 2009 we made a family pilgrimage down to Coral Gables, Florida to take Ethan to the University of Miami. We loaded up two cars with all his clothes, an old monster of a TV, more bathroom and cleaning supplies than he could use in a year, a twin-size

Tempur-Pedic mattress for his back, and drove the four hours to the school that was willing to give him a chance to prove himself once again.

Even this move was not without difficulty. We had to move him into the dorms not once, but twice. He was first assigned to room with Ryan Perry, a soft-spoken 22 year old fifth year senior. Ryan had been living in the room all summer long, and was already well-established and comfortable, his bed, books, clothes all orderly, organized, well set up long before we arrived. We had some concerns about how he would meld with haphazard freshman Ethan, but that was a decision that was way beyond our control.

And then, don't ask me why, but we checked downstairs at the information desk for the dorms about something – his mail, his keys – and found out the coaches had switched him to another room, this time with sophomore Teddy Blackman, an outfielder who had played for the Scorpions. Ethan and Teddy already knew each other from Central Florida baseball, and we immediately thought this was a good move, with reservations. The boys were more simpatico. They would get along easier than Ethan would with a more mature student. We also had some concerns, since Teddy came with a reputation as a fun-loving ballplayer and a partier more than a student. But the boys hit it off right away, and we hoped for the best. We packed Ethan up again, and moved him a second time in a matter of hours into the room he would remain in for the rest of his first year. For whatever reason, Ethan and Teddy were the only baseball players in the Mahoney Residential Tower that year. Everyone else was in the adjacent Pearson Residential Tower, and the isolation was another cause for concern, but we were happy Ethan had landed at such a prestigious university and great baseball school, and weren't about to fuss about a little matter like that.

We'd been warned not to be helicopter parents, hovering around campus while our son acclimated to his new environs, outstaying our welcome and checking in on him too many times, trying to cling to the last strands of childhood we felt slipping through our fingers. So we left a day earlier than we'd planned, making sure Ethan had everything he needed to succeed – his room set up, clothes unpacked, bed made, TV hooked up, a pair of headphones with a long cord so he could watch TV while Teddy studied (if that was ever the case), and we all took the elevator downstairs to say goodbye. Another baseball player took a picture of all of us outside the Miami dorms, and

Ethan walked us to our cars. We hugged, happy and proud that Ethan had landed in the right place at last, sad to say farewell, at least for now, to our oldest, talented, complicated boy.

"Don't cry, Dad," Ethan said to me. "Don't you dare cry. This is a good time."

Goodbyes never came easily to me. He'd caught me tearing up. "All right," I told him. "I promise. No tears." We hugged one final time, and he turned his back and walked towards the dorms, refusing to turn around even though I hoped he would as I watched every step he took. He raised his hand and, without looking, flicked a backwards wave to us, and disappeared inside.

26512600R10160

Made in the USA
Charleston, SC
10 February 2014